FINDING THE WILD WEST: THE GREAT PLAINS

Own the Complete Finding the Wild West Series:

The Great Plains: Oklahoma, Kansas, Nebraska, and the Dakotas
Along the Mississippi: Louisiana, Arkansas, Missouri, Iowa, and Minnesota
The Southwest: Arizona, New Mexico, and Texas
The Mountain West: Colorado, Nevada, Utah, Wyoming, and Montana
The Pacific West: Alaska, California, Oregon, Washington, and Idaho

FINDING THE WILD WEST: THE GREAT PLAINS

OKLAHOMA, KANSAS, NEBRASKA, AND THE DAKOTAS

MIKE COX

TWODOT®

GUILFORD, CONNECTICUT
HELENA, MONTANA

A · TWODOT® · BOOK

An imprint and registered trademark of Globe Pequot, the trade division of
The Rowman & Littlefield Publishing Group, Inc.
4501 Forbes Blvd., Ste. 200
Lanham, MD 20706
www.rowman.com

Distributed by NATIONAL BOOK NETWORK

British Library Cataloguing in Publication Information available

Library of Congress Cataloging-in-Publication Data

Names: Cox, Mike, 1948– author.
Title: Finding the Wild West. the Great Plains : Oklahoma, Kansas, Nebraska, and the Dakotas / Mike Cox.
Other titles: Great Plains : Oklahoma, Kansas, Nebraska, and the Dakotas
Description: Guilford, Connecticut : TwoDot, [2022] | Series: Finding the Wild West | Includes index.
Identifiers: LCCN 2021042848 (print) | LCCN 2021042849 (ebook) | ISBN 9781493034284 (paperback) | ISBN 9781493034291 (epub)
Subjects: LCSH: Historic sites—Great Plains—Guidebooks. | Great Plains—History, Local—Guidebooks. | Great Plains—History—19th century.
Classification: LCC F590.7 .C69 2022 (print) | LCC F590.7 (ebook) | DDC 978—dc23
LC record available at https://lccn.loc.gov/2021042848
LC ebook record available at https://lccn.loc.gov/2021042849

∞™ The paper used in this publication meets the minimum requirements of American National Standard for Information Sciences—Permanence of Paper for Printed Library Materials, ANSI/NISO Z39.48-1992.

Writers typically dedicate their books to a particular person, but this book is dedicated to a singularly spiritual moment in the once Wild West and the three people who shared it with me. On June 20, 2016, on our way to the annual Western Writers of America conference, Beverly Waak and I, along with our friends Preston and Harriet Lewis, visited the Little Bighorn Battlefield National Monument. In this historic place where two cultures collided so violently, what we perceived, lingering over the still-remote landscape like traces of gun smoke, was an overwhelming sense of peace. At the circular memorial commissioned by the Lakota to honor their fallen warriors, I happened to look up into a dark blue Montana sky. Having traveled to a lot of places over many decades, I had never seen anything like this: a long, high, thin cloud that looked very much like a giant eagle feather. Beverly, Harriet, and Preston saw it too. Freak of weather? Somehow, it didn't feel like that. Rather, it was as if the sky, in concert with the wind and the sun, wanted to remind us with its rendering of such a sacred American Indian icon that no matter what, all of us are connected—to each other, to the past, and to the land.

—Mike Cox

CONTENTS

Kansas

PREFACE: FINDING THE WILD WEST

Ain't nothing better than riding a fine horse in a new country.
—Gus McCrea in *Lonesome Dove*

Like most Baby Boomers, I learned about the Old West in the mid-1950s and early 1960s watching black-and-white television westerns and John Wayne movies in color. But that was Hollywood's Old West.

Thanks largely to my late granddad, L.A. Wilke, I began to learn about the real Old West. He was born in Central Texas in the fading days of that era, just long enough ago to have learned how to ride a horse well before he ever got behind the wheel of an automobile. Too, as a youngster and later as a newspaperman, he met some notable Wild West figures, from Buffalo Bill Cody to old Texas Rangers who had fought Comanches. A fine storyteller, he shared his experiences with me. Also, he passed his copies of *True West* and *Frontier Times* on to me. At the time, his friend Joe Small published both magazines in Austin, where I grew up.

Even before I started reading nonfiction Western magazines and books, again thanks to Granddad, I got to visit some Old West historic sites when they were still just abandoned ruins. With him, as a first grader I prowled around old Fort Davis in West Texas well before the federal government stabilized it as a National Historic Site. Later, Granddad took me to several southwest New Mexico ghost towns, including Shakespeare, Hillsboro, and Kingston. This was in 1964, when many of that state's roadways were not yet paved. In that desert high country, I experienced for the first time the still-vast openness of the West and the sense of adventure in exploring an old place new to me.

So why was the West wild?

I think you will come to understand the "why" when you experience the "where" of the Wild West. Though many of the sites described in these books are in populated areas, some are as remote or more remote than they were back in the Wild West's heyday. In visiting these sites, say a ghost town well off the beaten path, you should be able to feel the reason why the West was wild. When I stand in the middle of nowhere, distant from nothing, I feel the sense of freedom that must have driven so much of human behavior in frontier times. In such emptiness, usually scenic, it's easy to believe you can do anything you, by God, want to, be it bad or good.

Some see the West as being all the states west of the Mississippi, which includes twenty-three states. Others maintain that the West begins at the ninety-eighth meridian. My belief is that the Mississippi River is what separates the East from the West in the US.

Accordingly, moving from east to west, this series of travel guides divides the West into five regions: along the Mississippi (Louisiana, Arkansas, Iowa, Minnesota, and Missouri); the Great Plains (Oklahoma, Kansas, Nebraska, South Dakota, and North Dakota); the Southwest (Arizona, New Mexico, and Texas); the Mountain West (Colorado, Montana, Nevada, Utah, and Wyoming); and the Pacific West (Alaska, California, Idaho, Oregon, and Washington).

Having described what I consider the West, what constitutes "wild?"

Former Wild West History Association president Robert G. (Bob) McCubbin, a history buff who acquired one of the world's most inclusive collections of Western photographs, ephemera, books, and artifacts, a few years back offered his take on the matter.

"The Wild West was a time and place unique in the history of the world," he wrote. "It took place on the plains, prairies, mountains, and deserts of the American West, from the Mississippi River to the Pacific Ocean. It began about the time of the California gold rush and was at its height in the 1870s through the 1890s, fading away in the decade after the turn of the twentieth century—as the automobile replaced the horse."

He went on to explain that Wild West does not mean wilderness wild. It means lawless wild. While untamed grandeur was certainly a part of the Wild West, it was the untamed men and women who made the West wild.

"Of course," McCubbin continued, "during the Wild West period there were many good and substantial citizens who went about their business in a law abiding and constructive way. Most of those are forgotten. It's the excitement of the Wild West's bad men, desperadoes, outlaws, gunfighters, and lawmen—many of whom were also, at times, cowboys, scouts, and buffalo hunters—and the dance hall girls and 'shady ladies,' who capture our interest and imagination."

While mostly adhering to McCubbin's definition of the Wild West, I could not stick to it entirely. Some things that happened prior to the California gold rush—Spanish and French colonial efforts, the Louisiana Purchase, the Lewis and Clark Expedition, the exploits of mountain men, the development of the great western trails, and the Mexican War of 1846 to 1848—were critical in shaping the later history of the West. That explains why some of the sites associated with these aspects of history needed to be included in this book.

For the most part, 1900 is the cut-off date for events related in this series of books. But the Wild West did not end at 11:59 p.m. on December 31, 1899. Some places, particularly Arizona, Oklahoma, New Mexico, and far west Texas stayed wild until World War I. Sometimes, events that occurred in the nineteenth century continued to have ramifications in the early twentieth century. An example would be the life and times of Pat Garrett, who killed Billy the Kid in 1881. Garrett himself was shot to death in 1909, so his death site is listed.

The Finding the Wild West series is not intended as a guide to every single historic site in a given city, state, or region. Some towns and cities had to be left out. It would take an encyclopedic, multi-volume work to cover *all* the historical places throughout the western states. I have tried to include the major sites with a Wild West connection, along with some places with great stories you've probably never heard.

These books focus primarily on locations where there is still something to see today. Those sites range from period buildings and ruins to battlefields, historical markers, tombstones, and public art. In addition to historic sites, I have included museums and libraries with collections centered on "those thrilling days of yesteryear." Again, I have *not* listed every museum or every attraction.

A note on directions: Since almost everyone has access to GPS applications or devices, locations are limited to specific addresses with "turn here" or "until you come to" used only when necessary, with the exception of block-row-plot numbers of graves (when available). GPS coordinates are given for more difficult to find locations.

The Wild West has long since been tamed, with nationally franchised fast-food places and big-box stores standing where the buffalo roamed and the deer and the antelope played. Considered another way, however, the Wild West hasn't gone anywhere. It still exists in our collective imagination—a mixture of truth and legend set against the backdrop of one of the world's most spectacular landscapes.

Wild Bill Hickok, Jesse James, George Armstrong Custer, Billy the Kid, Wyatt Earp, and others received a lot of press and rose from the dead as Western icons, but there were many more characters—from outlaws to lawmen, drovers to cattle barons, harlots to preachers—whose stories are yet to be brought to life. Indeed, every tombstone, every historical marker, every monument, every ghost town, every historic site, every place name, every structure, every person has a story to tell. Like a modern-day prospector, all you need to do is pack these books in your saddlebag, mount up, and ride out in search of the Wild West.

—Mike Cox
Wimberley, Texas

INTRODUCTION TO THE GREAT PLAINS

For centuries the province of the buffalo and the Native Americans who depended on the shaggy animals for everything from food to shelter, the mostly flat, grassy Great Plains region includes five states: Oklahoma, Kansas, Nebraska, South Dakota, and North Dakota.

What is now Oklahoma traces to the US government's creation of the Indian Territory in 1830. The territory lay above the Red River, which was then the northern boundary of the Mexican province that would become Texas, and immediately west of Arkansas. The government then proceeded to uproot five Southern Indian tribes and move them to the new territory.

The first political subdivisions established in the region were the territories of Kansas and Nebraska, born of the 1854 Kansas-Nebraska Act. Under the law, Congress designated the land north of the thirty-seventh parallel as Nebraska Territory while land north of the fortieth parallel became Kansas Territory.

Creation of the two territories, an action primarily motivated by the slavery issue, triggered bloody conflict along the Missouri-Kansas border that amounted to a dress rehearsal for the looming Civil War. It also led to the first significant wave of white settlers on land that by treaty had been reserved for Indians. That would bring the first major conflict between the Plains tribes, newly arrived settlers, and the US military forces that came to protect them.

The map changed again in 1861, when Congress took land from the western portion of Minnesota Territory and some from northern Nebraska Territory to create Dakota Territory. The new territory

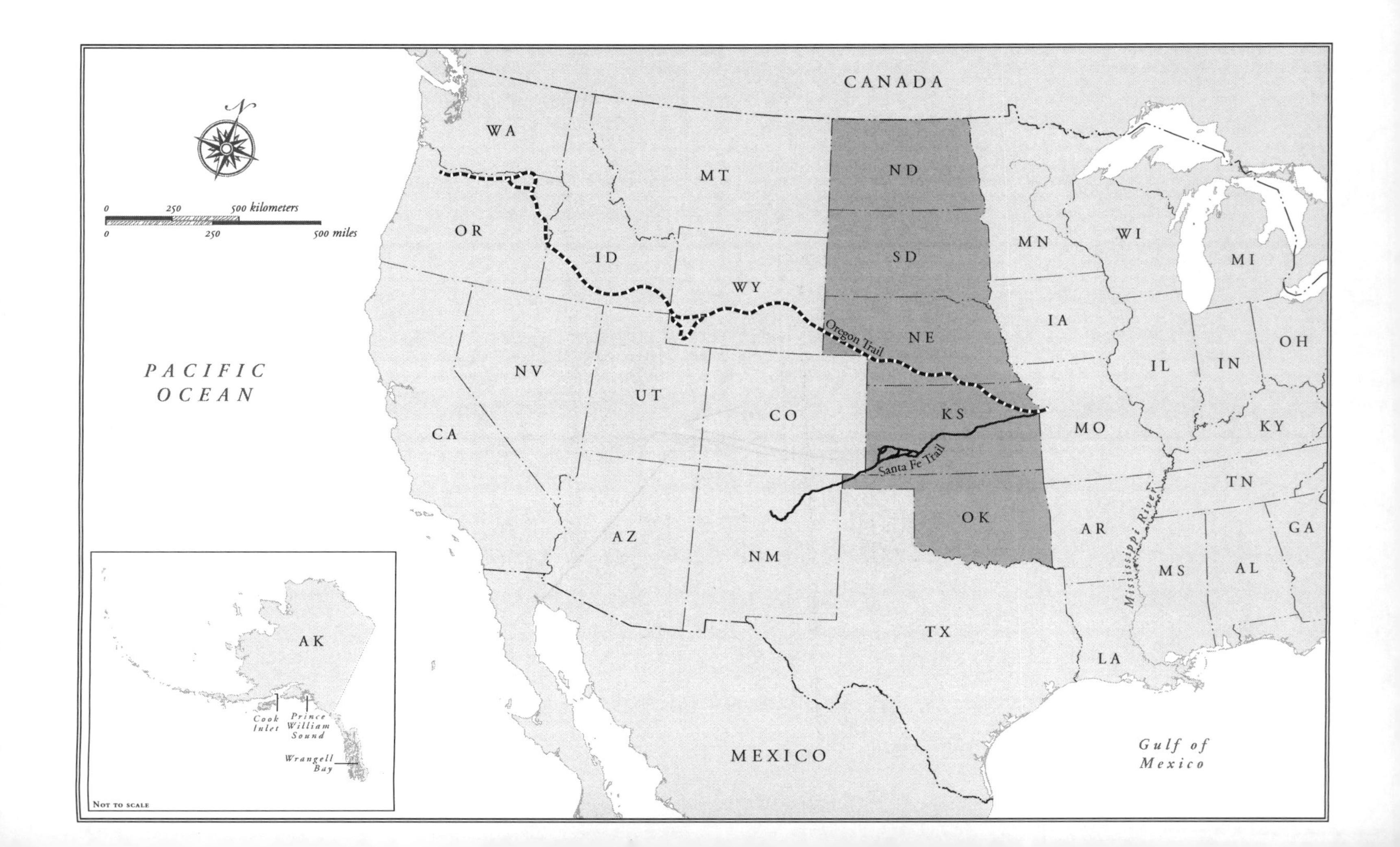
CANADA
WA
MT
ND
OR
ID
WY
SD
MN
WI
MI
NE
IA
OH
IL
IN
NV
UT
CO
KS
MO
KY
CA
TN
AZ
NM
OK
AR
GA
MS
AL
TX
LA
MEXICO
Gulf of Mexico
PACIFIC OCEAN
Oregon Trail
Santa Fe Trail
Mississippi River
0 250 500 kilometers
0 250 500 miles
AK
Cook Inlet
Prince William Sound
Wrangell Bay
Not to scale

extended westward to include much of the land that would later become Montana and Wyoming.

With the passage of the Homestead Act in 1862, Americans hungry for the free land the new law allowed began staking claims in Dakota Territory and elsewhere on the Great Plains. A treaty in 1868 reserved Dakota Territory west of the Missouri River for the Indians, but when gold was discovered in the Black Hills, miners and others descended on the region, no matter the treaty. That brought about a war with the Sioux that lasted through the 1870s into the early 1880s. In 1889 the Indians relegated to reservations and the buffalo virtually extinct, Congress created the new states of North and South Dakota.

The rest of what would become Oklahoma was designated as Oklahoma Territory in 1890. Seventeen years later, Congress combined the Indian and Oklahoma Territories and made Oklahoma a state in 1907.

OKLAHOMA

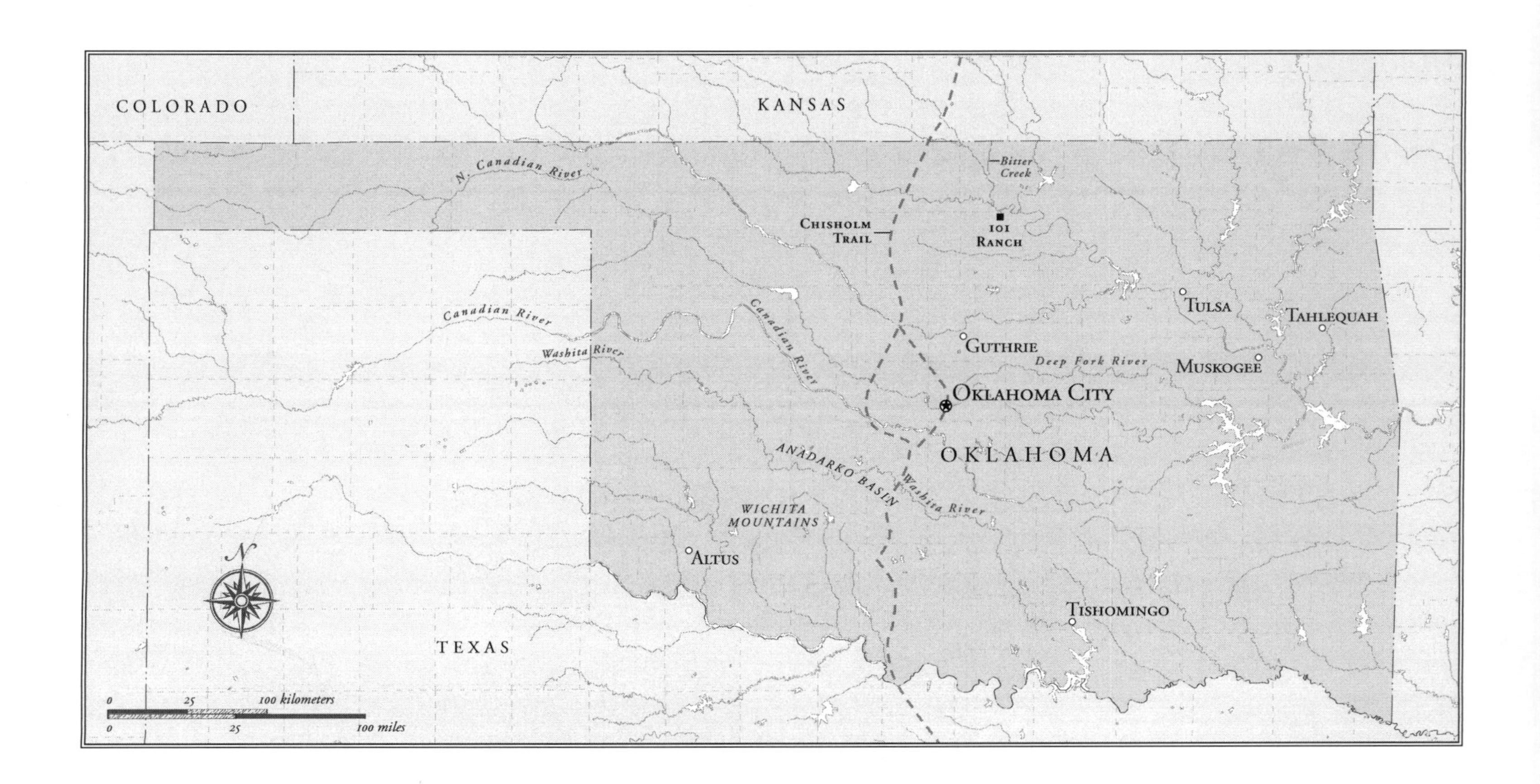

COLORADO
KANSAS
N. Canadian River
Bitter Creek
Chisholm Trail
101 Ranch
Canadian River
Washita River
Canadian River
Tulsa
Tahlequah
Guthrie
Deep Fork River
Muskogee
Oklahoma City
OKLAHOMA
Anadarko Basin
Washita River
Wichita Mountains
Altus
Tishomingo
TEXAS
N
0
25
100 kilometers
0
25
100 miles

Ada (Pontotoc County)

A crossroads in the Cherokee Nation looked like a good place to start a business, so William J. (Jeff) Reed built a store and a log cabin for his family there in 1890. The next year, when the government approved a post office at his store, he named it Ada for his daughter. Sales picked up considerably when the Frisco Railroad arrived in 1900 and the town grew from there.

The Night the Lights Went Out in Ada

The Old West and twentieth-century technology intersected at 2:00 a.m. on April 19, 1909, when suddenly Ada's electric grid and telephone system went dead. A mob led by some of the town's most respected citizens had cut off power and communication and then proceeded in the dark to the county jail, where four murder suspects lay asleep in their cells. The vigilantes easily took charge of prisoners, ordered them to dress, and marched them to the nearby vacant Frisco Livery Stable where they were hanged from the rafters. They had been accused of killing popular Ada resident **A. A. "Gus" Bobbitt**, a rancher and deputy US marshal. Later that day Justice of the Peace H. J. Brown ruled that Joe Allen, B.B. Burrwell, Jim Miller, and Jesse West came to their deaths "by strangulation by a rope tied around their necks . . . administered by the hands of unknown persons." Of the four accused, the best known was Miller, a professional hit man known for or suspected of killing a dozen people. A religious man despite his violent occupation, Miller did not fight for his life. All he asked was that his hat be placed on his head after he was gone. After the four quit kicking, someone obliged his final request.

The frame structure on Main Street where the mass lynching occurred has long since been razed and the old Pontotoc County courthouse and jail were replaced in 1926. But in 1997, the Oklahoma Outlaw and Lawman Association (now defunct) placed a shiny black granite marker on private property not far from the scene of the quadruple hanging. Engraved at the bottom of the marker, beneath 119 words describing the lynching, is the notation that it had been erected "As a memorial to the end of the Old West and the struggle for law and order." There it stood, to the annoyance of many locals who would just as soon not have Ada remembered for a lynching, until it was placed in storage in 2009. In 2015 the marker was moved to the **Box X Cemetery** (5251 County Road 1470; GPS coordinates: N34° 51.37', W96° 48.37'), 9.2 miles northwest of Ada.

Altus (Jackson County)

In the 1870s a buffalo hunter named Frazer hollowed out a dugout near Bitter Creek in what was then Greer County, Texas. He left when the buffalo did, but a small community that bore his name remained in the vicinity of his dugout. When a flood swept over the settlement in 1891, a new town was laid out on higher ground. Someone familiar with Latin suggested the place be called Altus, meaning high. The town grew as a railroad and agricultural center, with cotton-growing initially driving the economy. Altus has six buildings listed on the National Register of Historic Places.

The Western Cattle Trail from Texas to Dodge City entered Oklahoma at **Doan's Crossing** in Jackson County. Some nineteen million cattle splashed across the river at this point until the crossing was abandoned in 1895. The **Museum of the Western Prairie** (1100 Memorial Dr., Altus; 580-482-1044) covers the full range of southwest Oklahoma's history, including the story of this old cattle "highway." A historical marker summarizing the history of the Western Trail stands just off US 62, two miles east of Altus. Another historical marker is located southwest of Tipton on County Road East 159.

Anadarko (Caddo County)

An Indian agency opened in 1871 north of what would become Anadarko, but thirty years passed before the city came into being.

That happened when the various Indian reservations surrounding the agency were opened to white settlement. As with the previous, larger-scale land openings in Oklahoma, lots became available on a set day, which for Anadarko was August 6, 1901. In anticipation of the land auction, in which no one could buy more than one business and one residential lot, twenty thousand people showed up. By December only three thousand or so remained in the new town, but it grew into an agricultural trading center.

Seven tribes have their headquarters in the Anadarko area and two museums focus on Native American culture: **Southern Plains Indian Museum and Craft Center** (715 East Central Blvd.; 405-247-6221) and the **National Hall of Fame for Famous American Indians** (851/901 East Central Blvd.; 405-247-5555).

One of the West's more interestingly named museums is also located in Anadarko: The **Philomathic Museum** (311 East Main St.; 405-247-3240). Dating from 1935, when women of the Anadarko Philomathic Club began working to establish a local history museum, the collection has been housed in the old Rock Island Railroad depot since 1975. (A philomath is someone who enjoys learning, as in a person who would be curious to know the definition of "philomathic," the adjective used to describe the enjoyment of learning.)

Ardmore (Carter County)

Until shortly before the Santa Fe Railroad came through in 1887, the area around what would become Ardmore was open range land in the Chickasaw Nation. The only structure was the 700 Ranch headquarters. But the railroad changed all that. First in tents, then in frame buildings, businesses popped up near the tracks to cater to railroad men, travelers, and the Chickasaw people. A fire in 1895 wiped out much of the town, but it was rebuilt with mostly brick buildings. In the early twentieth century, Ardmore boomed as an oil town.

The career of one of the Wild West's most notorious outlaws, **Bill Dalton**, ended near Ardmore on June 8, 1894. That's about the only undisputed fact about what happened that day. At first, many found it hard to believe that Dalton had been killed at all. Of course, some newspaper readers could be forgiven for being a bit skeptical of the news. After all, Dalton had been reported dead or dying three times previously after encounters with law enforcement. But after the outlaw's widow formally identified his body, and his corpse went on display at a funeral home in Ardmore, most folks accepted that his run had finally ended. But there was still the matter of who killed him. The historical marker at the site of the shootout says deputy **US Marshal Selden Lindsey** fatally shot Dalton when he resisted arrest. But **Caleb "Loss" Hart**, another deputy US marshal who was there that day, claimed he killed Dalton, not Lindsey. It should be noted that the historical marker later erected at the site of the shooting was paid for by Harrell McCullough (1913–1999), grandson of Selden Lindsey.

The shooting took place on a farm west of the small community of Elk, now known as Poolville. The site is 6.2 miles north of State Highway 53 off Poolville Road. From I-35 take exit 42 to State Highway 53, and travel 12.8 miles to Poolville Road. Turn right (north) and follow to the marker.

Pat Garrett of Billy the Kid fame was not the only notable Wild West sheriff with that last name. In Carter County, Buck Garrett (1871–1929) had a long and distinguished career as a lawman, as Ardmore police chief from 1905 to 1910 and sheriff from 1910 to 1922. He seldom carried a gun. Considering the record of his longtime deputy **David M. "Bud" Ballew** (1877–1922), going around unarmed may have been a good idea. In separate line of duty incidents, Ballew killed six men in Ardmore. The first was a man he shot while trying to make an arrest with Garrett. On his own, Ballew killed a former deputy US marshal and prohibition agent named Dow Braziel (1881–1919), a would-be robber, and two other men. The body count ended when Ballew moved from Ardmore to the Texas oil boomtown of Wichita Falls. There, on May 5, 1922, when he got drunk and caused a disturbance in a saloon there, Police Chief J.W. McCormick and another officer tried to arrest him. Ballew reached for a concealed handgun but the chief put five bullets in him before he could pull the weapon.

Ballew is buried seven miles from Ardmore in **Lone Grove Cemetery**, near the intersection of Church and North Memorial Roads. Garrett and former deputy US Marshal Braziel are buried in Ardmore's **Rose Hill Cemetery** (1604 C St. Southeast).

"Gainesville Shoes"

Before Oklahoma statehood, federal law prohibited distribution of alcohol in the five nations of Indian Territory. Ardmore was in the Chickasaw Nation and the most common criminal charge was bootlegging. However, only thirty-nine miles down the tracks in Gainesville, Texas, whiskey selling was legal. Consequently, Ardmore residents not willing to give up their ardent spirits often found it necessary to take the Santa Fe to Gainesville to "buy shoes." Of course, each shoe box they returned with held a bottle of booze, not new footwear.

The ready availability of "shoes" south of the Red River, coupled with other smuggling methodologies, kept Ardmore rough around the edges until World War I. The only difference between the town's saloons and bawdy houses and other Wild West venues was the necessity of being less conspicuous. The **Dew Drop Inn**, one of the toughest dives, operated wide open, if discreetly, in the basement of a two-story brick building. A pharmacy occupied the ground floor while Dr. Walter Hardy had a sanitarium, or hospital, on the second floor. The saloon had a less-visible side entrance that made it easier for customers to drop in the Dew Drop. The low-key approach also put less pressure on local or federal authorities to shut it down. The arrangement also proved handy for Dr. Hardy, who did not have to go far to treat fistfight and gunshot victims.

The building at 125 Main Street in which the Dew Drop Inn did business has since been razed, but during a 2018 renovation of a retail shop at 117 Main Street, workers found evidence of a long-rumored tunnel believed to have connected bars and bordellos to a respectable hotel. Most of the vice-related businesses were along Caddo Street, which intersects Main. For years, the district was known as "Bloody Caddo."

Housed in a former National Guard armory built with federal Works Progress Administration money in 1935–1936, **Greater Southwest Historical Museum** (35 Sunset Dr.; 580-226-3857) covers the social, cultural, and economic history of south-central Oklahoma.

Thirty-two miles from Ardmore is the **Chickasaw Cultural Center** (867 Cooper Memorial Dr., Sulphur; 580-622-7130).

Bartlesville (Washington County)

When Jacob Bartles married Delaware Chief Charles Journeycake's daughter, it entitled him to settle in Indian Territory. He and his wife built a cabin at Silver Lake, a natural body of water in future Washington County, but they soon moved to Turkey Creek, where, in 1873, Bartles opened a trading post. A year later he bought and expanded a grist mill at a third location, this one on the Caney River. There Bartles opened a general store, a blacksmith shop, livery stable, and inn. The community that came to be called Bartles Town developed around the pioneer entrepreneur's businesses. Later the name was changed to Bartlesville. The Santa Fe Railroad came through in 1899, but it was the discovery of oil two years earlier that shaped the town's future.

Frank Phillips wasn't doing badly as the owner of several barber shops in Creston, Iowa, when he learned in 1903 that an oil boom was underway in Bartlesville. Phillips sold his businesses and came to the new oil patch. With his barber shop sales profits, Phillips bought a bank, and from there expanded into the oil business. In 1917, he and his brother incorporated the Phillips Petroleum Company.

By 1925 Phillips had ample money to buy a ranch where he built a substantial lodge as a retreat for family and friends. Four years later Phillips had a stone pavilion built nearby for storage of the Woolaroc, an airplane he had entered in a 1927 air race between California and Hawaii. (*Woolaroc* is a fabricated word standing for woods, lakes, and rocks common to the surrounding Osage Hills.) In addition to his airplane, Phillips had a growing collection of Native American artifacts, Western art, and Colt firearms. From 1929 on, his collection grew, and the pavilion was expanded into a large museum he named after his airplane. Since the early 1930s the museum has been the home to a bronze statue, ***The Outlaw, Belle Starr***, believed to be the only sculpture of a female outlaw. A 3,700-acre wildlife refuge surrounds the lodge and **Woolaroc Museum** (1925 Woolaroc Ranch Rd.; 918-336-0307), located ten miles southwest of Bartlesville. The **Bartlesville Area History Museum** (401 South Johnstone Ave.; 918-338-4290), covers ten thousand square feet on the top floor of Bartlesville City Hall. Twenty-five miles south of Bartlesville is the **Osage Nation Museum** (819 Grandview Ave., Pawhuska; 918-287-5441). Established in 1938, it is the oldest tribally owned museum in the nation.

Boise City (Cimarron County)

Fittingly enough for a town lying at the heart of the once outlaw-infested real estate that used to be called No Man's Land, Boise City began in 1908 with a fraudulent development scheme that sent two of its founders to federal prison for mail fraud. Long before Boise City, however, the Cimarron cutoff of the Santa Fe Trail passed through the desolate area that is now the Oklahoma panhandle. Composed of eight historic structures on three and a half acres, the **Cimarron Heritage Center** (1301 North Cimarron Ave.; 580-544-3479) has exhibits on the Santa Fe Trail and other aspects of the area's history. At Goodwell, sixty miles southeast in Texas County, is the **No Man's Land Museum** (207 Sewell St.; 580-349-2670). Operated by Oklahoma Panhandle State University, the museum has been an area fixture since 1934.

Cache (Comanche County)

Quanah Parker, the last war chief of the Comanches—well regarded by his people as well as citizens of the nation that subjugated him—had risen in status and wealth to the extent that by 1890, he felt he should have a home befitting his position. A warrior who had become a man of peace, he built a two-story, eight-room house on his people's reservation. Once it had been completed, in further recognition of his status, Parker had fourteen large white stars painted on the house's red roof, including two on a smoke house and two on a summer house. The chief got the idea after observing a pompous army general with stars on his epaulets. With his seven wives and twenty-five children, Parker lived in the house until his death in 1911. During that time, he entertained fellow tribesmen, wealthy cattlemen, and President Theodore Roosevelt in the house.

The residence remained in the Parker family until 1958, when the chief's daughter Linda Parker Birdsong traded it to Herbert T. Woesner, who planned to restore it and make it the centerpiece of Eagle Park, an amusement venue west of Cache he'd opened in 1957. Woesner had the house moved from its original location to the park and stabilized, but never got around to a major renovation. In 1985 the park ceased operation and the old house slowly began to fall into disrepair. The Comanche Nation has expressed interest in restoring the house, which is listed on the National Register of Historical Places.

Star House and six other historic structures that had been moved to the amusement park sit on 260 acres owned by Wayne Gipson and his sister. Time and weather permitting, Gipson accepts donations for providing tours of the property. To arrange a tour, contact Gipson at his business, the Trading Post (810 North 8th St.; 580-429-3420).

Chandler (Lincoln County)

Lying midway between Tulsa and Oklahoma City, Chandler was settled in 1891. Nearly destroyed by a tornado in 1897, it became an agricultural shipping center with the arrival of the St. Louis and San Francisco Railroad (better known as the Frisco) in 1898.

Today, with eight thousand square feet for artifacts, historical records, and exhibits, the **Museum of Pioneer History** (717 Manvel Ave.; 405-258-2425) occupies Chandler's two oldest commercial structures, matching (and now adjoined) two-story sandstone buildings dating to 1897 to 1898. The museum features a Bill Tilghman exhibit with memorabilia associated with the famed lawman, including an original copy of the 1915 movie Tilghman did with partner Benny Kent, *The Passing of the Oklahoma Outlaw.* Tilghman is buried in **Oak Park Cemetery** (Block 16, Lot 18, Space 1; GPS coordinates: N35° 42.00', W96° 54.17').

Cheyenne (Roger Mills County)

When Lt. Col. George Armstrong Custer and four brigades of the Seventh Cavalry charged over snow-covered ground toward the sleeping Cheyenne village early on the morning of November 27, 1868, it was so cold that the regimental band's instruments froze halfway through the "Gary Owen," the unit's fighting song. But the fighting was hot. The soldiers killed some sixty men, women, and children while losing twenty of their own. As the Washita Battlefield National Historic Site website notes, "The event was an example of the tragic clash of cultures during the Great Plains Wars." Part of the National Park System since 1996, the 315-acre **Washita Battlefield National Historic Site** (18555 State Highway 47 Alt.; 580-497-2742) is located along the Washita River within the US Forest Service's Black Kettle National Grassland, two miles west of Cheyenne. The visitor's center features an interpretative film and exhibits that tell the story of the battle.

Claremore (Rogers County)

Rogers County is named for one of its earliest settlers, Clem Rogers. He came to the area in 1856 and went on to establish the sixty-thousand-acre **Dog Iron Ranch** (9501 East 380 Rd.; 918-275-4201), located two miles east of Oologah. The rancher played an important role in pushing for Oklahoma statehood and served on the new state's constitutional convention in 1907, but he would not be the best-known Rogers in the family. His son Will, born in 1879, became a world-famous rodeo performer, movie star, and pundit.

First known as Clermont for an Osage chief, the town got a post office in 1874 and became county seat with the later organization of Rogers County. As often happened, a post office error resulted in

Clermont becoming Claremore. A railroad crossroads, the town grew as a trade center.

The nineteen-thousand-square-foot **Will Rogers Memorial Museum** (1720 West Will Rogers Blvd.; 918-341-0719) tells the story of Rogers's transition from cowboy to comedian to commentator with artifacts, memorabilia, photographs, films, and documents. The museum opened in 1938, three years after Rogers and Wiley Post died in a plane crash in Alaska. Rogers's tomb is on the twenty-acre site, which along with Rogers's birthplace on the Dog Iron Ranch is managed by the Oklahoma Historical Society. An eleven-thousand-square-foot addition to the museum in Claremont was built in 1983.

Take Your Medicine Like a Good Boy

Young John Monroe Davis lay dangerously ill but refused to take any medicine. If he'd change his mind, Davis's father told his son, he'd give him a shotgun. Not only did the father's bribe work, it kindled a life-long passion for firearms that led to Davis's development of the world's largest privately held gun collection. Already a gun collector, Davis bought Claremont's Hotel Mason in 1916 during the Tulsa-area oil boom. He later branched out into other business endeavors, but early on that hotel was both his means of making a living and a place to display his growing gun collection. As he did better in business, he continued to acquire individual firearms and the collections of others, his holdings growing faster than cartridges ejected from a Gatling gun. Davis transferred ownership of his collection to a non-profit foundation in 1965. The foundation then leased the guns to the Oklahoma Historical Society for ninety-nine years, with the stipulation that the society build and maintain a museum to conserve and display his collection. The **J.M. Davis Arms and Historical Museum** (330 North J.M. Davis Blvd.; 918-341-5707), opened in Claremore on July 27, 1969, Davis's eighty-second birthday. When he died in 1973, he was buried on the museum grounds, eternally close to his twelve-thousand-plus guns.

Cromwell (Seminole County)

The violent death of Cromwell town marshal Bill Tilghman on November 1, 1924, had a Wild West connection, even if it was related to Prohibition. When a drunken and reportedly corrupt federal prohibition agent named Wiley Lyn shot and killed Tilghman, an era ended along with his life. At seventy, the oil boomtown marshal was a legend in his own time, though recent scholarship shows his badge wasn't quite as shiny as is usually portrayed. Even so, Tilghman was a lawman in Dodge City in the 1870s and 1880s, a contemporary of people like Wyatt Earp and Bat Masterson. Then, in the 1890s, he became known as one of the "Three Guardsmen," the trio of deputy US marshals who did much in ridding what is now Oklahoma of its more infamous outlaws.

A historical marker stands at the site of **Murphy's Dance Hall**, where Tilghman had been before going outside to investigate a gunshot and finding agent Lyn, whom he tried to arrest. The marker was placed in a park off Shawnee Avenue between Jenkins and Hall Streets in Cromwell. A fire whipped through town about a year after Tilghman's killing and destroyed most of the wood frame buildings and tar paper shacks that constituted the town, including Murphy's Dance Hall.

Dewey (Washington County)

When Admiral George Dewey defeated a Spanish fleet in Manilla Bay in 1898, it seemed fitting to name the new town then being developed in Washington County in his honor. The community could as well have been named for the man who founded it, rancher-entrepreneur Jacob H. "Jake" Bartles. First, he surveyed a rail route from Caney, Kansas, to his store at Silver Lake. Next, he contracted to have the right-of-way graded, and then he induced the Santa Fe Railroad to take over the project and lay tracks. The railroad followed most of the route Bartles had laid out, but when the company decided to bypass where he had his store, he laid out a townsite along the Santa Fe's route. Bartles vacated Silver Lake and moved his store to Dewey. He didn't just build a new store, he literally moved the old one on rollers, with oxen doing the pulling. Mindful of cash flow, he kept the business open during the five months it took to move it.

The next thing Bartles needed for his new town was a fine hotel. In 1899 he started construction of an ornate, three-story Victorian building with wide porches and a distinctive cupola. The thirty-one-room **Dewey Hotel** (801 North Delaware Ave.; 918-534-0215) opened a year later and was the social center of the town for decades. Over the years it accommodated cowboys, ranchers, railroad men, outlaws, and just plain folks. In 1964 it was donated to the Washington County Historical Society, which renovated it and opened it as a museum.

In the latter part of 1911, Dewey city fathers hired a thirty-two-year-old Pennsylvania-born cowboy and Army veteran to serve as night town marshal. He was married to a local woman and their daughter was born in Dewey. That man was Tom Mix. Mix had performed in Zack Miller's 101 Wild West Show, had already had a few parts in silent Western movies, and didn't tote a real gun in Dewey for long before he returned to Hollywood and became a screen legend. He starred in almost three hundred movies before his death in a car crash in 1940. In 1965, a group of local businessmen realized that a Tom Mix museum would be good for the local economy. They negotiated to buy a large collection of items that had been in his estate and rented and remodeled a building to house the artifacts. Later, the Oklahoma Historical Society took over operation of the **Tom Mix Museum** (721 North Delaware St.; 918-534-1555). A replica of the concrete jail in which Mix would have booked prisoners stands behind the Dewey Hotel Museum.

A Shooting Starr Goes into the Ground

Era-spanning outlaw **Henry Starr**, who transitioned from horseback to automobile, is buried in the **Dewey Cemetery** (Lot 18, Space 6; 411 East Don Tyler Ave.). For years his grave was unmarked, findable only because it lay next to the marker for one of his two children, marked simply if incorrectly, "Baby Star." A gray granite tombstone has since been placed over his grave. Inscribed on the bottom of the tombstone are some of Starr's own words: "I've robbed more banks than any man in America." The cemetery is on the east side of US 75, just north of town.

Duncan (Stephens County)

The Chisholm Trail made money for Texas cattlemen, but others benefited from it as well. In 1872, William Duncan married a Chickasaw woman and soon opened a store on the trail. He did well supplying food and other provisions to trail drivers and did even better when he moved his store to be near the approaching Rock Island Railroad. His wife exercised her tribal rights to a five-hundred-acre tract and selected land along the railroad right-of-way. The Duncans had a townsite plotted, donated land for a depot, and the town of Duncan came to life in 1892.

The storied Chisholm Trail, which originated in South Texas, entered what is now Oklahoma after crossing the Red River near present Terral. The trail cut north-south across Oklahoma for 180-plus miles. Today US 81 generally follows the old trail. Construction of the **Chisholm Trail Heritage Center** (1000 Chisholm Trail Pkwy.; 580-252-6692), began in 1997. With expansions in 2003, 2005, and 2007, the center has been named one of the top ten Western museums.

Oklahoma oilman-philanthropist Thomas H. McCasland, Jr. funded an impressive monument telling the story of the Chisholm Trail. McCasland commissioned sculptor Paul Moore, then an artist-in-residence at the University of Oklahoma, to do the piece. Standing nearly fifteen feet high atop an immense base and extending almost thirty-five feet across, the **Chisholm Trail Monument** is titled *On the Chisholm Trail*. In August 2014, *Oklahoma Magazine* included the massive piece of public art in its "20 Objects that Shape Oklahoma."

Founded in 1967, the **Stephens County Museum** (Fuqua Park, US 81 and Beech St.; 580-252-0717) now occupies the old National Guard armory built in 1936–1937 as a federal Works Progress Administration project. While the Chisholm Trail Heritage Center focuses on the famous cattle trail, this museum covers the rest of the county's history.

Durant (Bryan County)

Founded in 1870 by Choctaw Tribe member Dixon Durant, whose French-Choctaw family had settled in the area in the 1830s, the community became known as Durant Station when the Missouri, Kansas, and Texas Railroad (the Katy) came through and built a depot. A decade later, the word "Station" was dropped and the town developed as an agricultural center. Durant is home to the Choctaw Tribal Headquarters.

Fort Washita and Aunt Jane

The US Army established Fort Washita just east of the Washita River and eighteen miles north of the Red River in 1842 to protect the Choctaw and Chickasaw Nations from hostile Plains Indians. During the California gold rush, the fort became an important waypoint on the trail westward from Fort Smith, Arkansas. The post was abandoned at the beginning of the Civil War but served as a Confederate supply depot. After the war, most of the fort's buildings burned, but the government transferred the property to the Chickasaw Nation. Later the Dawes Commission allocated the old fort site to Charles and Abbie Colbert. The Chickasaw couple rebuilt some of the buildings and began farming the land but moved on after a few years.

That's about the time rumors of hauntings arose, the main story centering on the supposed ghost of one Aunt Jane, possibly a freed slave. According to legend, she had been murdered in the vicinity of the fort at some point prior to 1861 when she refused to reveal the location of her hidden money stash. As with most ghost stories, more fanciful details seem to be added with each telling, but accounts of strange manifestations at the old fort have persisted. The Oklahoma Historical

Society acquired the property in 1962 and began operating it as the **Fort Washita National Historic Site** (3348 State Highway 199; 580-924-6502). In 2016 the society partnered with the Chickasaw Nation, which now manages the site. The old fort is sixteen miles west of Durant.

Elk City (Beckham County)

The Great Western Cattle Train from Texas to Dodge City, Kansas, passed near the future site of Elk City, but settlement in the area did not begin until the opening of the Cheyenne-Arapaho Reservation in 1892. The town—named for nearby Elk Creek—developed with the arrival of the Choctaw, Oklahoma, and Gulf Railroad in 1901. But Elk City wasn't its first name, it was Busch, as in brewing magnate Adolphus Busch. The overly optimistic developers hoped the St. Louis–based co-founder of Anheuser-Busch would be so honored that he'd invest in the town, and hopefully open a brewery there. That didn't happen, and since hardly anyone in the new community liked the name, it died out and Busch officially became Elk City in 1907. The **Elk City Museum Complex** (2717 West 3rd St.) encompasses five different museums, with the **Old Town Museum** focusing on the area's history. The other museums include the **Farm and Ranch Museum**, the **Blacksmith Museum**, the **National Route 66 Museum**, and the **National Transportation Museum**.

El Reno (Canadian County)

El Reno got its name from Fort Reno, but the town did not come into existence until the April 1889 land run. The same day people staked claims in what would become El Reno, those claiming lots on the other side of the Canadian River decided their coming community would be Reno City. When the forerunner of the Rock Island Railroad began laying rails in the direction of Reno City, its residents refused to lay out cash or donate any lots to assure the railroad's continued interest in serving the community. Accordingly, the railroad bypassed the new town and went straight to El Reno, whose citizens had been more than happy to deal. Their hopes for a town dead, Reno City residents moved their wooden buildings and homes to El Reno, which, with rail service, grew steadily from there.

Established in 1874 during the Indian Wars to guard the nearby Cheyenne-Arapaho Reservation, Fort Reno, six miles northwest of El Reno, served the military in various capacities through World War II. It had been soldiers stationed at the fort who oversaw the April 22, 1889, land rush, firing the shots that signaled its frenetic beginning.

Of the stone and brick post buildings of **Fort Reno** constructed from 1876 to 1890, sixteen still stand. Since 1946 the US Department of Agriculture has used the old fort as an agricultural extension station. A visitor's center and museum (7107 West Cheyenne St.; 405-262-3987) is operated by the non-profit Historic Fort Reno, Inc.

A man reported to have stood up twice to the blustery Lt. Col. George Armstrong Custer over issues they disagreed on—and kept his job—is fittingly buried in **Post Cemetery** (7107 West Cheyenne St.; 405-262-3987) at Fort Reno, given his long connection to the post. Ben Clark (1842–1914) was a scout who spent much of his career attached to Custer's Seventh Cavalry regiment. In 1868 he led Custer to Chief Black Kettle's camp on the Washita River, resulting in the controversial Battle of the Washita. Married into the Cheyenne Tribe, Clark came to Fort Reno from Fort Supply in January 1878 as an interpreter and later served as chief of scouts. In 1888 Clark hosted artist Frederic Remington who produced several drawings and paintings inspired by his three months at Fort Reno. Still at Fort Reno after thirty years, Clark was left in temporary charge of the post in 1908 during its transition from an active garrison to a remount station. Clark and his wife and children lived in the remodeled former post school and chapel, now Building 10.

Operated by the Canadian County Historical Society, the **Canadian County Historical Museum** (300 South Grand Ave.; 405-262-5121) is in the old Rock Island Railroad depot. Several historic structures from elsewhere in the county have been moved to the museum grounds and restored, including an 1869 jail from the Darlington Indian Agency, the 1876-vintage cabin Gen. Phil Sheridan lived in while stationed at Fort Reno, and the 1892 Hotel El Reno.

Enid (Garfield County)

Trail drives along the Chisholm Trail used to stop at a water hole where Enid eventually developed, but the town did not come into existence until the September 16, 1893, Cherokee Strip land run. Someone suggested naming the new townsite Skeleton, for the nearby Skeleton Ranch, but a railroad official thought that sounded too off-putting and countered with Enid, the wife of Geraint in "Idylls of the King." Another version of the story of how the town got its name is that in the tent city that arose following the land rush, the owner of a newly opened eating place put his sign that said "Dine" upside down.

A historical marker in **Government Springs Park** (400 block El Owen K. Garriott Rd.; 580-234-0400) stands near the Chisholm Trail–era water source. Enid's oldest park, it was founded in 1911.

The Cherokee Strip

The US government ceded much of northern Oklahoma to the Cherokee Nation so the Cherokee people could have access to hunting grounds to the west. Officially labeled the Cherokee Outlet, the area came to be more commonly known as the **Cherokee Strip**. When Texas cattlemen began driving large herds of longhorn cattle through the land to get to the railheads in Kansas, the Cherokee started leasing some of the land for grazing. But squatters, better known as "boomers," began encroaching on the land. In frustration, the Cherokee sold the land back to the federal government for $8.5 million—roughly $1.40 an acre. At noon on September 16, 1893, the government opened the land for settlement, triggering the largest land rush in US history. That day—known as the **Cherokee Strip Land Rush**—more than one hundred thousand would-be landowners raced on foot, horseback, in wagons, and on trains to claim forty thousand parcels of land. Enid has had a museum dedicated to the history of the Cherokee Strip since the early 1960s. First located on the campus of Phillips University, the museum moved to a new, larger building in 1975 and soon became an Oklahoma Historical Society property. The next expansion came in 1993 with the opening of the adjoining **Bill Humphrey Heritage Village**, a collection of historic structures that includes the only surviving US land office, where land run participants had to register their claims. In 2005 the Oklahoma Historical Society, the Sons and Daughters of the Cherokee Strip Pioneers Association, and the Phillips University Legacy Foundation partnered to create the **Cherokee Strip Regional Heritage Center** (507 4th St.; 580-237-1907), which opened in 2011.Two other **Cherokee Strip Museums** can be found in Alva (901 14th St.; 580-327-2030) and in Perry (2617 West Fir Ave.; 580-336-2405).

Geronimo, whose hard-resisted final surrender in 1886 finally ended the Indian Wars in the Southwest, had only been dead eight years when a company in Enid entered the fast-growing American automobile market. Unlike Henry Ford and many other early-day manufacturers of "motor cars," the Oklahoma car maker named their company and their new product after Geronimo. From 1917 to 1920 the company produced hundreds of four- and six-cylinder **Geronimos** that sold for $895 and $1,295. But before the brand had time to catch on, a fire gutted the factory, and the company went out of business. For decades antique car collectors thought none of the Oklahoma-made Geronimos had survived, but in 1972 someone discovered one sitting in a field in Kansas. The vintage Geronimo was restored and is on display at **George's Antique Car Museum** (508 South Grand St.; 405-242-6815). Though Geronimo the car has been mostly forgotten, Geronimo the Apache lives on as a Wild West legend.

Located in the old Santa Fe Railroad freight depot, the **Railroad Museum of Oklahoma** (702 North Washington St.; 580-233-3051), is operated by the Enid chapter of the National Railroad Historical

Association. The collection includes two rooms with working model railroads, railroad artifacts, a reference library, and sixteen pieces of vintage rolling stock.

Fort Gibson (Cherokee County)

Established in 1824 where the Arkansas, Grand, and Verdigris Rivers meet, a crossroads known as Three Forks, Fort Gibson was the first federal garrison in future Oklahoma. Troops occupying log buildings surrounded by a log stockade kept busy during the Indian removals of the 1830s and the post was a waypoint along the Texas Road. The army abandoned the fort in 1857 but reoccupied it during the Civil War. In 1890 the post was abandoned for the final time. The community of Fort Gibson, which developed near the fort, is considered Oklahoma's oldest town.

The federal Works Progress Administration reconstructed the old fort in 1937. With state and federal funds, the buildings and stockade were refurbished starting in 2013 and the **Fort Gibson National Historic Landmark** (907 North Garrison Ave.; 918-478-4088) reopened in 2016. A visitor's center in the old post commissary building on Garrison Hill has interpretive exhibits on the history of the fort. The Oklahoma Historical Society manages the fort as a state historic site.

Fort Towson (Choctaw County)

Technically it stood in Arkansas Territory, but for all practical purposes Fort Towson was in Texas. Established on the north bank of the Red River in 1824, the garrison lay just across the river from the Mexican province of Texas. The post became a waypoint for Anglo settlers on their way to Texas, which only twelve years later they would wrest away from Mexico. Key Texas figures like Stephen F. Austin, Sam Houston, and Davy Crockett all stopped at the fort on their way south. Relocated six miles farther north of the river to be above the flood plain, the fort saw the largest number of soldiers when it was used as a staging point from 1846 to 1847 during the Mexican War.

The post was abandoned in 1854 but was used for a time by Confederates during the Civil War. Only scattered remnants of stone foundations remained when the state of Oklahoma acquired the site in 1960. The ruins were stabilized and the post's sutler store was reconstructed to house the **Fort Towson Museum** (896 North 4375 Rd.; 580-873-2634) managed by the Oklahoma Historical Society.

Geary (Blaine and Canadian Counties)

Geary appeared on the Oklahoma map when the Rock Island Railroad came through western Oklahoma in 1898, but what happened near there thirty years earlier ties it to the Old West. On March 4, 1868, Jesse Chisholm died at Raven Spring, about eight miles east of what would become Geary. The man who gave the legendary Chisholm Trail its name, and helped blaze it, had been visiting an Arapaho chief named Left Hand when he fell ill. Chisholm's grave has been lost, but a red granite historical marker was placed at the approximate location. The **Jesse Chisholm Monument** (GPS coordinates: N35° 43.57', W98° 17.45') stands on a hill overlooking the north Canadian River off US 281 between Geary and Greenville.

Gene Autry (Carter County)

Gene Autry has not always been named for the famous cowboy crooner. C.C. Henderson founded the town in the 1880s, naming it Lou after his wife. For whatever reason, in November 1883 the name of the post office was changed to Dresden. When the Santa Fe Railroad came through in 1887, the town got its third name: Berwyn. In 1939, at the peak of his career as an entertainer, Gene Autry bought a 1,200-acre ranch just outside town and a couple of years later the community decided it was time to recognize the county's most famous property owner. Berwyn would officially become Gene Autry. Thousands came for the November 16, 1941, ceremony marking the name change, an event carried live on Autry's Melody Ranch radio program. Local officials believed Autry intended to make his home at the ranch, but the Japanese attack on Pearl Harbor changed all that. In 1942

Autry joined the military. After the war, having transitioned from movie making to business enterprises, Autry sold the ranch. But the town kept the name Gene Autry and now is home to the **Gene Autry Oklahoma Museum** (47 Prairie St.; 580-924-3276). Operated by a foundation, the museum covers Autry's life (he grew up in Oklahoma) and cowboys as stage or movie performers and is home to the world's largest private collection of vintage black-and-white B-Western movies and memorabilia connected to cowboys in entertainment.

Guthrie (Logan County)

Just a water-stop on the Santa Fe Railroad prior to the April 22, 1889, land rush, by nightfall that day Guthrie had become Oklahoma's largest city, albeit one of white canvas tents. With the organization of Oklahoma Territory in 1890, Guthrie became the capital and retained that status with statehood in 1907. Three years later, however, voters elected to move the seat of government to Oklahoma City and Guthrie nearly became a ghost town.

Guthrie may have lost its status as capital, but it remains one of the Old West's best-preserved collections of Victorian architecture. The National Register of Historic Places lists 2,169 structures over a 1,400-acre downtown that is the largest contiguous historical district in the nation.

Built in 1892 with private capital and leased out as a federal prison, a two-story sandstone and brick lockup located at the northeast corner of the intersection of 2nd and Noble Streets was often referred to by criminals as the **Black Jail**. With nineteen-inch walls and state-of-the-art cell blocks, the facility was proudly touted as escape-proof by its builders. Arkansas-born outlaw and former Dalton gang member **Bill Doolin** (1858–1896) disproved that assertion on July 5, 1896, when he and more than a dozen other inmates broke out. After the government abandoned the building, a church held services there until the 1970s. A religious cult occupied the property until 1995 when the state's Department of Human Services took the old building and used it for low-rent housing. Now privately owned, the former territorial prison stands vacant and deteriorating, though a new roof has been added as a first step toward future renovation.

Previous to his stay in the Black Jail, Doolin had moved on from the Dalton gang and went on to organize his own outlaw cabal. He and his cronies specialized in bank robbery until deputy US Marshal Bill Tilghman arrested him in Eureka Springs, Arkansas. After escaping the Black Jail, Doolin remained on the lam until cornered on August 25, 1896, on a farm near Lawson. A seven-man posse led by another noted federal officer, Heck Thomas, had tracked him down. When the outlaw opted for shooting over surrender, Thomas cut loose on him with a shotgun. Counting rifle fire from deputy Bill Dunn, Doolin ended up with twenty holes in him. That made for one of the Wild West's most iconic photographs, a postmortem image of the outlaw on an undertaker's slab taken by a Guthrie photographer. To help defray funeral expenses, the outlaw's widow wrote a poem about her late husband and had it printed on cards that she sold for a quarter along with a print of her late husband's death photo. Doolin's grave, under a red-granite tombstone, is in Section 1000, better known as **Boot Hill**, in **Summit View Cemetery** (1808 North Pine St.; 405-282-0064).

A former associate of Doolin, **Richard "Little Dick" West** was laying low, working on a farm near Guthrie when he tried to recruit his boss for a train robbery. The farmer's wife told a friend in Guthrie, who told another lady whose husband was county district clerk. He in turn notified the US Marshal's Office and soon two of the West's more famous lawmen—Heck Thomas and Bill Tilghman—rode with three other officers (plus Thomas' son) to the farm eager to "harvest" West. When they confronted the outlaw outside a barn, he started shooting at the officers, but it turned out the deputies were better marksmen. The shootout took place April 13, 1898. West was buried not far from Doolin in the **Summit View Cemetery**.

Future Western movie star Tom Mix tended bar at the **Blue Bell Saloon** (224 West Harrison; 405-466-8400) from 1902 to 1904. The two-story brick building, dating from 1889, which hosted a bordello called Miss Lizzie's on the second floor, was renovated in 2012 and reopened as a restaurant. A historical marker on the brick sidewalk in front of the building relates its history and the fact that one of its best customers had been **Temple Houston**, the colorful Woodward attorney who was Sam Houston's son.

When Guthrie's public library moved into a new building in the early 1970s, the 1902-vintage **Carnegie Library** for a time stood vacant. But local history lovers thought their city needed a museum, and a $350,000 donation by area farmer-rancher Fred Pfeiffer in memory of his wife and brother funded a two-story addition to the old library for use as the **Oklahoma Territorial Museum** (406 East Oklahoma Ave.; 405-282-1889). Opened in 1974, the museum documents land usage in Oklahoma from the arrival of the first reservation Indians during what came to be known as the Trail of Tears up through the land rushes that opened much of the area to settlement. The museum also has an exhibit devoted to noted outlaws Bill Doolin and Belle Starr as well as the deputy US marshals who played such a vital part in bringing law and order to the territory. Another display tells the story of bad man mummy Elmer McCurdy (see sidebar).

The Dummy Was a Mummy

Thirty-one-year-old bank and train robber Elmer McCurdy died in a shootout with law enforcement officers on October 7, 1911, at Okesa in Osage County. His body was taken to a funeral home in Pawhuska, Oklahoma, where the owner infused it with arsenic (a practice that became illegal in 1922) and waited for relatives to claim the remains and, more importantly, pay him for his services. When no one showed up, the undertaker stuck a rifle in McCurdy's hands and put the body on display, charging a nickel a look. The mortician eventually sold the well-preserved remains and McCurdy embarked on a new career as a carnival sideshow attraction.

With the passage of time, the belief arose that McCurdy (having changed hands numerous times) was just a wax dummy, not a real outlaw. Following his accidental rediscovery in 1976 at a Long Beach, California, amusement venue, forensic experts and Oklahoma historians confirmed he was McCurdy and his remains were returned to Guthrie for burial. Some three hundred people showed up for his graveside services on April 22, 1977. Just to make sure he stayed put this time, two feet of concrete was poured over his coffin before the grave was covered. McCurdy's grave is in the **Boot Hill** section of **Summit View Cemetery** (1808 North Pine St.; 405-282-0064), next to outlaw Bill Doolin's final resting place.

Ingalls (Payne County)

No longer even on the Oklahoma highway map, the ghost town of Ingalls had more residents than Stillwater in the 1890s. But lacking a rail connection, and not being on the way to anywhere, it went nowhere as a town. It might have been completely forgotten had it not been for what happened there in the late summer of 1893.

Arizona's famed OK Corral gunfight was not the only gunpowder "gala" in which the letters "OK" figured. On September 1, 1893, tipped that federal officers intended to descend on Ingalls to round up the Dalton gang, the outlaws got their horses ready and played poker in Ransom's Saloon until the lawmen arrived, concealed in two covered wagons. The wanted men made it out of town in a flurry of gunfire that left two of them with minor wounds. An ailing "Arkansas Tom" Jones was too sick to escape, but he was not so ill as to impair his shooting. From his second-floor room in the **OK Hotel**, he shot and killed three of the marshals. One innocent bystander was killed, and three townspeople wounded. Bill Dalton's horse also died in the shootout.

Ingalls is eight miles east of Stillwater off State Highway 51, on the south side of the roadway. A stone marker at the approximate spot that one of the gunfight victims fell stands on Ash Street near the volunteer fire department. Placed there in 1938, the monument's bronze plaque was later stolen, but a replacement was added in the 1990s. The ghost town is a National Historical Site.

Kingfisher (Kingfisher County)

Kingfisher Station was only a remote stagecoach stop along the Chisholm Trail until April 22, 1889, the day the government opened the Cherokee Strip for settlement. When a pistol shot started the land rush at noon on the big day, claims staked in the vicinity of the station developed as two separate townsites, Lisbon and Kingfisher. The communities later merged as Kingfisher. The famous cattle trail was no longer being used, but it still had an impact on the day of the run. Over the years, hundreds of thousands of cattle, along with horses and wagons, had worn deep ruts across the prairie. Unfortunately for the thousands making the land run, a wet spring filled the old trail with high grass that concealed its footprint. Consequently, some horses suffered broken legs. The sudden drop also wrecked wagons and buggies.

The **Chisholm Trail Museum** (605 Zellers Ave.; 405-375-5176) is the nearby, architecturally distinct, three-story mansion built by Abraham Jefferson Seay, the third governor of Oklahoma Territory, in 1892. Several other restored historic structures are also part of the museum complex. ***Ambassador of the Plains***, a bronze statue of Jesse Chisholm astride a horse stands on a large stone base at the intersection of US 81 and State Highway 33 downtown.

Emmett Dalton

Though wounded, Emmett Dalton survived the wild twelve-minute gun battle that broke out when he and two of his older brothers tried to rob both of Coffeyville, Kansas's, banks on October 5, 1892. (It's often reported that Dalton sustained twenty-three gunshot wounds that day, and while that's technically correct, most of those wounds were from shotgun pellets.) Following his release from prison in the fall of 1907, Dalton wrote two books about the exploits of the Dalton gang and produced a movie on the Caldwell shootout. The movie was a flop, but he did well in real estate and the construction business. He died in 1937 at sixty-six of natural causes in Los Angeles. His remains were cremated and later buried in the Dalton family plot in **Kingfisher Cemetery** (14214 State Highway 3), at the intersection of North 2830 Road and State Highway 33. His mother, Adeline Lee Younger Dalton (1835–1925), and other Dalton family members are also buried here.

Lake Eufaula (McIntosh County)

Belle Starr, having done time for horse theft, lived in a cabin at Younger's Bend along the North Canadian River with her son and whatever man she happened to be married to or seeing at the time. Though she had no trouble making male friends, she had at least one enemy. On February 3, 1889, someone armed with a scattergun lay in ambush for her. When she rode into range, he blew her off her horse and she would not be getting back up. While more outlaw associate than outlaw, in death Starr was transformed by the *Police Gazette* and sensational newspaper articles into the "Bandit Queen." No one was ever charged with her murder, though historians believe it was either a neighbor who feared Belle would expose him as a murderer or her own son, whom she had recently whipped for mistreating a horse. Shortly after Starr's burial, her grave was robbed and vandalized. Belle's daughter, Pearl, then a high-class Fort Smith, Arkansas, madam, used some of her bordello income to commission a tombstone featuring an engraved bell, a horse, and a star. In addition, she composed this epitaph: "Shed not for her the bitter tear, Nor give the heart to vain regret; 'Tis but the casket that lies here, The gem that filled it sparkles yet."

Starr's grave is on private property 1.1 miles east of Lake Eufaula Dam (2910 State Highway 71, Porum). In 2010 the property owner restored the grave. The nearby cabin Starr lived in prior to her murder was razed in 1933, and only remnants of the stone foundation remain. The property owner allows visitors, but requests they come only during daylight hours, not during hunting season, and not on Halloween. A state historical marker (GPS coordinates: N35° 18.07', W95° 20.37') giving the history of Younger's Bend stands off State Highway 71.

A life-sized bronze statue of Starr created by artist Joe Mora in 1929 stands outside the Woolaroc Museum near Bartlesville.

Lawton (Comanche County)

Promoted early on as the only town to ever begin already having twenty-five thousand residents, Lawton came into existence in 1901 with Oklahoma's last land rush. Soon after both the Santa Fe and Frisco Railroads began serving the city. With its rich Kiowa, Apache, and Comanche heritage, Lawton is considered one of the most diverse communities in the US. It is also home to one of the nation's largest and oldest military posts. **Lawton Fort Sill Convention and Visitor's Bureau** (302 West Gore Blvd.; 580-355-3541) has a visitor's guide, maps, and brochures on local historic sites and other attractions.

Established in 1869 just below the Wichita Mountains in southwestern Oklahoma on a site selected by Gen. William T. Sherman, **Fort Sill** was one of the most strategically important cavalry posts on the Southern Plains during the Indian Wars. Its troops participated in the Red River War of 1874–1876 that finally subdued the Comanches and later guarded the adjoining Kiowa, Comanche, Apache, and Wichita Indian reservations. Fort Sill continues in operation as an artillery training installation, the third-largest US Army post in the nation.

Considered the best-preserved of all the Indian War–era military posts, Fort Sill has fifty historic buildings around its quadrangle, two museums relating to the fort's history, and one museum dedicated to the story of army field artillery. Non-military personnel must check in at the Fort Sill Visitor Control Center (T6701 Sheridan Rd.; 580-442-9603). Civilians need to fill out a one-page form and show some form of legal identification. After a security check, visitors are issued passes allowing access to the post at the Sheridan Road gate.

General Sherman's Close Call

Only one general died violently in the line of duty during the Indian Wars, but if not for a deflected arrow Gen. William T. Sherman might have become the second. It happened not in an ambush or battle, but on the front porch of Fort Sill commander Col. Benjamin Grierson's quarters. The close call came as the army's highest-ranking officer personally saw to the arrest of three Kiowa headmen responsible for the May 18, 1871, attack on a wagon train in Texas that left seven teamsters dead and mutilated.

Learning that Satank, Santana, and Big Tree had openly boasted of the raid after returning to the Fort Sill Kiowa reservation, the general devised a plan to get the three men back to Texas to face murder charges. Since the military had no authority on the reservation, Sherman had the civilian Indian agent inform tribal leaders that he wished to have a council with them at Grierson's quarters. When the Kiowas showed up, Sherman intended to question the three men and, if satisfied that they were involved in the raid, have them taken into custody. To that end, he hid soldiers inside the residence and had three squads of cavalry on standby, but out of view, at strategic points near the house.

Sherman, Grierson, an interpreter, subordinate officers, and soldiers were gathered on the front porch of Grierson's quarters when the three Kiowa headmen arrived along with other tribal leaders, including Kicking Bear, Lone Wolf, and Stumbling Bear. Kicking Bear brought rifles, pistols, and bows and arrows, which he distributed to the other Kiowa leaders. After hearing that Sherman intended to send Satank, Santana, and Big Tree back to Texas, an enraged Stumbling Bear notched an arrow and pulled back his bow clearly intending to sink a barbed shaft into Sherman's chest. Just as he released the draw string someone grabbed his arm and the arrow flew off target. Grierson signaled for the concealed troops to emerge and the three Indians were restrained and manacled without further incident. Twelve days later, the three prisoners left under escort for Texas. Not far from the post, Satank tried to escape and was killed. Santana and Big

Tree stood trial, were found guilty of murder, and were sent to the state prison in Huntsville.

Long since known as the **Sherman House**, the 1871 post commander's quarters still stand on the fort's quadrangle. The historic one-and-a-half story structure (the military designates it as Hamilton Road Building 422) continues as the residence for the post's top officer and his family. It is not open to the public but can be seen from outside.

One of the Wild West's most gripping sagas is represented by two graves in the **Fort Sill Post Cemetery**. On May 19, 1836, a band of Comanches attacked a log-walled compound in central east Texas known as **Fort Parker**. The Indians captured several children, including nine-year-old Cynthia Ann Parker. She later adapted to Comanche ways and became the wife of Chief Pete Nocona. Their son, Quanah, would become the last great chief of the Comanches. The story is told in numerous non-fiction books and novels, and was the basis of the John Wayne classic movie *The Searchers*. Recaptured by Texas Rangers in 1860 in an operation that took the life of Chief Nocona, Cynthia Ann never readjusted and died in 1871. While the chief's final resting place is unknown, his wife was buried in Anderson County, Texas. In 1910 Quanah had her remains removed to Post Oak Mission Cemetery on the Comanche reservation outside Fort Sill. When Quanah died in 1911, he was buried next to his mother.

An expansion of Fort Sill in 1957 necessitated the relocation of Post Oak Mission Cemetery and Quanah's remains were exhumed and reburied in the Post Cemetery. His mother's remains, ceremonially escorted by Texas Rangers, also were removed and reinterred adjacent to her son's new grave.

Quanah's epitaph is poetry in stone:

Here Until Day Break And Shadows Fall And Darkness Disappears Is Quanah Parker Chief Of The Comanches Born - 1852 Died Feb 23, 1911.

Two other notable burials are those of Kicking Bird and Geronimo.

On the morning of May 3, 1875, **Chief Kicking Bird** emerged from his teepee on the bank of Cache Creek, bathed in its waters, and had a cup of coffee. A short time later, only forty years old, he collapsed and died. The popular story is that someone in his own tribe, possibly one of his wives or a malevolent medicine man, poisoned him. Certainly no shortage of people had a motive to murder the chief. The government had compelled him to decide which of his tribesmen should be imprisoned at Fort Marion, Georgia, for participating in the 1874–1875 Kiowa uprising, and those he selected had been shipped out only the day before. A more prosaic possibility is that he suffered a stress-induced heart attack, having complained the night before that "his heart felt . . . like someone had a hold of it pulling it out."

Chief Kicking Bird's grave is in the Fort Sill Post Cemetery (Section 4, Grave 1078B) in an area known as Chief's Knoll, just east of where Quanah Parker would later be laid to rest. The graves of fifteen significant Indian headmen are in this area.

The seventy-nine-year-old Apache **Chief Geronimo** died February 17, 1909, of pneumonia and was buried at Fort Sill. Whether he rests in peace—or pieces—became a matter of contention in the early 1980s when Ned Anderson, then chairman of the San Carlos Apache Nation in Arizona, began an effort to have Geronimo reburied in his ancestral homeland. That generated nation-wide publicity and inspired a particularly bizarre story. Anderson received an anonymous letter reporting that Geronimo's grave had been robbed and his skull removed during World War I by six Fort Sill soldiers—all members of Yale University's Order of the Skull and Bones, a secret society founded in 1832. Though generally dismissed as a hoax, the stolen skull story led to a federal lawsuit in 2008 seeking to recover the skull (if it indeed had been taken) and have the chief's remains removed to his native New Mexico. Two years later the lawsuit was dismissed on a technicality.

Today, Chief Geronimo lies beneath a stone pyramid in the **Apache Cemetery** on the Fort Sill military reservation (GPS coordinates: N34° 41.79', W98° 22.25').

Founded by the Comanche County Historical Society, the **Museum of the Great Plains** (601 Northwest Ferris Ave.; 580-581-3460) opened in 1962, with an additional twenty-five thousand square feet of exhibit space added in 1997. Now operated as a public trust by the non-profit Museum of the Great Plains Authority, the museum focuses on the people, animals, and things that shaped the history of the Great Plains and Lawton—the Indians, the buffalo, cattlemen, farmers, and town builders. The influence of everything from barbed wire and windmills to newspapers is also shown.

In 1902, two years after the end of his illustrious career as a deputy US marshal, Heck Thomas became Lawton's first police chief. He reigned as the city's top cop until his health began to fail in 1909. The Museum of the Great Plains displays the two badges Thomas wore during his time in Lawton. One showed he was city police chief, the other identified him as chief of the volunteer fire department. The archives maintained at the museum by the Institute of the Great Plains have a substantial Thomas collection. The lawman died of Bright's disease on August 14, 1912, at the age of sixty-two and was buried in **Highland Cemetery** (2201 Northwest Fort Sill Blvd.).

Comanche national leadership had discussed the need for a museum for twenty years before obtaining a National Endowment for the Humanities grant in 2000 to develop one. The **Comanche National Museum and Cultural Center** (701 Northwest Ferris Ave.; 580-353-0404), covering the history of the Comanche people, their twentieth-century role as code talkers during World War II, and their religion, opened in 2007. The museum has more than three thousand artifacts and the largest collection of Comanche art in the world.

Mangum (Greer County)

For thirty-six years all of what are now the Oklahoma counties of Greer, Harmon, and Jackson, plus the southern half of Beckham County, were part of Texas. Created by the Texas legislature in 1860, Greer County, Texas, covered more than 1.5 million acres, an area larger than Rhode Island and Delaware combined. Many of Greer

County's early settlers came from elsewhere in the Lone Star State and by one estimate, at least half of Greer County, Oklahoma's, current residents have Texas ancestry. One of those settlers was A.S. Mangum, who, in 1882, donated the land for a townsite named in his honor.

The well-worn Western Cattle Trail cut through the county and Texas Rangers provided law enforcement. But Texas's claim to Greer County, based on its belief that the north fork of the Red River constituted the boundary between Texas and what is now Oklahoma, led to a lawsuit that went all the way to the US Supreme Court before being decided against Texas in 1896. Proof enough of the complicated nature of the land dispute is the length of the lawsuit—1,400 pages.

Mangum's Border-McGregor Hospital handled the medical needs of the people of Greer County for more than six decades. The hospital moved to a new facility in 1967, and in the early 1970s the three-story brick building became the home of the **Old Greer County Museum and Hall of Fame** (222 West Jefferson St.; 580-471-9917). Each of the museum's sixty-plus rooms holds either artifacts or archival material related to the history of what the local newspaper still calls "The Empire of Old Greer County." The Hall of Fame is a unique outdoor memorial adjacent to the museum with scores of engraved pink granite slabs dedicated to the county's pre-1907 pioneers. Each marker bears an image of the individual followed by a brief biographical sketch.

Marlow (Stephens County)

Dr. Wilson Williamson Marlow and wife Martha Jane, kin to Daniel Boone, homesteaded in what is now Stephens County in the early 1880s. The physician offered his services to cowboys pushing cattle up the nearby Chisholm Trail and augmented his medical practice by farming. The Marlows' five sons, George, Charlie, Alfred, Lewellyn, and Boone, gathered and sold wild horses, a business model they soon modified by stealing someone else's horses. Or at least that's what some people said. The doctor died in 1885, three years before his boys violently earned their place in Wild West history down in Texas. No matter how his sons turned out, when a town was laid out near the former Marlow place in 1891, the community was named in his honor.

The original Marlow family home no longer stands, but it is believed to have been just north of present **Redbud Park** (112 North Elm St.), where a large red granite marker erected in 1998 tells what became of the Marlow boys. Local legend, supported by some early newspaper articles, has it that the Marlow boys used a cave along Wild Horse Creek as a hideout. However, there is no known "smoking gun" connecting them to the cave. No one even knew of the cave until 2004, when a Marlow city worker discovered it accidentally. The cave is located just northwest of Redbud Park and maintained by the city. It is open to visitors.

The **Marlow Area Museum** (127 West Main St.; 580-658-2212), has an exhibit on the Marlow brothers. The starkest artifact related to the Marlows is the original tombstone of Alfred, Boone, and Lewellyn. Their mother and other women in the family carved the lettering in the stone.

Muskogee (Muskogee County)

Merle Haggard's 1969 country western classic "Okie From Muskogee" made Muskogee a household word across the nation, but it was the **Missouri, Kansas, and Texas Railroad** (nicknamed the Katy) that put the town on the map. Building from Kansas toward Texas, in the fall of 1871 Katy track layers reached a point just above the Arkansas River before having to stop so a bridge could be built across the river. During the three months that took, a tent town flourished at the end of the line. In addition to rail workers, the camp swarmed with whiskey peddlers, professional gamblers, and prostitutes, as well as more traditional businesspeople. Once the river had been spanned, in January the railroad built a depot three miles south of the Arkansas and named it for the Muskogee (Creek) Indians. In 1889 a federal court was seated there. Ten years later Muskogee was incorporated.

In the early 1870s, the federal government opened the Union Agency of the Five Civilized Tribes to centralize services for the Cherokee, Choctaw, Creek, Chickasaw, and Seminoles, the tribes removed from their Southeastern homelands in the 1820s and 1830s. Those tribes, though they had varying cultures, were referred to as "civilized" because the members seemed to be assimilating to American ways, from developing written languages and adopting a republican form of government to practicing Christianity. Initially each of the tribes had their own Bureau of Indian Affairs agency except the Chickasaws and Choctaws, who shared an agency. Construction began in the summer of 1875 on a two-story sandstone building to house the new entity. When it was completed, the agency superintendent and his family occupied the second floor with the ground floor serving as the agency headquarters.

After the agency ceased operations, the building saw various uses until the 1940s, when it fell into disrepair. In 1951 the Da-Co-Ta Indian Club developed a museum in the building, an effort that culminated in its opening in 1966. Listed on the National Register of Historic Places, the **Five Civilized Tribes Museum** (1101 Honor Heights Dr.; 918-683-1701) is devoted to the history and culture of the five tribes that are such an integral part of the Oklahoma story.

The life of famed African-American lawman Bass Reeves, who served as a deputy US marshal and closed out his long and legendary career as a Muskogee police officer from 1907 to 1909 is honored at the **Three Rivers Museum** (named for the nearby Arkansas, Neosho, and Verdigris Rivers), housed in the 1916 Mission Valley Railroad Depot (220 Elgin St.; 918-686-6624). The museum opened in 1998 and is operated by the Muskogee Historic Preservation Commission. Reeves is buried in **Union Agency Cemetery** (GPS coordinates: N35° 47.44', W95° 24.04'), 1.5 miles east of Fern Mountain, just east of US 69. The grave is unmarked but in the 1990s the since-disbanded Oklahombres organization placed a small stone for him in the general vicinity of his burial place. Though located on public property, private land must be crossed to get to the cemetery, which has not been used since 1930 and is poorly maintained.

Norman (Cleveland County)

A prank pulled by a surveying party member in 1870 is behind the name of the state's third-largest city. The man in charge was Kentuckian **Abner E. Norman**. At one of their camps in what is now the central part of the state, for whatever insider reason, one of his underlings peeled bark from a large elm and branded the words "Norman's Camp" into the tree. The tree is long gone, but the place name stuck, minus the "Camp" part.

Settlement in Norman began with the Oklahoma land run of April 22, 1889. And in what may have been a law enforcement first, on one occasion the town marshal had to deputize twenty able-bodied men to pick up a newly constructed frame building and carry it to another lot, its original location having been deemed in violation of a city ordinance.

When the University of Oklahoma was established by the territorial legislature in 1890, Norman was designed as its home. Today, the university's library has one of the nation's largest collections of vintage photographs and archival material related to the Old West. OU's **Western History Collection** (630 Parrington Oval; 405-325-3641) is on the university campus.

The **Fred Jones Jr. Museum of Art** (555 East Elm Ave.; 405-325-3272) has one of the nation's most significant collections of American Indian and Southwestern art.

The **Jacobson House Native Art Center** (609 Chautauqua Ave.; 405-366-1667) is located in the former residence of Swedish-born Oscar Jacobson, who put together a major collection of Kiowa and other American Indian art.

The **Moore-Lindsay Historic House Museum** (508 North Peters Ave.; 405-321-0156) occupies a Queen Anne Victorian–style home built in 1899 and focuses on the history of Cleveland County.

Oklahoma City (Oklahoma County)

Most western states settled town by town, city by city, county by county. But not Oklahoma. At noon on April 22, 1889, the federal government opened to settlement roughly two million acres known as the Unassigned Lands and tens of thousands of people rushed in to claim homesteads. Two years earlier, the Southern Kansas Railroad had established a water stop and depot near the North Canadian River in central Oklahoma called Oklahoma Station. Overnight the land around the railroad stop became a city of more than five thousand. In 1910, three years after Oklahoma gained statehood, the capital was moved from Guthrie to Oklahoma City.

Nothing like the sudden availability of a couple of million acres of free land to inspire disagreements over ownership. By 1891 enough claim disputes had piled up since the 1889 land rush for President Benjamin Harrison to appoint a special land commissioner to settle the issues. That person was William Harn who, with his wife Alice, moved to Oklahoma City and got to work. When her husband's appointment ended two years later, Mrs. Harn assumed they would be moving back to Ohio, but William wanted to stay. Being a professional dispute resolver, he told his wife that if she agreed to remain in Oklahoma, he'd build her a fine home. She accepted the deal and within a few years they lived in an elegant Victorian house on a 160-acre farm. In addition to farming, Harn invested in real estate and did well at it. After Oklahoma became a state and the seat of government moved to Oklahoma City, Harn donated half the land—forty acres—for the new state house. The couple stayed in their house for the rest of their lives and Mrs. Harn's niece lived there until 1967. That year she donated the property to Oklahoma City, and the **Harn Homestead** (1721 North Lincoln Blvd.; 405-235-4058) became a museum and living history venue operated by a non-profit group.

The largest museum in the state, the **Oklahoma History Center** (800 Nazih Zuhdi Dr.; 405-521-2491) is just across from the state's capitol. With four permanent galleries, the 215,000-square-foot museum focuses on all aspects of Oklahoma's past, including its rich American Indian heritage, the land rushes, outlaws and lawmen on up to the modern era. As the state's travel website proclaims, the center "is the preeminent destination for those seeking a key to Oklahoma's historical wealth and an excellent one-stop-shop experience for both the novice and advanced historian."

Founded in 1955, the **National Cowboy and Western Heritage Museum** (1700 Northeast 63rd St.; 405-478-2250) has a world-renowned collection of more than twenty-eight thousand Western artifacts and art. Galleries are devoted to Native Americans and their art, Western expansion, cowboys, rodeos, Western performers, and more.

Opened in 2000, the **Oklahoma Railway Museum** (3400 Northeast Grand Blvd.; 405-424-8222) has a large collection of vintage rolling stock and a restored Kansas City, Mexico, and Orient Railroad depot built in Oakwood, Oklahoma, in 1905.

The Man Who Killed the Man Who Killed Jesse James

Missouri-born **Joseph "Joe" Grant Burnett** (1867–1917) joined the Oklahoma City Police Department as a patrolman in 1901. On January 13, 1904, he said hello to a man and ended up in a desperate fight for his life.

Edward "Red" Kelley (1857–1904) did ten years of a ninety-nine-year-sentence for shotgunning Bob Ford, the man who killed Jesse James. Following his release from prison in Colorado in 1900, Kelley went to Oklahoma City. The twentieth century had begun, but Oklahoma City's tenderloin was as rough as any of its nineteenth-century Wild West predecessors. Naturally, that's where Kelley hung out. In January 1904 Kelley became offended after being stopped and questioned by a police officer. Nothing came of it, but Kelley didn't think the man who killed the man who killed Jesse James should be treated that way.

The next day, January 13, a different officer, Joe Burnett, was walking his beat in the red-light district when he saw Kelley and politely said hello. A man of extremely ill temperament, Kelley drew a pistol with evident intent to kill the policeman. Burnett grabbed Kelley's wrist trying to get his gun and that triggered a vicious, running fight. Kelley fired several times at the officer who was too busy tussling with him to pull his own weapon. Kelley kept missing but the muzzle blasts set Burnett's clothes on fire. Then Kelley started biting Burnett, excising chunks of flesh. Finally a bystander ran to the officer's assistance and Burnett was able to get his revolver out and fatally shoot his attacker.

Kelley was buried in an unmarked grave in **Fairlawn Cemetery** (2700 North Shartel St.; 405-524-2559). The Oklahoma Outlaw and Lawman Association later placed a flat stone at the site, and a larger monument was subsequently added. Burnett, the man who killed the man who killed Jesse James, is buried in the same cemetery. Outlaw-lawman Joe Horner, alias Frank Canton (1849–1927) is also buried in Fairlawn.

Okmulgee (Okmulgee County)

Since 1868 Okmulgee—the Creek word for "bubbling water"—has been the headquarters of the Muskogee (Creek) Nation. For decades tribal leaders met in a council house that still stands. The community changed drastically in 1907 with the discovery of oil nearby and the boom that followed. In addition to that seismic shift, Oklahoma also became a state that year.

The old council house, built in 1878 and used until 1906, is now the **Creek Council House Museum** (106 West 6th St.; 918-756–6172). Capped by a wooden cupola, the two-story stone structure underwent major renovation in 1993 with more work done in 2017.

Pawnee (Pawnee County)

Beginning in 1873 the Pawnee Tribe was moved by the federal government from their Nebraska homelands to Indian Territory. After the opening of the Cherokee Outlet in 1893, promoters laid out the town of Pawnee near the Pawnee Indian Agency and boarding school. The town developed as an agricultural center after getting its first rail connection in 1902.

Pawnee Bill

Born in Illinois, Gordon W. Lillie (1860–1942) came to Kansas with his family in 1875 and soon became friendly with the Pawnee people, then being removed to a reservation in Indian Territory. Lillie had learned the Pawnee language and later taught at the Pawnee agency, also serving as interpreter-secretary for the Indian agent. In 1883, by then nicknamed **Pawnee Bill**, he joined Buffalo Bill Cody's newly organized Wild West show as an interpreter for its Pawnee performers. Five years later and newly married, Lillie formed his own show, Pawnee Bill's Wild West. The venture failed, but he soon went back on the road with an exhibition he called Pawnee Bill's Historical Wild West, Indian Museum and Encampment. In 1908 he merged his production with Buffalo Bill's show, a venture renamed Buffalo Bill's Wild West and Pawnee Bill's Great Far East. Lillie made his living selling the past, but as a businessman he stayed in the present and looked to the future. He profited in oil, banking, and real estate. Realizing the growing importance of motor vehicle transportation, he promoted the development of US 64 in Oklahoma. He also worked to help save the buffalo.

Pawnee Bill Ranch and Museum (1141 Pawnee Bill Rd.; 918-762-2513) is composed of the five-hundred-acre **Lillie Ranch**, where he based his traveling Wild West show, the fourteen-room Lillie mansion, the ranch's original blacksmith shop, a 1903 log cabin, a large barn, and an Indian flower shrine. Lillie is buried in the Lillie family mausoleum at **Highland Cemetery** (State Highway 18 at E0450 Road).

Perkins (Payne County)

The community that became Perkins began less than a month after the 1889 land rush when an application for a forty-acre townsite was filed at the land office in Guthrie. That town was to be called Cimarron, but approval was delayed because not enough people claimed lots. A few months later an application was filed for a town at the same location that would be named Italy, but when the new town got a post office, it was named Perkins for the congressman who pushed through the necessary legislation. Soon townspeople wanted more—county seat status. To that end, an armed delegation descended on Stillwater and attempted to seize the county records and take them to Perkins. A larger number of armed men rebuffed the attempt and Stillwater is still the county seat. Later, Perkins tried to get the territory's newly authorized Agriculture and Mechanical College (now Oklahoma State University) but that, too, went to Stillwater.

Opened as part of the Oklahoma statehood centennial celebration, the six-acre **Oklahoma Territorial Plaza** (750 North Main St.; 405-547-2777) features two twelve-foot statutes by sculptor Wayne Cooper, one of Frank "Pistol Pete" Eaton, and the other of Iowa Indian Chief Nachineninga. Three historic structures moved from their original locations to the site include Eaton's restored 1900 residence, a 1901 log cabin, and a 1907 barn. Eaton is buried in **Perkins Cemetery** (525 West Knipe Ave.). The **Iowa tribal headquarters** (335588 750 Rd.; 405-547-2402) is three miles south of Perkins.

Ponca City (Kaw County)

With the opening of the Cherokee Outlet, Michigan furniture plant owner Burton Barnes sold out and came south to found New Ponca City on September 16, 1893. (The Indian agency at the Ponca reservation was known as Ponca.) New Ponca was incorporated two months later and by January 1894 had a post office. What it did not have was a railroad connection. Residents of the new town had to travel a mile to the town of Cross to catch a train. Barnes and others began a campaign to convince the Santa Fe Railroad to open a depot at New Ponca and they succeeded. Cross faded and New Ponca City grew. Twenty years after its founding, the "New" had worn off the town's name and from then on it was simply Ponca City.

101 Ranch

George Washington Miller registered the now famous 101 as a brand in Kansas in 1881, but when the Cherokee Outlet opened in 1893, he established a ranch called the 101 southwest of New Ponca City. The same year, the nation slid into a financial depression only exceeded in severity by the Great Depression of the 1930s. To survive, Colonel Miller diversified by growing wheat, corn, alfalfa, and other crops. When the economy recovered, the **101 Ranch** remained in business. After their father's death in 1903 sons Joe, George, and Zack Miller took over management of the 101, which at its high point was a farming and ranching operation covering 110,000 acres of owned and leased land.

In 1905 the 101 staged a Western exposition and rodeo for hundreds of newspaper editors gathered in Oklahoma for their association's annual convention. The show went so well, and got so much publicity, that the Miller brothers began a traveling production called the **101 Wild West Show**. The ranch also pioneered in the making of Western movies. The silent films and the Wild West show further contributed to the already growing Old West mythology and opened the figurative livestock chute for performers like Tom Mix; bulldogger Bill Pickett; and a cowboy, comedian philosopher named Will Rogers.

The 101 made it through the 1893 depression, but not the next financial downturn. The 101 Wild West Show ended in 1932 and the ranch went out of business four years later. After failing, the 101 Ranch was divided into smaller parcels and sold.

In 1973 the site of the former ranch headquarters was listed on the National Register of Historic Places and two years later accorded National Historic Landmark status. A non-profit foundation acquired eighty-two acres of the old headquarters in 1976. Before the few surviving ranch structures could undergo planned restoration, they were lost when the nearby Salt Fork River flooded. The last remaining building, a ranch store built in 1918, was destroyed by fire in 1987. All that remains at the site, thirteen miles south of Ponca City off State Highway 156, is the massive concrete foundation of the once-expansive Miller residence (called the White House), two silos, and a few other foundations and remnants. Just south of the river is **Cowboy Hill**, the cemetery where Zack Miller (1877–1952) is buried, along with former 101 cowboys. Farther down State Highway 156, one mile north of the Marland community is **Monument Hill**, burial site of Bill Pickett (c. 1870–1932). Rising fifteen feet from the top of the hill is a round cairn built by the Miller brothers as a monument to Ponca chief White Eagle. A white stone eagle sits atop it. The Oklahoma legislature designated State Highway 156 as the 101 Ranch Memorial Road.

When someone suggested to Ponca City oil man and future Oklahoma governor E.W. Marland that he commission a monument to the vanishing American, a Ponca, Otoe, or Osage Indian, the wealthy former Pennsylvanian replied, "The Indian is not the vanishing American, it's the pioneer woman." While that could have been argued either way, in 1927 Marland commissioned a dozen artists from the US and abroad to submit three-foot models of a statue honoring pioneer women. When completed, the miniatures were exhibited in twelve cities across the nation for public input. Reserving the final decision for himself, Marland selected ***Confident***, the piece sculpted by British artist Bryant Baker. Dedicated April 22, 1930 (the forty-first anniversary of the 1889 land rush), the statue depicting a bonneted pioneer woman holding her son's hand weighs six tons and is seventeen feet tall. On its stone base, the work Marland paid $300,000 for rises thirty-three feet, Oklahoma's tallest statue. The **Pioneer Woman Museum** (701 Monument Rd.; 580-765-6108), opened in 1958 and expanded in 1996, is directly across the street from the statue.

Begun in 1925 and completed three years later, the **E.W. Marland Mansion** (901 Monument Rd.) sits on thirty-four acres and is a huge (3 stories, 55 rooms, 43,561 square feet) artifact of Oklahoma's oil boom era, but there is a Wild West tie in that Marland funded Ponca's Pioneer Woman statue.

Marland's first Ponca City residence, known as the **Marland Grand House** (1000 Grand Ave.; 580-767-0420) was completed in 1916. The restored two-story house now exhibits an extensive 101 Ranch collection on the first floor and a large collection of Native American artifacts upstairs.

A committee of Ponca tribal and local leaders met in 1993 to plan for a center dedicated to the history and culture of the Ponca people. But before turning to bricks and mortar, the group commissioned a statue to honor **Standing Bear**, the chief who pleaded in federal court for his people and ultimately won a Supreme Court decision that American Indians were entitled to protection under US law. (See Omaha, Nebraska.) The twenty-two-foot bronze was dedicated in 1996 and the **Standing Bear Museum and Education Center** (601 Standing Bear Pkwy.; 580-762-1514) opened in 2007.

Poteau (Le Flore County)

Poteau, established in 1887 in the Choctaw Nation, is named for the Poteau River. The place name is a relic of early French exploration, the word meaning "post." After the town gained rail service it was a coal-mining center until supply and demand declined. Timber harvesting continued to drive the local economy.

The **Kerr Legacy and Historical Center** (23009 Kerr Mansion Rd.; 405-429-8530) focuses on the history of eastern Oklahoma and the career of former Oklahoma governor and US Senator Robert Kerr. Built in 1957, the Kerr family home was deeded to the state by the late senator's family in 1978 and transformed into a museum. Three miles west of Poteau on US 59 in Heavener is the restored 1894 **Peter Conser House** (47114 Conser Creek Rd.; 918-653-2493). Peter Conser (1852–1934) was a noted captain with the Choctaw Lighthorsemen—a legendary Old West law enforcement body.

Stillwater (Payne County)

Stillwater was born of the 1889 land run, its developers selling one business lot or two residential lots for $5.00. Two years later residents voted to incorporate their city. The next election was to determine if Stillwater should issue $10,000 in bonds to fund a portion of the construction costs if the territorial legislature chose Stillwater as the home for the planned Agriculture and Mechanical College. Voters said yes and so did the legislature. Later the college became Oklahoma State University.

Pistol Pete

Almost all college mascots are animals or, if a person, not a real person. Not so for Oklahoma State. The school's **Pistol Pete**—a six-shooter-packing, chap-wearing, tough-looking guy with a big hat and droopy mustache—honors Old West character Frank "Pistol Pete" Eaton. In reality, there were two Frank Eatons—the fake one and the real one. The made-up Pistol Pete lost his father to ex-Confederates in Kansas and as a young man revenged his papa's murder by hunting down and killing the six perpetrators. Naturally, a man that handy with a gun would go on to an action-packed career as a scout for the US Cavalry and later as a frontier lawman. The real Pistol Pete (1860–1958) made up much of his story for a book brought out by a respected Boston publishing house in 1952, *Pistol Pete: Veteran of the Old West.* The bibliographer Ramon Adams called the book a "preposterous tale," saying it read more like Wild West fiction than factual memoir. Eaton did live in the days of the Wild West and the book about him may contain some truth, but the story Eaton told is considered about as genuine as the over-sized plastic mask and giant orange cowboy hat worn by the Oklahoma State student chosen to be Pistol Pete. Eaton is buried in **Perkins Cemetery** (530 Knipe Ave.), 11 miles south of Stillwater.

The **Stillwater History Museum at the Sheerar Center** (702 South Duncan St.; 405-377-0359) has exhibits relating to the history of Stillwater and Payne County from the land rush to the twentieth century. The best-selling book at its gift shop is Pistol Pete's autobiography.

The **Washington Irving Trail Museum** (3918 South Mehan Rd.; 405-624-9130) in Ripley focuses primarily on Irvin's 1832 trek through Indian Territory but has an exhibit on the Doolin-Dalton gang with artifacts from the Ingalls gunfight.

Tahlequah (Cherokee County)

Forced from their homeland along what they would call "The Trail Where They Cried" (more generally known as the Trail of Tears), the Cherokee people were resettled by the military in 1838 and 1839 in the northeastern part of what became Oklahoma. Sixteen years before their removal from their homeland in Georgia, an event that claimed hundreds of lives, the Cherokee had established a republican form of government based on the US. Following their relocation to the West, they established their capital in the Illinois River Valley and called it Tahlequah. After Oklahoma statehood in 1907, Tahlequah became the seat of Cherokee County but remains the location of the Cherokee tribal headquarters.

Built in 1869 on the Tahlequah town square, the Cherokee national capitol accommodated the tribe's executive, legislative, and judicial branches until 1906. After that, the Cherokee Nation Supreme Court used the building for more than a century. In 2019 the **Cherokee National History Museum** (101 South Muskogee Ave.; 918-456-0671) opened in the building. The five-thousand-square-foot museum has permanent and rotating exhibits on the history of the Cherokee people. The two-story brick capitol is listed on the National Register of Historic Places and is a National Landmark.

Located in a two-story red brick building constructed in 1844, the **Cherokee National Supreme Court Museum** (122 East Keetoowah St.; 918-207-3508) was the original home of the Cherokee National Supreme Court. The oldest government building still standing in Oklahoma, it housed the nation's district and Supreme Court as well as the office of the *Cherokee Advocate*, the first newspaper in Indian Territory. Exhibits focus on Cherokee law and education. Regarding tribal law, interpretive displays show the progression of the tribe's enforcement of behavioral norms from clan practices to its court system. How the Cherokee developed a written language and the evolution of tribal journalism is also explored.

Forty-two miles south of Tahlequah is **Sequoyah's Cabin Museum** (470288 State Highway 101; 918-775-2413). Sequoyah (c. 1770–1843) developed the written Cherokee language in 1821 and lived in this cabin following the tribe's removal to future Oklahoma.

Fangs Bared in Going Snake

Cherokee **Ezekiel "Zeke" Proctor** (1831–1907) rode to the Hildebrand Mill on Flint Creek in what is now Delaware County on February 13, 1872, to confront his former brother-in-law Frank Kesterson. Whether Proctor intended to kill Kesterson, whip him, or merely remonstrate with him for leaving his wife (Proctor's sister) for Pauline "Polly" Beck is still argued all these years later. Whatever led to it, Proctor shot and wounded Kesterson and, he claimed, accidentally killed Polly. Charged with murder in the Cherokee judicial system, he would be tried in the Going Snake District (a pre-statehood Cherokee political subdivision). With feelings running high among the two Cherokee families involved, the judge decided to hear the case in the more secure Whitmire School rather than the Going Snake courthouse. The judge feared violence because the Beck family believed the trial would be a sham, with Proctor's innocence a foregone conclusion. To hedge their bet, Kesterson and some of the Becks traveled to Fort Smith, Arkansas, on April 11 to get Proctor charged in federal court with assault with intent to kill. The US commissioner issued a warrant for Proctor's arrest and on April 14 dispatched deputy US marshals to take him into custody. The following day, when a dozen federal officers showed up at Proctor's trial, a shootout ensued. The result was eight dead lawmen and three dead Cherokees. As the Beck family had expected, Proctor was acquitted the next day. He also left the territory, heading through Texas to Mexico. Meanwhile, federal charges were filed against those suspected of killing the deputy US marshals and a posse rounded them up six days after the shooting. All charges were eventually dismissed for lack of evidence. Known as the Going Snake Massacre, the event marked the deadliest day in US Marshal Service history, the worst incidence of Cherokee inter-tribal violence, and resulted in more deaths than any other non-military gun battle in the Old West.

The original Hildebrand Mill, also known as Beck's Mill, was located near US 412 close to Flint. It no longer stands, but in 1900 another mill was built at the same location and its ruins remain. The site, listed on the National Register of Historic Places, is ten miles west of West Siloam Springs in Delaware County. The Whitmire Schoolhouse was near present Christie in Adair County. Proctor is buried in **Johnson Cemetery** (7727 Cedar Dr., Colcord), just behind Calvary Baptist Church, about 42 miles northeast of Tahlequah. The cemetery is commonly shown in West Siloam, but the church's address is in nearby Colcord. Both are only small communities.

After the capitol and the supreme court building, the third building put up by the Cherokee government was a two-story cut sandstone jail opened in 1874. During Reconstruction and for years afterward, the Indian Territory was a particularly violent place and the prison saw numerous offenders. The facility served as the Cherokee national prison until 1904 when the nation sold it to Cherokee County. The county continued using the old lockup until 1970. The building was later renovated and opened as the **Cherokee National Prison Museum** (124 East Choctaw St.; 918-207-3640), which focuses on the history of Cherokee crime and punishment. A reproduction of the prison's original gallows stands on the museum grounds.

Established in 1963, the **Cherokee Heritage Center** (21192 South Keller Dr., Park Hill; 918-456-6007) is devoted to the history and culture of the Cherokee people. Six miles south of Tahlequah, the center has a permanent exhibit on the Trail of Tears as well as other displays. The Cherokee Family Research Center is also housed at the center.

Tulsa (Tulsa County)

Founded in 1898, Tulsa is Oklahoma's second-largest city. Most of Tulsa's history happened after the Wild West era, but the discovery of oil in the area in 1901 brought the standard boomtown riffraff and rowdiness.

Tulsa's oil town status led to a museum that some have called the Smithsonian of the Old West. The **Gilcrease Museum** (1400 Gilcrease Museum Rd.; 918-596-2700) was founded in 1949 by Thomas Gilcrease (1890–1962), a Tulsa oilman who wanted a place for his extensive collection of Western art, artifacts, and archival material, including some one hundred thousand books related to Western history. In 1958 Gilcrease donated the museum, its collections, and thirteen acres to the City of Tulsa. The University of Tulsa manages the museum.

Tuskahoma (Pushmataha County)

The 1830 Treaty of Dancing Rabbit Creek guaranteed, among other things, that as compensation for leaving their homeland in Mississippi the Choctaw people would receive money from the US government to build a council house in the center of their new land in Indian Territory. The council house—called **Nunih Wayah** for a sacred mound in Mississippi—went up a mile and a half northwest of present Tuskahoma. In 1884 the nation built a more substantial two-story brick structure that now houses the **Choctaw Capitol Museum** (163665 North 4355 Rd.; 918-569-4465).

Woodward (Woodward County)

Woodward developed when the first rail line came through the so-called Cherokee Outlet in 1887. Having railroad service made Woodward an important supply point for nearby Fort Supply and turned it into Oklahoma's wildest cow town as cattle began arriving up the Great Western Trail from Texas for shipment to market. After the trail-driving days ended, Woodward continued as a ranching and agricultural center.

Established as Camp Supply in 1868 at the beginning of the army's winter campaign against the Plains Indians in western Indian Territory, the post remained active, renamed Fort Supply, until 1894. Its soldiers escorted cattle drives and protected stagecoaches, freight haulers, and other travelers as they moved along the trails. Until the opening of the Cherokee Strip, Camp Supply troops patrolled the area to keep out trespassers and contain the tribes. Lt. Col. George Armstrong Custer departed from this post on the mission that culminated in the Battle of Washita.

Managed by the Friends of Historic Fort Supply, **Fort Supply** (1 William S. Key Blvd.; 580-256-6136) is located 14 miles north of Woodward. Five original buildings still stand, including the 1875 ordnance sergeant's quarters and the 1882 civilian employee quarters. Both are picket-style log buildings, common at the time. Not many have survived. The 1879 commanding officer's quarters and the duplex 1882 officers' quarters also are original. The only brick building at the post was the 1892 guardhouse. This restored structure houses exhibits dealing with the post's history.

Temple Lea Houston

His famous father Sam played a critical role in Texas history, but **Temple Houston** (1860–1905) spent the last eleven years of his life in Oklahoma. After participating in the 1893 Oklahoma land run, a year later Temple moved his family to the relatively new town of Woodward from Canadian, in the Texas Panhandle. He served as legal counsel for the Santa Fe Railroad and soon garnered a reputation as a topnotch if flamboyant trial lawyer. On October 8, 1895, following an argument at the Cabinet Saloon, Temple shot and killed Ed Jennings, a brother of Oklahoma outlaw Al Jennings. Authorities duly charged Temple with murder, but a jury acquitted him. Intelligent and well read, Temple knew the law. He also knew how to put on a good show in the courtroom.

In 1899 a newspaper reporter happened to be in the courtroom when a routine case against a local prostitute came up on the docket. Houston volunteered as Minnie Stacey's attorney since she had no legal representation or money to hire counsel. By most accounts, Houston's extemporaneous plea on behalf of the soiled dove—its verbiage preserved for posterity by a fast-scribbling journalist—had most of the all-male jury weeping before he concluded. They quickly found the young woman not guilty. Political observers saw Houston as a possible candidate to be the first governor of the about-to-be-created state of Oklahoma, but he suffered a debilitating stroke and died at age forty-four on April 15, 1905.

Much of old Woodward was destroyed in a devastating killer tornado on April 9, 1947, including any structures once associated with Temple Houston. But tornadic winds could not blow away the flat gray granite tombstone marking the colorful lawyer's final resting place in **Elmwood Cemetery** (2755 Downs Ave.).

A bronze statue of Houston by sculptor John Gooden dedicated in 2016 stands in front of the **Plains Indians and Pioneers Museum** (2009 Williams Ave.; 580-256-6136), which has a room devoted to Houston. In it, his law office has been recreated as well as the parlor of his Woodward residence. Two of the more striking artifacts on display are a cane presented to him by one of Geronimo's wives and a volume of the *1893 Statutes of Oklahoma Territory* he happened to have been carrying when he was wounded in the 1895 saloon fight. The law book slowed the bullet and likely saved the lawyer's life.

KANSAS

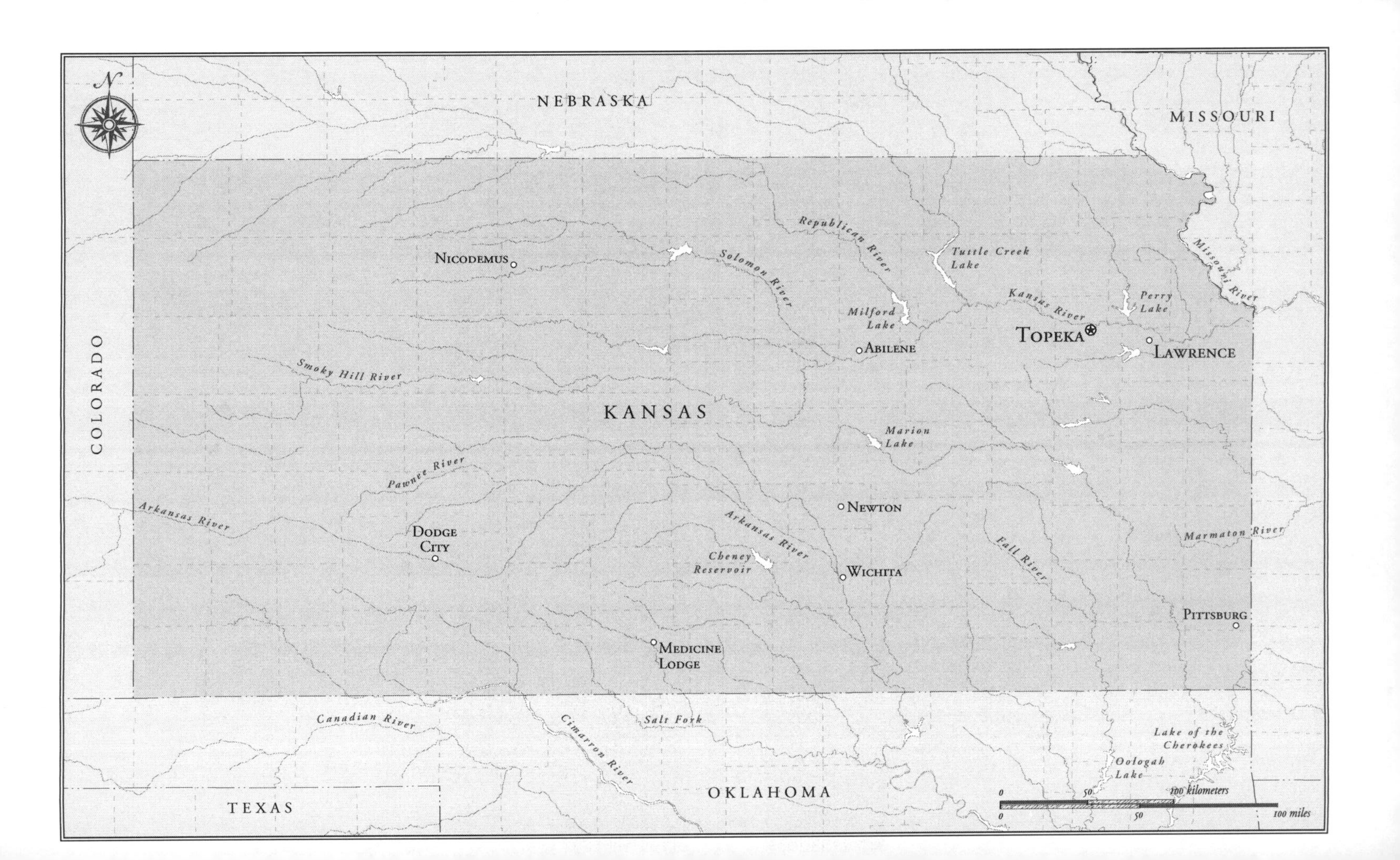
N
NEBRASKA
MISSOURI
COLORADO
KANSAS
OKLAHOMA
TEXAS
Nicodemus
Abilene
Topeka
Lawrence
Newton
Wichita
Dodge City
Medicine Lodge
Pittsburg
Republican River
Solomon River
Smoky Hill River
Kansas River
Missouri River
Tuttle Creek Lake
Milford Lake
Perry Lake
Marion Lake
Pawnee River
Arkansas River
Arkansas River
Cheney Reservoir
Fall River
Marmaton River
Canadian River
Cimarron River
Salt Fork
Lake of the Cherokees
Oologah Lake
0
50
100 kilometers
0
50
100 miles

Abilene (Dickinson County)

Abilene's first settlers arrived in 1857, but another decade passed before it became the first of the Wild West's rowdy cow towns. Two factors contributed to that—industrial progress and one man's idea. First came the Union Pacific Railroad, enough to give any town a surge in vitality. But it was **Joseph G. McCoy**, an Illinois cattle shipper and promoter, who had the idea of developing still-sleepy Abilene as a destination for Texas cattle. The Lone Star State did not yet have any interstate rail lines, so it made economic sense to drive cattle to the rail head at Abilene and ship them to market from there. To that end, McCoy purchased land outside town near the tracks and built pens and other infrastructure, including an office and a three-story hotel he named **Drover's Cottage**.

The first herd, 2,400 head driven north from San Antonio, hit town in late summer 1867 and the boom began. So, too, began a pattern that would be repeated elsewhere in Kansas for nearly the next twenty years: After a hard trip up the trail, Texas cowboys—then more commonly called drovers—celebrated the completion of their journey and concomitant earnings in the town's saloons, gaming establishments, and bawdy houses. By the end of Abilene's heyday, three million head of cattle had been shipped from there.

The **Dickinson County Heritage Center** (412 South Campbell St.) displays a pair of revolvers Wild Bill Hickok sold to his friend C.W. Peterson before Hickok moved to Ellsworth, Kansas. Peterson bought both pistols for $16, selling one and keeping the other. Peterson later passed the gun on to his son, who lived in Pasadena, California. Following his death in 1936, Peterson's son stored the weapon in his attic until his death, when Peterson's granddaughter inherited it. She conveyed it to the museum in 1970.

Long-since razed, the **Alamo Saloon**, where Wild Bill Hickok shot two men in October 1871, stood on Cedar Street just south of its intersection with Texas Street. A mural depicting Hickok is at 203 North Buckeye Avenue.

Old Abilene Town (502 Northwest 21st St.) was developed by the town business community in 1958 as a publicly held tourist destination. Vintage structures were moved in from elsewhere in the county and replicas representative of a typical Western town were added to the site. The venue was the centerpiece of the 1967 centennial of Abilene's emergence as a cow town. After the celebratory trail dust settled, Old Town continued in operation until 1981 when it was sold to private interests. The site was heading toward its last roundup when the non-profit group Historic Abilene bought it in 2004 and began renovations as funding allowed. Wild Bill Hickok may not have wet his whistle in the tourist town's Alamo Saloon, but visitors with imaginations can get a feel for what the real old Abilene must have been like. The marketing slogan on the Old Abilene Town website says it all: "Abilene: Where the Chisholm Trail Ends and the Legends Begin."

Bear River Smith and Wild Bill Hickok

Abilene's town fathers generally sought to achieve a balance between outright lawlessness and allowing visitors an opportunity to have a good time while supporting the local economy. They looked around for lawmen with a reputation or ones itching to gain one. The first man they hired had an ordinary name made distinctive by a nickname, **Bear River Tom Smith**.

Marshal Smith quickly proved his worth by successfully using his fists rather than a six-shooter to convince a couple of rowdies that he really meant it when he told them they were under arrest. But on November 2, 1870, when he and a sheriff's deputy tried to serve a warrant on a farmer outside town, the man pulled a pistol and shot Smith twice. Though seriously wounded, Smith managed to take down the man and handcuff him. Meanwhile, a friend of the farmer, and clearly no supporter of law enforcement, attacked Smith with an axe. No help came from the deputy, who had fled at the first shot. When he returned with a posse, they found the marshal's body, his head nearly severed. Marshal Smith was first buried under a wooden marker on a hill near town, but his remains were exhumed in 1904 and reburied in **Abilene Cemetery** (513 Northwest 14th St.). A large granite rock with a metal plaque marks his grave.

Abilene's second and best-known marshal was Wild Bill Hickok. He started on April 15, 1871, and by early fall had killed two men. Both deaths occurred on October 9 that year near the Alamo Saloon. Hickok fatally shot special deputy Mike Williams by accident while trying to subdue a boisterous gambler named Phil Coe. Coe ended up dead with two bullets in his belly. Hickok paid for Williams' funeral and visited the man's widow. While Hickok did keep the town relatively quiet, he spent much of his time playing cards. Town officials cashiered him in December 1871.

Atchison (Atchison County)

Founded in 1854 by pro-slavery Missourians where Independence Creek meets the Missouri River, Atchison—named for Missouri senator David Rice Atchison—developed as a steamboat town and departure point for west-bound travelers. The Pony Express had a stop here during its short life, as did the Overland Mail Company. Atchison never became a major city, but in 1859 Cyrus K. Holliday coupled its name to one of the West's more important and long-lasting rail lines, the Atchison, Topeka, and Santa Fe (popularly known as the Santa Fe Railroad). The line would begin at Atchison, but no tracks were laid until 1868. Four years later the railroad had only gone as far as Topeka, but the Santa Fe grew into one of the nation's largest carriers.

Fittingly located in the restored stone 1880 Santa Fe freight depot, the **Atchison County Museum** (200 South 10th St.; 913-367-6238) focuses on a history that dates to the arrival of the Lewis and Clark Expedition in 1804.

Athol (Smith County)

A physician with a penchant for poetry, **Dr. Brewster M. Highley** scratched out a piece in 1872 he called "My Western Home." The doctor didn't consider it any great literary work, but when a neighbor read the poem, he talked Highley into submitting it for publication. The piece appeared in the *Smith County Pioneer* in December 1873 under a new title, "Oh, Give Me a Home Where the Buffalo Roam." A local fiddler put the poem to music and the tune grew increasingly popular. Other musicians began adding verses and the derivative song that began with Highley's poem evolved into the anthem of the West, "Home on the Range."

The **small log and stone cabin** (773 90 Rd.) on West Beaver Creek where Highley wrote his poem survived into the twenty-first century and was restored in 2011. There's a modest exhibit inside and a one-page history of the song is available for a quarter on the honor system. Located eight miles north of Athol off State Highway 8, the cabin is on private property but is open to the public.

Baxter Springs (Cherokee County)

Reverend John Baxter, his wife, and eight children traveled from Missouri in the spring of 1849 to settle near a robust mineral spring long used by passing Osage Indians. The old Indian trail had evolved into a military road connecting Fort Smith, Arkansas, with Fort Gibson in Indian Territory and Baxter opened a general store and inn to cater to travelers. First known as Baxter's Place, the community that developed there became Baxter Springs. But the preacher, shot to death in 1859 during a property dispute, never got to enjoy the honor. During the Civil War, in what became known as the **Baxter Massacre**, guerilla fighter William Quantrill slaughtered a hundred Union soldiers just outside of town. After the war, Baxter Springs boomed as Kansas's first cattle town when the Missouri, Kansas, and Texas Railroad came through in 1870.

The town saw the usual rowdiness stirred up by passing trail drivers, but it was a falling out between two local officials that led to a particularly notable killing. That happened on July 1, 1872, when town marshal C.M. Taylor confronted Mayor J. R. Boyd with an arrest warrant for assault. When the marshal ordered Taylor to hand over his weapon, the lawman discovered too late that his honor had been carrying a derringer as well as a revolver. The mayor pulled the small pistol from his coat, pressed the firearm against the marshal's chest and shot him in the heart. Taylor fell dead without a word. Charged with murder, Boyd was freed on $10,000 bond and later acquitted. A **historical plaque** (1024 Military Ave.) marks the site of the shooting.

A few years later, on April 19, 1876, two gunmen stuck up the Crowell Bank, escaping with $3,000. Western historians believe the robbers were Charlie Pitts and Bill Chadwell, members of the James-Younger gang. However, Jesse and Frank James are not thought to have taken part in the heist. Occurring long before the advent of federally insured deposits, the holdup was bad for the bank, but blaming it on the James boys turned into an asset for Baxter Springs tourism.

Long since out of business, **Crowell Bank** (1101 Military Ave.) occupied a two-story brick building constructed in 1870 that still stands. Visitors can learn more about the area at the **Baxter Springs Historical Center and Museum** (740 East Ave.). Operated by the Baxter Springs Historical Society, the two-story museum has twenty-three thousand square feet of exhibit space covering every aspect of the town's rich history, including its Wild West era.

Belleville (Republic County)

For generations, the Pawnee reigned as the dominant power of the Central Plains. The Kitkehahki band settled along the Republican River around 1820 and lived in a walled community of forty-plus earthen lodges. A decade after coming to the river, a shortage of wood combined with a loss of fertility in the river valley forced the Indians farther north. Opened in 1967, the **Pawnee Indian Village State Historic Site** (480 Pawnee Tr.; 785-361-2255) is nineteen miles northwest of Belleville and is built around an archeological excavation of one of the larger lodges.

The "Belle" in Belleville came from Arabelle Tutton, wife of A.B. Tutton, one of the men who settled the town in 1861.

Caldwell (Sumner County)

Founded in 1871 on the Chisholm Trail just above the Kansas state line, Caldwell was the first town Texas drovers reached after pushing their herds through sparsely populated Indian Territory. And that made for a lively community. The cow town grew even faster after the Santa Fe Railroad arrived in 1879. That allowed cattlemen to ship their beeves to market from there instead of having to walk their cattle all the way north to Abilene. Nicknamed the "Border Queen," Caldwell offered Texas trail hands all the usual amenities, from whiskey to women. While pleasure came at a price, life was cheap in Caldwell. At least thirty-two killings took place in Caldwell from 1871 to 1891.

When Oklahoma's Cherokee Strip opened in 1893, Caldwell experienced a second boom as a gathering point for those eager to stake their claim. When the land rush began at noon on September 16 that year, thousands of men and women stampeded southward from the border town. After that, no longer a significant waypoint, Caldwell fell into decline though it stopped short of becoming a ghost town. Fortunately for history lovers, most of its nineteenth-century architecture has survived.

The **Trail, Rails & Scales** visitor's center (intersection of East Central Avenue and Arapahoe Street; 620-845-6666) has interpretive displays explaining Caldwell's boisterous past. A brochure with a map showing the locations of Caldwell's seventeen historical markers can be picked up here.

A large work of public art commemorating the trail-driving era called ***Ghost Riders of the Chisholm Trail*** stands on the east side of US 81, two miles south of town. Built with local donations and labor, and completed in 1995, the piece is a series of life-sized cut metal silhouettes of cattle, drovers on horseback, and a chuckwagon. Nearby is a state historical marker giving the history of Caldwell and the Chisholm Trail.

The **Caldwell Cemetery**, begun in 1879, had a Boot Hill section believed to be the final resting place of some eighty individuals but many of their markers have disappeared. Overall, the cemetery has more than five thousand burials, but unlike the Boot Hills in Dodge City and Tombstone, Arizona, no cheesy tombstones with fake names and funny inscriptions. The cemetery is a half-mile north of town off South Sunflower Road (GPS coordinates: N37° 03.25', W97° 36.89').

Other attractions include **Heritage Park** (102 South Main St.), where a three-story brick building built in 1887 on Main Street stood for 102 years. Formerly the tallest privately owned structure in the county, when the building was razed, the lot was turned into a small park featuring a statue of a longhorn steer. There's also an early stone **Chisholm Trail marker** and a historical marker outlining Caldwell's development. The north wall of the building adjoining the park has a mural depicting the town's colorful history. Finally, the **Border Queen Museum** (2 South Main St.) is highlighted by a detailed model of Caldwell in the 1880s built by Texas historian and writer Bill O'Neal to tell this old cow town's story. The 1881 opera house in which the museum is housed had been condemned and was about to be torn down when the Caldwell Historical Society purchased it for back taxes in 2002. Four years later the building was reopened as a museum and venue for cultural events.

Marshal Henry Brown

On New Year's Day 1883, the grateful citizens of Caldwell gave their newly appointed town marshal a gold- and silver-inlay Winchester rifle. Affixed to the stock of the weapon, a small silver plate bore this inscription: "Presented to City Marshall H.N. Brown for valuable services rendered on behalf of the Citizens of Caldwell Kas., A.N. Colson, Mayor, Dec. 1882."

Caldwell had hired Brown as assistant marshal in October 1882. Town officials liked the way the quiet, no-nonsense lawman did his work and soon promoted him to the top job. The *Caldwell Post* touted Brown as "one of the quickest men on the trigger in the Southwest" and suggested that "a little bit of fine shooting" might be in order to settle things down in the boisterous cow town.

Soon enough, Brown did find it necessary to kill two men in the line of duty. The town's other newspaper, the *Caldwell Commercial* called the marshal "cool, courageous and gentlemanly, and free from . . . vices."

Turned out the solid citizens of Caldwell were a bit off the mark in their assessment of Marshall Brown. Not only did he have a past of which they were not aware, he had a problem that a year-and-a-half later would become tragically evident. (See Medicine Lodge.)

Cherryvale (Montgomery County)

What became of the Benders? Most Wild West homicides, excepting occasional assassinations from ambush, involved known parties and generally occurred in front of witnesses. Mysterious murders were far less common but did sometimes happen. A particularly bizarre and gruesome case unfolded near newly founded Cherryvale beginning in 1871 and continued through the spring of 1873.

John Bender and wife Kate, who had come west with their son and daughter (also John and Kate), operated an inn and store catering to west-bound travelers. For some, rather than a waypoint, the Benders' place turned out to be a final destination. As it later developed, the Benders were robbing and killing selected customers and burying them in the orchard near their place of business. During an intensive search for one missing traveler, the Benders apparently realized they were about to be found out and decamped during the night. When searchers checked their house not long after, a terrible stench led them to the basement, where they found a large amount of clotted blood. Someone noticed a depression in the earth in the family's orchard and soon uncovered the bludgeoned body of the most recent victim. Horrified volunteers and lawmen eventually discovered from eight to eleven sets of human remains, the exact count impossible to determine because of decomposition. Authorities charged all four Benders with murder, but like their victims, they were never seen again. Numerous theories have been advanced over the years, but no one has ever been able to document what happened to the early-day serial killers.

Located in a roadside rest area just northeast of the intersection of US 169 and US 400, a state historical marker (GPS coordinates: N37° 20.93', W95° 31.67') summarizes the Bender family story. The Benders lived in Labette County about eight miles from Cherrvale. Nothing remains of their house—a frame structure with stone-lined basement—or the orchard where they planted bodies among the fruit trees. The **Cherryvale Historical Museum** (215 East 4th St.) has three hammers on display said to have been found at the crime scene. Supposedly the hammer heads matched indentations found in some of the victims' skulls. Another surviving Bender relic is a butcher knife picked up at the scene by the brother of one of the victims. Since 1923 it has been in the collection of the **Kansas Museum of History** (6425 Southwest 6th Ave., Topeka).

Cimarron (Gray County)

Settled in 1879 on the Santa Fe Trail only seventeen miles west of Dodge City, Cimarron is the seat of Gray County—but that was not always a given. From 1887 to 1893, whether Cimarron or Ingalls would be the county capital was bitterly contested. The matter reached a climax on January 12, 1889, in what came to be called the **Battle of Cimarron**. Cimarron had received the most votes in an election supposed to decide the issue, but a contingent of hired guns, including former and future lawman Bill Tilghman and Bat Masterson's brother Jim, raided the courthouse to seize county records. That unsuccessful effort led to a wild gunfight between many Cimarron citizens and the Ingalls faction. Despite hundreds of gunshots, only one person, a pro-Cimarron man, was killed. Three to seven of the raiders suffered wounds, but all survived. The gunfight marked the last bloodshed connected to the issue, but the matter remained in contention for another four years. Estimates of the number of shots fired that day range from 1,000 to 1,600—either number made it the largest post–Civil War gunfight in Wild West history. In addition to the trouble surrounding its status as county seat, on June 10, 1893, outlaw Bill Doolin and three of his associates robbed a Santa Fe train just west of town. They netted $1,000.

The old depot is gone, and the robbery site is unmarked, but several buildings that figured in Cimarron's Wild West history still stand. Built in 1880 as a store, the two-story brick **Gray County Courthouse** (117 South Main St.), ground zero of the gun battle, continued in use until 1927. Listed on the National Register of Historic Places, it is open to the public. Bullet holes are still visible in the tin ceiling upstairs and in the window and door frames. The lone victim of the battle, John Wesley English, lies in the **Cimarron Cemetery** (901 North 5th St.; Old Section 1, Lot 17, Space 2). The Gray County Historical Society placed a modern tombstone on his grave. Aside from the historic courthouse, the most impressive (and un-altered) building in town is the **Cimarron Hotel** (203 North Main St.), a three-story brick accommodation built in 1886 as the New West Hotel.

Coffeyville (Montgomery County)

James A. Coffee and a partner opened a trading post in far southeastern Kansas to do business with the Osage and Cheyenne Indians in 1869. Just above the Indian Territory boundary, the trading post flourished and the small settlement that developed around it came to be called Coffeyville. When rail service arrived in 1871, Coffeyville relocated about a mile and became yet another rambunctious cow town. But not for another two decades would the event that put Coffeyville on the map in the figurative sense occur.

Intending to prove they were tougher and smarter than the late Jesse James and his gang, on October 5, 1892, the Dalton gang hit their hometown planning to rob both its banking establishments at the same time. The gang consisted of Bob, Grat, and Emmett Dalton and two others, Dick Broadwell and Bill Power. But as the outlaws walked toward their targets, several townspeople recognized the Daltons (despite the fake facial hair they wore) and quickly mobilized to protect their uninsured bank deposits. While the robbers were inside the banks, many citizens armed themselves with firearms supplied by a local hardware store and waited for the men to emerge.

When the robbers came out of the bank, the lead began to fly. Eighty percent of the gang died on the spot or soon thereafter and Emmett Dalton fell severely wounded. But before they went down, the outlaws killed Marshal C.T. Connelly and citizens Lucius Baldwin, Charles Brown, and George Cubine. Three other locals suffered wounds.

Built in 1871, the two-story **Perkins Building** (807 Walnut St.) was the home of the C.N. Condon Bank. The building is now occupied by the Coffeyville Chamber of Commerce. The bank's lobby, teller counter, and vault have been restored.

Owned and operated by the nonprofit Coffeyville Historical Society, the **Dalton Defenders Museum** (113 East 8th St.) opened on October 5, 1963—the sixty-first anniversary of the bloody shootout. The museum has a variety of artifacts associated with the Daltons, including two of the gun belts taken from their bodies, a glove that belonged to one of the robbers, and even one of the grain bags the outlaws brought along to hold the cash they planned to take from the banks.

After the outlaw's bodies had been photographed, the bullet-punctured remains of Bob and Grat Dalton and Bill Power were placed in black wooden coffins and unceremoniously buried in **Elmwood Cemetery** (Elmwood and Eldridge Streets). For years, their only marker was a bent length of pipe taken from the hitching post to which they had tied their horses. Later, when Coffeyville began to realize the dead outlaws had some socially redeemable qualities as a tourist attraction, a red granite tombstone was placed over their burial plot. It lists only their names.

A fourth Dalton also lies in the cemetery. Brother Frank, who died in the line of duty while serving as a deputy US marshal, has a traditional period tombstone. He lies within sight of his brothers, but not next to them.

Two of the slain defenders, Charles Brown and George Cubine, also are buried here. In addition, Thomas G. Ayers, the cashier who survived a gunshot wound at the hands of Bob Dalton, is buried in the cemetery. Others buried here who played a role that day are H.H. Isham, who owned the hardware store across from the bank and supplied townsfolk rifles and ammunition, and his clerk at the time, Lewis A. Dietz. The Dalton Defenders Museum has a free brochure with a map showing the location of the grave sites associated with the botched robbery.

Concordia (Cloud County)

A lawyer and politician, James Hagaman was instrumental in the creation of Shirley County, later renamed Cloud County. In 1869 two towns—Clyde and Sibley—vied for the make-or-break status of county seat. Hagaman did not like either venue so he platted a townsite and got the non-existent place on the ballot. None of the communities received a majority vote, so a second election was set for early 1870. Concordia won that time and Hagaman formed a company to begin selling lots in his new town, a community he later served twice as mayor. The Santa Fe Railroad reached Concordia in 1887.

The **National Orphan Train Complex** (300 Washington St.) serves as a reminder that not every pioneer came west in a covered wagon or stagecoach. Starting in 1854 and continuing well into the twentieth century, more than a quarter million homeless children from the Northeast (mostly New York and Boston) arrived on what came to be called orphan trains. Charles Loring Brace's Children's Aid Society and New York's Foundling Hospital ran the placement program. While it marked the beginning of foster care in America, in some cases it was just another form of slavery. Some children found good homes and others became boarders, apprentices, or indentured servants. Exploited children often ran away.

An estimated one in twenty-five Americans has a family connection to an Orphan Train child. Two orphans who found new lives in the West later became governors, one in Alaska and the other in South Dakota, and many others had successful careers in other professions. Most of the children grew up to live good but ordinary lives. Some did not turn out so well. A few online sources say that Billy the Kid came west on an orphan train, but no documentation exists supporting that and even though little is known for sure about the Kid's early youth no serious student of the Wild West gives it credence.

Located in the renovated 1917 Union Pacific depot, the National Orphan Train Complex opened in 2007 and is the only museum and research center entirely devoted to the history of the movement.

The **Cloud County Museum** (635 Broadway St.), is housed in the 1908 former Carnegie Library and operated by the Cloud County Historical Society. The museum has exhibits and archival material related to the history of the county and surrounding area.

Coolidge (Hamilton County)

Coolidge is the closest community to the site of one of the Wild West's more unusual towns, **Trail City**, Colorado. Only two miles west of the Kansas border, Trail City developed as Congress debated, and for a time seemed likely to pass, a bill that would have created a National Cattle Trail from Texas to Canada. As envisioned, the trail would have been a narrow strip of no-man's land that would enable Texas cattlemen to circumvent quarantine laws in Kansas and other states in driving their herds north. The measure got out-lobbied and died, but in the summer of 1886, ranchers from Texas used the proposed route anyway, giving short-lived vitality to newly built Trail City, a place where cowboys could drink and carouse. Extreme weather—both a severe drought and a terrible winter—along with other factors, soon brought the trail-driving era to an end and Trail City quickly trailed off into the sunset. But during its short life, like other cow towns, it saw all the attendant Wild West rowdiness. One artifact of the area's wild days still exists in Coolidge's town ordinances: It is illegal for women to ride horseback with no clothes on.

Only a few foundation remnants mark the site of Trail City. A Colorado historical marker at the rest area on US 50 just before the Kansas state line tells the story of the town. The only surviving Trail City structure is an old saloon, built in 1886 and moved to Coolidge a year or so later. Listed on the Kansas Register of Historic Places, the wood-frame structure at 110 Walnut Street was converted into a bed and breakfast in 2011. Insight into the area's history can be gained at the **Hamilton County Museum** (102 North Gates St.) in the county seat of Syracuse.

Prosperous cattleman Martin Culver and several investors from Garden City and Dodge, banking on congressional approval of the National Trail, platted Trail City in 1885 to capitalize on the expected influx of cattle and cowboys. They figured the new town would be the next Dodge, but they figured wrong. Despite the boomtown's rapid bust, Culver and his family remained in Coolidge. The rancher served as county treasurer and was well-regarded by the community but died of a ruptured appendix on October 5, 1887. Culver is buried in the **Coolidge Cemetery** (GPS coordinates: N38° 03.42', W102° 00.08'), two miles northwest of town.

Council Grove (Morris County)

Four years after William Becknell blazed the Santa Fe Trail, Congress in 1825 authorized the president to appoint three commissioners to better mark the trade route. At the Neosho River, about 150 miles along the trail from Independence, Missouri, the commissioners met with the Osage to negotiate a treaty allowing travel through their land. The gathering, or council, took place in a stand of trees that commissioner George Sibley named **Council Grove**. Once the treaty had been signed, the commissioners and their escort continued along the trail to New Mexico. A town developed at the site and took Council Grove as its name.

A large oak, on which trail commissioner Sibley had someone carve "Council Grove" in 1825, stood for years and—protected by a fenced-in overhead shelter just east of the Neosho River Bridge at 3rd and Main Streets—its stump remains. Knowing the old tree wouldn't last forever, in 1931 the local chapter of the Daughters of the American Revolution planted an acorn harvested from the historic tree before it had to be cut down. That new tree grew and now stands at the corner of Adams and Columbia Streets.

The stump of what's left of an oak that local lore says served as an unofficial post office where travelers could leave notes in a stone cache at its base is still in place and can be found in front of the **Post Office Oak Museum** (22 East Main St.). Operated by the Morris County Historical Society, the museum occupies an 1864 stone building that once housed a brewery.

The stump of an elm under which Lt. Col. George Armstrong Custer supposedly camped in 1869 (and which survived until Dutch Elm disease claimed it in 1990) stands in Custer Elm Park (490–502 South Neosho St.). The **Council Grove/Morris County Chamber of Commerce and Tourism** (207 Main St.; 620-767-5413) has a self-guided tour of the more than twenty-five historic structures or sites in the area.

Also in Council Grove is the **Kaw Mission State Historical Site** (500 North Mission). Kansas is named for the Kansa or Kaw Indians, who long held land in eastern Kansas. With increased trade along the Santa Fe Trail and Euro American encroachment, the tribe ceded most of their land in an 1846 treaty that moved them to a twenty-square-mile reservation that included present Council Grove. In 1851 the Methodist Church opened a mission near the trading post of Seth M. Hays, Council Grove's first settler. The mission taught Kaw boys basic academics and farming but was not popular with the tribespeople. The school's costs led to its closure in 1854. Five years later the Kaw land was reduced to a nine- by fourteen-mile tract and in 1872 the tribe was relocated to Indian Territory. The eight-room, two-story native stone building remained in the family of Thomas Huffaker, one of the mission teachers, until 1951. That year the Kansas Historical Society acquired the building and opened it as a museum telling the story of the Kaw people.

Nearby is the **Unknown Kaw Indian Monument**, where in the early 1920s erosion in a stream bed exposed Native American remains in the vicinity of an old Kaw village. Council Grove residents funded a thirty-five-foot limestone tower to memorialize the area's Kansa heritage. The unidentified remains and the possessions found with them were reburied at the monument in what is now **Allegawaho Heritage Memorial Park** (South 525 Rd.). In addition to the monument, visitors can view the ruins of three of the original 138 huts the US government built in 1862 at the Kansa reservation.

In 1928 the Daughters of the American Revolution placed one of their ***Madonna of the Trail*** statues (there are a dozen across the West depicting a pioneer mother and her two children) just outside Council Grove at the northeast corner of the junction of US 56 and K-177. On the other side of town, a new statute, ***The Guardian of Council Grove***, depicts a Kaw Indian. The **Neosho Riverwalk** connects the *Madonna of the Trail* statue to the Kaw Indian statue, which stands on the walk's southeast side.

Dodge City (Ford County)

The "Queen of the Cowtowns," Dodge City was the wild child of the Atchison, Topeka, and Santa Fe Railway, which reached a point just east of the Arkansas River in 1872. Located near the US Army's Fort Dodge, a buffalo hunter's camp called "Buffalo City" was the first settlement in the area. Its principal amenity was a tent saloon where a shot of whiskey sold for a quarter. With the railroad on the way, a group of investors formed a town company and laid out Dodge City in the late summer of 1872.

In 1875 the Santa Fe built cattle pens adjacent to its tracks in Dodge. A few months later the *Topeka Daily Commonwealth* reported, "The people of Dodge City differ from those of most places. They don't want settlers on the plains around them. They want to make their place the great cattle mart of the West." And that, for a time, is what happened. Soon, along the Western Cattle Trail, drovers began herding longhorns by the multiple thousands up from Texas. From Dodge, the cattle would be shipped east to the newly opened stockyard in Kansas City, Kansas.

Dodge's early businessmen knew that soldiers, buffalo hunters, and Texas cowboys constituted the town's economic lifeblood, but they didn't want their visitors to get too rowdy. Many of the Wild West's more legendary characters—from John Wesley Hardin to Bat Masterson to Wyatt Earp—spent time here. The town developed quite a reputation, and in the mid-1920s finally began to capitalize on it, but it was not until a fictional lawman named Matt Dillon began enforcing the law in the popular and long-lived TV Western aptly named *Gunsmoke* that Dodge acquired its international reputation. Only Deadwood, Lincoln County's Fort Sumner, and Tombstone rank with Dodge City as the Wild West's most iconic towns.

Dodge City's first museum was the private collection of Merritt Beeson, whose father Chalkley had been co-owner of the Long Branch Saloon during Dodge's tenure as "cattle mart of the West." The younger Beeson inherited the Dodge City–related artifacts his father had acquired and continued to collect. Initially he kept the stuff in his basement, but, in 1932, as the number of people who asked to see his collection increased, he opened a museum. When he died in 1956, his widow continued to run the museum and did so until 1964.

By that time, the **Boot Hill Museum** (500 Wyatt Earp Blvd., formerly Front Street) had been a downtown fixture since 1947. Located near the site of the original Boot Hill Cemetery, this non-profit museum includes a 1958 recreation of Dodge's 1870s Front Street. (Additional reconstructions were added in 1964 and 1970.) In addition to its exhibits and recreated Old West false-front structures, the museum maintains five restored historic buildings moved to the site from Dodge City or the general area. The first was the old Fort Dodge guardhouse, acquired in 1953. Since then, the museum has added an 1870s blacksmith shop; a Santa Fe Railway depot from Sitka, Kansas;

the First Union Church dating from 1900; and the 1879 R. J. Hardesty house. The museum curates roughly sixty thousand artifacts and archival items. A $6 million, free-standing addition to the museum, complete with permanent and temporary exhibit halls and other state-of-the-art amenities, opened in 2020.

Fort Dodge (228 Custer St.) is five miles east of Dodge on US 400. The military post that gave the town its name began as a collection of dugouts halfway between Fort Leavenworth and Santa Fe. The crude shelters were uncomfortable, unhealthy, and unsightly. When scouts found ample rock for quarrying twelve miles from the fort, construction of stone buildings began in 1867. In 1868, troops from the post began a concerted fall and winter offensive against Plains Indians who had been raiding in Kansas. That fall, Lt. Col. George Armstrong Custer and his Seventh Cavalry spent some time at the fort before moving out as part of that campaign. By the early 1880s most of the buffalo and all the hostile Indians were gone from western Kansas and the army abandoned the fort in 1882. Eight years later, the government conveyed the former military reservation to the state of Kansas for use as a veteran's home, a function that continued into the twenty-first century.

In a building dating from 1867, the **Fort Dodge Library and Museum** (218 Pershing St.) has exhibits on the fort's history and archival material. A self-guided tour of the old post is available at the museum. Buildings dating to the fort's military days include the Pershing Barracks (1867), Nimitz Hall (formed from three buildings dating to 1867), a building at 105 MacArthur (1870), and the Sutler's Store (1870). The most historic building still standing is the former post headquarters, its second floor having served as the commanding officer's residence. The building is now the veteran facility's superintendent's residence.

The **Dodge City Convention and Visitor's Bureau** (400 West Wyatt Earp Blvd.) offers a self-guided walking tour of the Dodge City area that explains the history of seventy-seven points of interest, including attractions, historical content storyboards, and **Dodge City**

Trail of Fame medallions and pole banners. The Trail of Fame, a series of bronze sidewalk medallions and statues in the National Historic District, allows visitors to walk where some of the Wild West's most storied figures once put down their boots. The trail also recognizes many of the actors who had parts in television or movie portrayals of Dodge City over the years. Statuary includes Wyatt Earp; Doc Holliday; the late actor James Arness, better known as Marshal Matt Dillon; and *El Capitan* (the Captain), a bronze of the critter that made the boomtown possible, a longhorn steer.

"On the Ashes of My Campfire . . ."

Tallies vary, but during the twenty-year life of television's *Gunsmoke* series (the longest-running TV show ever), at least 138 men and seven women died violently over the course of 635 episodes. As for the real level of violence in early Dodge City, historians have documented roughly thirty homicides between 1872 and 1885. Though few in number compared with Dodge's television death toll, some of the cow town's actual killings were among the most storied shoot-'em-ups in Wild West history.

While *Gunsmoke*'s crusty Doc Adams treated or pronounced dead many of the show's casualties, Dodge City had a real-life doctor who played a little-known role in keeping the whole town alive. Dr. Oscar Simpson, a dentist, arrived in Dodge in 1885, just as the town's rowdy era was winding down. But Front Street still had numerous saloons, and as an ardent prohibitionist, Simpson worked to shut them down. (He didn't succeed, though national prohibition finally did.) By 1925, Simpson had been retired for a few years and had taken up sculpting. A history buff, he urged city officials to use Dodge's history to attract tourists. Otherwise, he believed, Dodge might atrophy business-wise. Some local businessmen felt the same way, but Simpson pushed the hardest. In 1927 the city commissioned Simpson to sculpt a statue of a cowboy to stand in front of the new city hall. Made of reinforced concrete, the piece depicted a drover in chaps, a six-shooter strapped around his hips. Of course, openly carrying a handgun was illegal in Dodge even during its heyday, but tourists wouldn't know that. The inscription on the base of the statue asserts "On the ashes of my campfire, this city is built." And beginning with that statue, dedicated in 1929, a new local industry arose—heritage tourism.

It wasn't that people didn't die in Dodge City, but townsfolks didn't bother with starting a cemetery until 1878. Most families used nearby Fort Dodge's cemetery. But the first time someone died bereft of friends, family, or money, something had to be done. Considering it the Christian thing to do, someone took it upon himself to bury the indigent man on a hill overlooking town. That was the genesis of **Boot Hill**, so named because most of its occupants died with their boots on, not of disease or old age. Before long, the hill was too valuable a piece of real estate to be used for a pauper's cemetery, so in the dead of winter in 1879 the bodies were removed to the new **Prairie Grove Cemetery**. By 1887 that property also was too valuable, so anyone with family to see to it got moved to **Maple Grove Cemetery** (1100 Matt Down Rd.). That cemetery continues as Dodge City's principal cemetery, with more than thirteen thousand burials. While none of early Dodge City's most famous residents ended up here, it still contains the graves of many of the town's earliest citizens and numerous notable figures.

The city built a school where Boot Hill had been. Later that building was razed and replaced with Dodge's city hall in 1929. A portion of the old cemetery ground lies adjacent to the Boot Hill Museum. For the benefit of tourists, fake grave markers dot the ground. A phony hanging tree, so labeled, adds to the faux Wild West ambiance. On the plus side, the markers are for people known to have been buried in Boot Hill back when.

Ellsworth (Ellsworth County)

Ellsworth got off to a slow start but made up for it a few years later. Six months after the establishment of **Fort Harker** in November 1866, just north of the Smoky Hill River, investors organized the Ellsworth Town Company. Surveyors staked out streets and lots on 320 acres a mile west of the post. The speculators sank their money into the open prairie because the Kansas Pacific Railroad was laying tracks in the direction of their new town. The railroad reached Ellsworth the summer of 1867, but a major flood, a severe cholera outbreak, and harassment by Plains Indians resentful of Euro American intrusion on their land stunted the town's growth despite the military presence. Determined to profit from their investment, the new town's boosters sought to convince Texas cattlemen to start shipping their beef from Ellsworth rather than Abilene. The company built a stockyard and the railroad put in a siding for cattle loading, but Abilene remained the primary shipping point. Two things finally worked in Ellsworth's favor. First, the railroad bought the stockyard and enlarged it. Second, fearing the tick-borne disease Texas longhorns often carried, Abilene made it plain that trail herds were no longer welcome. In the summer of 1871, Ellsworth became the new end of the trail for Texas drovers and another wild Kansas cow town was born. Within a year, the town experienced eight killings.

Ellsworth's historic downtown district was added to the National Register of Historic Places in 2007. A joint project of the Ellsworth-Kanopolis Chamber of Commerce and the Ellsworth Historical Society, seventeen metal silhouettes depicting various aspects of the town's history have been placed around the three- by four-block downtown area. An interpretive sign matches each silhouette, but a self-guided tour is available at the **Ellsworth County Historical Society's** research center (104 West South Main St.; 785-472-3059).

"My God, Billy, You Have Shot Me!"

By the end of the 1872 trail driving season, more than one hundred thousand longhorns passed through Ellsworth. The steady stream of trail herds resumed in the spring of 1873. But in September a financial panic triggered a national depression and the cattle market withered like drought-parched grazing land. That situation—thousands of unsold cattle milling around outside town and several hundred far-from-home Texas cowboys with nothing else to do—led to even more drinking and carousing. That, in turn, often resulted in trouble. On August 15, 1873, a drunken Billy Thompson, younger brother of gambler-gunman Ben Thompson, mortally wounded unarmed county sheriff Cauncey Whitney (1842–1873) with a blast of buckshot.

"My God, Billy, you have shot me!" the lawman said as he went down.

The shooting was accidental, even Whitney said so before he died. Still, the sheriff was well-liked and had a lot of friends. Worried that a lynch mob might go after his brother, Ben gave Billy some money and hurried him out of town. He later showed back up, bewildered and hung over, and Ben sent him away again. After that, Ben left town as well, boarding a train for Kansas City. Indicted for murder, Billy Thompson stayed on the lam until Texas Rangers arrested him in October 1876 and he was extradited to Kansas to face trial. There, in September 1877, a jury found him innocent. Beneath a substantial marble gravestone, Whitney is buried in **Old Ellsworth Cemetery** (421 West Douglas Ave.).

By 1873, Ellsworth needed a larger and sturdier jail. Only ten days after Sheriff Whitney's death county commissioners received plans for a proposed new jail and approved it the following month. Within the year, at a cost of $4,600, the county had a new, two-story limestone lockup (6 North Court St.). John M. Gruder, arrested for theft on February 20, 1874, had the honor of being the jail's first prisoner. Eight days later, he had the honor of being the first prisoner to escape it. Apparently not all the locks had been installed yet. The county continued to keep prisoners in the jail until 1909. After that it saw a variety of uses before the Ellsworth County Historical Society acquired it in 1988.

Built in 1875 by prominent Ellsworth resident Perry Hodgen, his two-story house was the first private residence made of stone. His choice of building material had been influenced by a devastating fire in 1874 that destroyed much of the town's wooden buildings and houses. Another fire ravaged the town in 1876, but his house survived. By 1961, however, it was badly in need of renovation. The Ellsworth County Historical Society took care of that, and in 1963 opened the old house as the **Perry Hodgen House Museum** (104 South Main). Today it is listed on the National Register of Historic Places.

Fairway (Johnson County)

Beginning in the 1820s, many of the eastern tribes of American Indians were relocated to what is now Kansas. In 1839 Rev. Thomas Johnson opened a mission for the Shawnee people and other tribes. During its most active period, the mission consisted of sixteen buildings on two thousand acres. The mission, which included a training school, continued operation until 1862. Three large brick buildings once part of the mission still stand and are preserved by the Kansas Historical Society's **Shawnee Indian Mission State Historic Site** (3403 West 53rd St.; 913-262-0867). Exhibits explore the history of the so-called emigrant Indians, the overland trails that passed through Kansas, and more.

Fort Scott (Bourbon County)

The town of Fort Scott was laid out in 1857 on the original site of the Fort Scott military garrison, abandoned four years before. When the community gained a railroad connection in 1869 it grew as a transportation hub and supply point. For a time, the city rivaled Kansas City as a rail center. Named for Lt. Gen. Winfred Scott, the army's longest-serving general of the nineteenth century, Fort Scott was established in 1842. Soldiers from the fort guarded the Santa Fe and

Oregon Trails, sometimes campaigning as far as Wyoming. The fort also played a role during the bloody run-up to the Civil War in Kansas. The post remained active until 1853, saw use by both sides during the Civil War, and was re-garrisoned in 1869. After the war, its troops protected rail workers. The post was abandoned in 1873, the frontier having moved farther west. With twenty surviving original buildings, the old fort became the **Fort Scott National Historic Site** in 1978. It is located off US 69 at US 54.

The **Fort Scott Visitor's Information Center** (231 Wall St.) provides a self-guided walking tour of the city's historic downtown, which includes numerous Victorian structures. Near downtown, the **Fort Scott National Cemetery** (900 East National Ave.) is one of the first fourteen national cemeteries created by President Abraham Lincoln in 1862.

Garden City (Finney County)

Brothers William and James Fulton first saw this area of western Kansas as buffalo hunters. In 1878, they decided to put down roots in both a literal and figurative sense, starting a town and plowing the ground they had acquired. As other settlers arrived, someone surprised to see crops growing on the open plains named the place Garden City. Fifty-two miles from Dodge City, Garden City did not have good time-seeking soldiers or trail drivers to enliven things. Lacking those two populations, Garden City held saloons, gambling halls, and bordellos in check and as western towns went, was a law-abiding place.

Buffalo Jones

Charles Jesse "Buffalo" Jones helped develop Garden City and served as its first mayor. That would have been enough to get him locally remembered, but something else he did set him aside as one of the Wild West's more important figures. He helped save the buffalo from extinction.

Born in Illinois in 1844, he came west to Kansas in his early twenties. First settling in Troy in 1866, he had success growing Osage orange (a hedge with thorny branches that made good fencing before barbed wire and that also could be used as fence posts) and fruit. Tiring of the nursery business, he moved farther west in the state and became a buffalo hunter. He killed the shaggy animals by the thousands, but he and his fellow hide men were shooting themselves out of business. In 1879, the great buffalo herds decimated, Jones became involved in the development of Garden City. Instrumental in convincing the Santa Fe Railroad to serve the town, he helped get Garden City named county seat and even donated a courthouse and the land on which it stood.

A young dentist from Ohio who aspired to write Westerns, Zane Grey based his first novel, *The Last of the Plainsmen*, on Jones. Writing that killing buffalo had been "repulsive to him," Grey had his protagonist smashing his rifle on a wagon wheel and vowing to save the species. While that was clearly overblown, Jones did begin gathering buffalo wherever he could find them, hoping to save the animal from extinction. But his motivation was not completely altruistic. In 1886, an unusually severe winter left thousands of frozen cattle on the range. Knowing that buffalo, while not immune to .50 caliber Sharp's rifles, could easily withstand bitter cold, Jones had an idea: Breed buffalo and cattle to create a hardy hybrid. When he found that "catalo" could not reproduce, he continued to build his herd. But the national financial crash of the mid-1890s forced him to sell his stock. Even though his crossbreeding efforts didn't succeed, through his later work in establishing a protected buffalo herd in Yellowstone National Park, Jones contributed significantly to the preservation of the buffalo.

The Finney County Historical Society erected a statue of Jones on the courthouse grounds at 8th and Pine Streets in 1979. Six bronze plaques at the monument's base tell his story. Jones died in 1919 and is buried in Garden City's **Valley View Cemetery** (2901 North 3rd St.; Zone C, Lot 137, Space 5).

The **Finney Historical Museum** (403 South 4th St.) has exhibits on Jones and other aspects of the county's history.

One of the Wild West's most famous photographs, "Independence on the Plains," depicts a weary looking woman standing behind a wheelbarrow full of buffalo chips. (On the plains, dried buffalo dung was used in lieu of firewood.) Also shown in the photo is the woman's young daughter, clutching a doll. The woman was Ada McColl, who lived in Garden City. Taken in 1893, the image has often been used to portray the hardships faced by early settlers, especially pioneer women. While the image will always be striking, historians eventually called B.S., exposing the image as staged. McColl set up the shot and then got her mother to trip the shutter of her Rochester camera. In 1984 her granddaughter donated that photo and twelve others to the Kansas Historical Society.

Anyone who has ever stayed at a multi-story hotel with rooms built around an open atrium can thank John A. Stevens, who built Garden City's **Windsor Hotel** (421 North Main St.) in 1886. The four-story, fifty-five-thousand-square-foot Windsor had 125 rooms, a large restaurant, and ground-floor rental space to accommodate businesses. The atrium, believed the first-ever in a hotel, extended upward from the second floor and was capped with a vaulted skylight. Called the "Waldorf of the Prairies," the hotel served as a cattleman headquarters. The old hotel was added to the National Register of Historic Places in 1972. The Finney County Preservation Alliance owns the property, which has been renovated as a sixty-five-room boutique hotel.

Goodland (Sherman County)

Whatever Lt. Col. George Armstrong Custer's thoughts were on June 26, 1876, as he and his outnumbered Seventh Cavalry troopers made their desperate final stand at Little Big Horn, he knew what happened when Plains Indian warriors overwhelmed a military command. He had seen it first-hand. Nine years before, he and his men had discovered the remains of a massacred Second Cavalry detachment led by Lt. Lyman Kidder.

The twenty-five-year-old lieutenant, with ten troopers and a Sioux scout, left Fort Sedgewick in Colorado Territory on June 29, 1867, with dispatches for Custer from Gen. William T. Sherman. But Custer had moved his command from his last reported position, and before Lt. Kidder's patrol could find them, they were found and killed by a Sioux war party. Bristling with arrows, their mostly nude bodies had been mutilated and only their Sioux scout had escaped scalping. One soldier had been tortured by burning.

Custer had the remains buried in a mass grave at the scene of the massacre. As it turned out, the message Kidder had died trying to deliver to Custer was a rebuke from General Sherman for disobeying orders.

A historical marker erected near the site is at the intersection of County Roads 28 and 77. A stone monument marking the actual **Kiddeer Massacre** site stands on land owned by Kuhrt Farms. The area around the massacre site looks much as it must have in the late 1860s and is not easy to reach. The **High Plains Museum** (1717 Cherry St.) has a small-scale diorama depicting the Kidder fight as well as artifacts and exhibits related to Sherman County history.

Hays (Ellis County)

As the Union Pacific Railroad pushed west after the Civil War, the US Army established a military post in north central Kansas to protect railroad workers and early settlers from hostile Indians. First called Fort Fletcher, the post was renamed Fort Hays in 1866. The town of Hays City ("City" later was dropped from the name) followed in the summer of 1867.

Situated in the middle of nowhere on the Kansas plains, a town full of railroaders, soldiers, and buffalo hunters saw plenty of violence. From July 1868 to December 1869, the town recorded fifteen homicides. Two of those killings were by James Butler "Wild Bill" Hickok, who had been hired by the town's vigilance committee to maintain as much order as possible. Hickok moved on in 1870. The first Western graveyard for itinerants and paupers to be called Boot Hill was in Hays City, the earliest burials in 1867. The cemetery was abandoned in 1874, but it had seen a lot of funerals in its time. As the May 14, 1878, issue of Dodge City's *Ford County Globe* noted, "Hays has recorded the burial of the sixty-fourth victim of gunplay in her Boot Hill." Later research revealed there were around eighty burials in all.

In Hays City's rougher days, its drinking establishments were not a place to share a quiet glass of wine with a friend. Some who bellied up to the bar back then ended up in Boot Hill. On January 6, 1869, three Fort Riley soldiers killed James Hayes in front of the **Tommy Drum Saloon** (115 West 10th St.) and were in turn lynched from a railroad trestle west of town. In the same saloon on August 20, 1872, former state representative John F. Wright was shot to death by Bill McClellan.

Four doors down is the former **Waters and Murray Saloon** (119 West 10th St.). While this saloon, operated by Moses Waters and Henry Murray, did not see any murders, when a fellow named Jack Hill got arrested for stealing a mule belonging to Waters, he was shot to death as he was being returned to Hays City to face charges.

No murders occurred in "Dog" Kelley's **Faro House** (Main and West 10th Streets), but in another bar, Kelley got away with killing Sheriff Peter Lanahan and accidentally wounding another man on July 16, 1871.

While the building in which Kelley's saloon was housed still stands, two other downtown saloons do not, but their locations are identified by markers.

Moved to its current location four miles south of Hays City in 1867, Fort Hays (1472 US 183 Alternate) continued as an active military post until 1889. During its busiest years, troops from the fort took part in two significant Plains Indian battles and numerous skirmishes. Gen. Nelson Miles, Gen. Phil Sheridan, Col. Richard Dodge, and Lt. Col. George Armstrong Custer were among the noted officers stationed at the fort at various times. Wild Bill Hickok and Buffalo Bill Cody also spent some time at the post. In 1900 Congress conveyed the former military reservation to the State of Kansas for use as a college, agricultural experiment station, and park. The park opened in 1930 and has been operated by the Kansas Historical Society since 1965. Four of the original fort buildings still stand, including a distinctive two-story stone blockhouse built as a defensive structure with gun ports. It later became the army post headquarters. Today a visitor's center has interpretive exhibits on the fort's history.

Legacy in Limestone

Over a long career as a self-taught artist, Hays City sculptor Pete Felton, Jr. produced more than thirty limestone statues that stand in and around his hometown. His largest Wild West–related work is the twenty-four-ton ***Monarch of the Plains***, an eight-foot-high buffalo standing on an eight-foot-high base placed at Old Fort Hays in 1967. A **stone steam locomotive** at the corner of Old US 40 and Commerce Parkway symbolizes Hay City's beginning; **Wild Bill Hickok** protects Union Pacific Park at 10th and Main and a **bust of Buffalo Bill Cody**, completed in 1961, reminds passersby of frontier days outside the Hays Public Library (1205 Main St.). Fort Hays hospital matron **Elizabeth Polly** at 26th and Indian Trail reinforces that not all Western figures were men and ***The Homesteader*** greets visitors to **Boot Hill Cemetery** (18th and Fort Streets).

A brochure providing a self-guided walking tour of historic downtown Hays is available at the **Hays Welcome Center** (2700 Vine St.). The **Ellis County Historical Society Museum** (100 West 7th St.) holds archival material available for researchers as well as exhibits on the county's history.

Humbolt (Allen County)

A place name and a historical marker are all that remain of one of the Wild West's wilder—if wildly unsuccessful—ideas. Of course, in modern times the notion that attracted Henry S. Clubb to eastern

Kansas does not seem all that outlandish, but in the mid-1850s a man who believed in eating vegetables only came across as being several bushels of corn short of a full wagon load. Not only did Clubb eschew the consumption of meat or dairy products, he also believed everyone should abstain from three of the young nation's more popular habits: tobacco, coffee, and alcohol. In March 1856, selling farmland to true believers at $5 an acre, Clubb lured roughly 150 settlers to his vegetarian colony. But his utopian colony failed to take root. Poor crops led to starvation while disease brought more rapid death. Nearby Osage Indians tried to help these strange people who did not like buffalo, antelope, venison, or beef but only fifty of the vegetarians survived (including Clubb, who kept practicing what he preached and lived to be ninety-four), and only four stayed in the area. But the stream near which Clubb founded his colony has been known as **Vegetarian Creek** ever since.

A state historical marker (intersection of 1150 Street and Arizona Road; GPS coordinates: N38° 03.42', W102° 00.08') explains the before-its-time colony. Visitors can also learn more about the vegetarian colony at the **Humbolt Historical Museum** (2nd and Neosho Streets; 620-473-5055).

Kanopolis (Ellsworth County)

On the frontier, a post guardhouse typically held enlisted men arrested for drunkenness or desertion—not a ranking officer and Civil War hero. But on June 21, 1867, at **Fort Harker**, the cell door slammed on Lt. Col. George Armstrong Custer, second in command of the Seventh Cavalry. His superior had ordered the colonel's arrest for leaving his command without orders, Custer having traveled without permission to see his wife at Fort Riley. Custer spent less than a day locked up, but he was later court-martialed for being absent without leave and several other offences and relieved of his rank and pay for a year.

Though Custer did not spend much time at Fort Harker, for a time it was one of the military's most active and important posts. It had been established in November 1866 to protect west-bound travelers and guard Union Pacific rail workers as they laid track for the railroad's Eastern Division. Four Seventh Cavalry companies and eight companies of infantry filled the post's stone barracks. Indicative of how rapidly the young nation was expanding to the west, by the spring of 1872 the post was no longer deemed necessary, and the army abandoned the garrison.

Four of the fort's original buildings still stand, the post headquarters, two officer's quarters, and the guardhouse where Custer languished for a few hours. The Ellsworth County Historical Society operates the **Fort Harker Guardhouse Museum** (303 West Ohio St.; 785-472-5733) in the old lockup. The other three buildings are private residences.

Kansas City (Wyandotte County)

Kansas City, incorporated in 1872, grew on the west bank of the Missouri River at its confluence with the Kansas (or Kaw) River. While its across-the-river neighbor, Kansas City, Missouri, developed into a city known for its culture and refinement, the city on the Kansas side was known for decades as a cow town, thanks to its sprawling stockyards.

The oldest surviving structure in Kansas City, the 1857 **Moses Grinter house** (1420 South 78th St.), is representative of the city's pre-stockyards history. Married to a Shawnee woman whose people had been relocated to the area in the 1830s, Grinter operated a ferry across the Missouri River, ran a trading post, raised livestock, and grew apples. Following Grinter's death in 1878, his wife Annie stayed in the house until her death in 1905. The two-story brick house remained in the hands of descendants until 1950. The State of Kansas acquired the old house in 1971 and operates it as a historic site.

Early in the trail drive era, it occurred to cattlemen that they could make more money off their livestock if they sold their animals at auction rather than directly to the railroads, which was the initial business model. The complex of related business and industries that came to be collectively known as the **Kansas City stockyards** began developing in 1871.

What turned Kansas City into the largest meat market in the West was completion in 1869 of the Hannibal Bridge across the Missouri River, the span that first connected the West with the other half of the nation. In 1878 the stockyard expanded from thirteen acres to fifty-five acres, with additional loading docks constructed along the network of tracks that adjoined the yards. By the early 1900s the city's stockyards and meatpacking district meant jobs for some twenty thousand locals and immigrants. During its peak years, the yards covered two hundred acres and were served by sixteen rail lines. The pens could handle 170,000 animals a day. Only Chicago's Union Stockyards did more business. It wasn't just beef, pork, and mutton coming out of the stockyards. The **Peet Brothers Manufacturing Co.** used rendered fat to produce "fancy toilet and laundry soaps."

The stockyards never really recovered from a devastating flood in 1951 but kept going for another forty years. The growth of rural feedlots and local auction houses finally pole-axed the Kansas City stockyards after twelve decades of operation. The last animal sold in 1991.

The only reminder of the stockyards still standing is the 1910 **Livestock Exchange Building** (1600 Genessee St.). The largest livestock exchange in the world at the time, the nine-story building had 475 offices accommodating everything from telegraph offices to banks. An investor bought the building in 1991, remodeled it, and converted it for modern use. The new owner found nearly fifty boxes of old stockyard-related records and donated them to the **Kansas City Public Library** (14 West 10th St.) in 2008.

Lansing (Leavenworth County)

With convicts pressed into service as laborers, construction on the **Kansas State Prison** began in 1864. Delayed by the Civil War, the facility admitted its first prisoners in 1868. The stone lockup, a castle-like main building and two wings, is where Emmett Dalton ended up after being convicted of murder following the 1892 raid on Coffeyville, Kansas's, two banks. Though handed a life sentence, Dalton received a gubernatorial pardon after serving only fourteen years. The facility also held prisoners from Oklahoma Territory until 1909. The original turrets and the front facade over the main building have been removed, but the rest of the old prison still stands and remains in use.

The **Lansing Historical Museum** (115 East Kansas St.; 913-250-0203) occupies a restored 1887 vintage Atchison, Topeka, and Santa Fe Railroad depot. While most of the museum is dedicated to the history of Lansing, it does have an exhibit on the prison's history.

Larned (Pawnee County)

The US Army built eight temporary or permanent posts along the Santa Fe Trail between 1847 and 1865 beginning with Fort Leavenworth on the Missouri River and extending to Fort Union in New Mexico Territory. One of those garrisons was **Fort Larned**, established in 1860 at its current location in central Kansas along the Pawnee Fork of the Arkansas River. The fort's original adobe buildings were replaced with nine red sandstone and timber structures between 1866 and 1868. Of strategic importance during the Indian Wars in protecting travelers making their way west from Missouri to Santa Fe, the fort's final mission was guarding railroad workers laying tracks across Kansas during the building of the nation's first transcontinental railroad. The army abandoned the post in 1878. The National Park Service acquired the well-preserved old fort from its private owner in 1966 and opened it as a National Historic Site. Eight of its original buildings still stand. The ninth building, a distinctive six-sided blockhouse with rifle loopholes for defense, was reconstructed to original specifications where it stood prior to being razed in 1900.

Fort Larned National Historic Site (1767 State Highway 156) is six miles west of Larned. The Santa Fe Trail passed just west of present Larned, and the **Santa Fe Trail Center** (1349 State Highway 156), with ten buildings on a ten-acre site only four miles from the old fort, includes interpretive exhibits dealing with western expansion and an extensive research library. The library has more than 700 linear feet of archival material, 7,000-plus historic photographs, and 2,300 vintage magic lantern glass slides. The center is two miles west of Larned.

Who Was W.D. Silver?

When the Anthony and Northern Railroad was surveying its route through Pawnee County in 1916, it purchased right-of-way through the farm of C.C. Line. That meant the Line family had to relocate one of their fences. While digging a post hole for the new fence, brothers Everett and C.C. Line were surprised when they hit a rock about eighteen inches down. When they dug up the flat stone, they found it bore a crudely carved inscription that read: "June A.D. 1841 – W.D. Silver – Die – Shot With." Beneath that, someone had carved a crude arrow. Since the stone indicated the presence of a grave (though none was found), the railroad in 1917 encased the stone in a six-foot concrete monument and placed it at the site. Historians have never determined who W.D. Silver was—or *if* he ever was. Most suspect the stone is nothing but a one-hundred-year-old-plus hoax. On the other hand, Stone may be a long-forgotten early-day traveler killed by Indians, and friends or family took the time to memorialize him with a simple stone before they resumed their westward journey. The monument is fourteen miles northwest of Larned, on the old railroad right-of-way one mile east of the almost ghost town of Ash Valley, a community that developed when the railroad came through.

Lawrence (Douglas County)

With a hill first known as Hogback Ridge as a landmark, the Oregon Trail ran along the Kansas River through what would become Lawrence. For the next decade-plus following the organization of Kansas Territory in 1854, Lawrence saw terrible sectional violence over the slavery issue. Conflict along the Kansas-Missouri border, essentially the dress rehearsal for the Civil War, served as training for future Wild West outlaws. Near the end of the war, Lawrence got its first rail connection, and in 1866, became the home of the University of Kansas.

That academic institution is home to one of the Wild West's more unusual relics—a stuffed horse. When Captain Myles Keogh fell with most of the rest of the Seventh Cavalry on June 26, 1876, at the Battle of Little Big Horn, his horse, Comanche, survived. The captain had been riding Comanche since 1868, and it had been wounded in several earlier engagements with Plains Indians. The horse suffered another wound at Little Big Horn, but after discovering him at the battle site, troopers nursed him back to health and he spent the rest of his cavalry career as a beloved and pampered retiree. When he died of old age on November 7, 1891, the Seventh gave him a full military funeral. But rather than bury him, the regiment's commander sent the horse's carcass to the University of Kansas to be preserved by a taxidermist. Since then, Comanche has been on display at the university's **Natural History Museum** (Dyche Hall, 1345 Jayhawk Blvd.; 785-864-4450). Refurbished in 2005, the old war horse is kept in an airtight case.

Leavenworth (Leavenworth County)

On the west bank of the Missouri River in the northeastern corner of the state, south of Fort Leavenworth, the town of Leavenworth was founded in 1854. A year later, it became the first incorporated city in Kansas Territory. The city's roughest years came during the turbulent anti-slavery versus pro-slavery controversy, and violence in and around Leavenworth continued through the Civil War.

Established in 1827, Fort Leavenworth is the oldest military installation west of the Mississippi still garrisoned by the US Army. Soldiers from Fort Leavenworth protected overland trails, fought in the 1846–1848 Mexican War, and patrolled the Kansas frontier during the Indian Wars. In 1903 the Leavenworth federal prison began accepting inmates. Some of the earlier convicts incarcerated there had cut capers in the Old West, including Native Americans, whites who illegally sold liquor to Indians, and outlaw Al Jennings.

The **Frontier Army Museum** (100 Reynolds Ave.; 913-684-3191), operated by the US Army's Combined Arms Command, documents the history of the fort and the army in the West. Its collection includes more than seven thousand artifacts. Visitors must show a valid photo identification and present proof of vehicle insurance at the Visitor Control Center (8 Sherman Ave.; 479-466-4310) before they can go on the post. A self-guided driving tour available at the museum points out sites on the post associated with the frontier army's two black cavalry units, the Ninth and Tenth Cavalry regiments. The Indians called them Buffalo Soldiers.

When thirty-year-old Cpt. Colin Powell reported to the US Army's Command and General Staff College at Fort Leavenworth in 1967, he was only a year away from his second Vietnam tour and probably did not spend much time thinking about the history of the Buffalo Soldiers. But the next time he got orders for Fort Leavenworth, in 1983, Powell had risen in rank to brigadier general. Noting that the only recognition the Ninth and Tenth Cavalry Regiments had received on the post was the naming of two gravel roads in their honor, the one-star began pushing for a more appropriate memorial to the Buffalo Soldiers. In 1992, as chairman of the Joint Chiefs of Staff, Powell returned to the fort to dedicate an almost thirteen-foot-tall bronze statue of a mounted African American trooper. The **Buffalo Soldier monument** stands on the post at 290 Stimson Avenue.

House of the Harvey House Man

The West was still plenty wild in 1878 when English-born Fred Harvey opened his first **Harvey House** restaurant along the Santa Fe Railroad in Florence, Kansas. Catering to rail travelers, Harvey Houses constituted the nation's first restaurant chain. Harvey Houses served generous portions of good foods and became noted for efficient, friendly service. Part of that was due to Harvey's next innovation. In 1883, the entrepreneur began hiring respectable young women as waitresses for his growing string of eateries. They wore uniforms, had to stick to a strict set of rules, and came to be known as Harvey Girls. By the late 1880s, for every hundred miles of track on the Santa Fe system, a Harvey House welcomed Western travelers. Harvey's final contribution to the West was his pioneer efforts at promoting tourism. He built a series of what would now be called destination hotels and his company developed printed materials to encourage travel in the Southwest. Harvey and his family lived in Leavenworth in a two-story mansion. At the time of his death at age sixty-five in 1901, he owned forty-seven Harvey Houses, fifteen hotels, and thirty dining cars. The Harvey residence has been renovated and opened as the **Fred Harvey National Museum** (624 Olive St.; 913-682-7947).

Lecompton (Douglas County)

The Civil War and the settlement of the Wild West are two separate historical periods, but they are intertwined. The community founded on the south side of the Kansas River in 1854 on a 640-acre Wyandotte Indian land claim was originally named Bald Eagle. But the town was soon renamed for Samuel D. Lecompte, chief justice of the Kansas Territory supreme court. In 1855 Lecompte became the territorial capital. Much of the political discord that led to the war, and the regional conflict along the Kansas and Missouri borders that launched the careers of some of the West's most infamous outlaws, took place here. The **Territorial Capital Museum** (640 East Woodson; 785-887-6148) and **Constitution Hall** (319 Elmore St.; 785-887-6520) put into perspective the violent antebellum events that took place in Kansas.

Leoti (Wichita County)

As the West began to settle, two things made or broke a new town—having a rail connection or being a county seat. Both were best but either one was worth fighting for.

Leoti prevailed in gaining county seat status in newly created Wichita County, but partisan feelings surrounding the young town's competition with another new town called Coronado led to a shootout on February 27, 1887, that left three men dead and several wounded. It took the arrival of law enforcement officers from Dodge City, including Wyatt Earp and Bat Masterson, to calm things down.

With Leoti as county capital, Coronado and another contender, Farmer City, withered like a wheat crop in a bad drought.

Operated by the Wichita County Historical Society, the **Museum of the Great Plains** (201 North 4th St.) is the place to learn more about the war that made one town and turned two others into ghost towns. As a fundraiser, its gift shop sells limited edition prints of an old photograph showing a Who's Who of legendary Wild West figures during the war, including Luke Short, Bat and Jim Masterson, Wyatt Earp, Doc Holliday, Bill Tilghman, Red Loomis, and Pat and Mike Sughrue. The photograph was taken in the spring of 1887 in front of the Wichita County Bank in Coronado. While these men were not active participants in the combat, they had been brought in to intimidate voters on behalf of Coronado. That didn't work, but it did lead to a historic photograph.

Five years after the bloody conflict, attorney William B. Washington—who had been a member of the pro-Leoti faction—built a two-story, Victorian-style house that still stands. Following his death in 1934, the house passed to his son and subsequently had several other owners. The family of the last occupants, Oren and Margie Ames, donated the house and a collection of antique furnishings to the Wichita County Historical Society. The **Washington-Ames House** (J and 3rd Streets; 620-375-2316) is open to visitors.

Liberal (Seward County)

Generations before it would occur to anyone to sell bottled water, S.S. Rogers—who in 1872 built the first house in the vicinity of future Liberal—is said to have given free water to travelers. The story is that Liberal got its name because so many people, in the more formal language of the nineteenth century, often acknowledged Rogers's no-charge hydration with, "That's very liberal of you." When Rogers built a general store in 1885 and the government opened a post office there, he suggested it be called Liberal and postal authorities agreed. After the railroad came through in 1888, the town grew rapidly as a trade center.

Housed in a residence built in 1918, the **Coronado Museum** (567 Cedar St.; 620-624-7624) is home to an eight-foot statue of **Don Francisco Vasquez de Coronado**, who in 1540–1541 with thirty-six men traveled through the Southwest, including a portion of what is now Kansas. While the museum's primary focus is the Coronado expedition, the museum also has artifacts and exhibits on the area during its Wild West days.

Manhattan (Riley County)

To protect travelers along the Santa Fe and Oregon Trails, the army established **Fort Riley** (originally Camp Center) in 1853 at the junction of the Republican and Smoky Hill Rivers. Two years later a party of New Englanders organized as the New England Emigrant Aid Company started a community only eight miles from the fort at the confluence of the Big Blue and Kansas Rivers in the northeastern part of newly created Kansas Territory. Despite the noticeable difference in geography, they decided to call the settlement New Boston. But in June 1855, when a riverboat with emigrants from Ohio ran aground near the new community, the stranded settlers opted to stay as long as the New Englanders agreed to rename the place Manhattan.

The town became an important stop for west-bound travelers during the Colorado gold rush of 1859, and it got a further boost when the transcontinental railroad came through in 1867. The **Riley County Historical Museum** (2309 Claflin Rd.; 785-565-6490) focuses on Manhattan's history.

A key installation during the Indian Wars, Fort Riley was where the Seventh and Eighth Cavalry Regiments were formed on September 21, 1866. A young lieutenant colonel who had risen to general during the Civil War joined the Seventh in November that year and the following year, on February 27, 1867, he became regimental commander. His name was George Armstrong Custer.

In 1884 Gen. Phil Sheridan, in his annual report to Congress recommended that Fort Riley be designated as the army's cavalry headquarters and training school. Congress appropriated money for the expansion of the post, and it continued as the actual and spiritual home of the cavalry until the army dismounted that storied branch of the military after World War II.

Kansas travelers have not needed military protection for a long time, but with twenty-first-century duties Fort Riley remains an active military installation. Non-military visitors must show a photo ID and proof of vehicle insurance and undergo a brief background check before being allowed on post. The **US Cavalry Museum** (Bldg. 205, Huebner Rd.) is in the old post hospital, built in 1855 and remodeled in 1887 to host the newly created cavalry tactics school. A guide to other historic buildings and sites on the post is available at the museum. Also of historical interest is ***Old Trooper***, a statue of a mounted nineteenth-century cavalryman dedicated in 1961 to mark the grave of **Chief**, the last cavalry horse listed on government rolls. Another monument honors **Major Edmund Ogden**, who oversaw the post's construction in 1853 only to die in the cholera epidemic, which two years later claimed some seventy lives at the fort.

Marysville (Marshall County)

When trading post owner Francis Marshall opened the first post office in the Kansas Territory in 1854, he named it for his wife, Mary. In addition to his trading post, Marshall operated a ferry across the nearby Blue River catering to travelers on the Oregon-California Trail. He laid out the town in 1855 and it was incorporated in 1861, a year after the Pony Express established a relay station there.

Changing horses every twelve to fifteen miles, Pony Express riders traveled seventy-five to one hundred miles before handing over their *mochila* (a leather mail sack with four locked pockets) at what the company called a home station. The Marysville station was in a refurbished stone barn leased to the company by Joseph Cottrell. Forty home stations and 150 smaller relay stations lay along the long route from Missouri to California and the first of those stops was Marysville.

Sixteen miles northwest of town the express company set up another station at a log cabin built by German immigrant Geret Hollenberg, who with his wife Sophia Brockmeyer Hollenberg settled along the Little Blue River in 1857. Initially Hollenberg farmed and sold supplies, lodging, and meals to travelers on the Oregon-California Trail. After travel along the trail wound down, Hollenberg continued to support his family as a farmer. The State of Kansas purchased the property in 1941 and twenty years later opened it as a historic site. The **Hollenberg Station** (2889 23rd Rd.) is the best-preserved Pony Express structure still on its original site along the two-thousand-mile route. Located a mile east of Hanover off State Highway 243, the National Historic Site offers interpretive exhibits that focus on Native Americans, westward expansion—including settlers and early commerce—the Oregon-California Trail, and the Pony Express.

Marysville's **Pony Express Barn Museum** (106 South 8th St.) also has exhibits on the history of the Pony Express and Marysville's role as a waypoint in westward expansion.

Meade (Meade County)

An attractive young woman named Eva Dalton arrived in the new prairie town of Meade in 1886 to open a shop where she made and sold ladies' hats and other finery. She caught the eye of local merchant John N. Whipple and they married in the fall of 1887. A highly respected resident, Whipple had a small two-level home built for his bride on a hillside overlooking town. Mrs. Whipple came from a large family, having two sisters and nine brothers. Family tragedy struck in 1887 when her brother Frank was killed in the line of duty while serving as a deputy US marshal. But that was only the beginning. Soon brothers Bob, Grat and Emmett began operating on the other side of the law. When Bob and Grat were shot to death in 1892 in a failed bank robbery at Coffeyville, and Emmett wounded and arrested for murder and robbery, Eva and her husband quietly left Meade. Following their departure, the Whipple house's new occupants discovered a hidden ninety-five-foot tunnel leading downhill from the residence to the Whipple's barn. The belief arose, never proven or disproved, that Eva and her husband had periodically allowed the outlaw Daltons to hide out at their house.

The **Whipple House** (502 South Pearlette St.) was restored during the Depression, with National Youth Administration and Works Progress Administration funds used to line the tunnel with stone. Now the **Meade County Historical Museum**, the organization also maintains a local history research library at 200 East Carthage Street.

Medicine Lodge (Barber County)

Medicine Lodge was settled in 1873, five years after a historic gathering at a sacred Indian site on Medicine Lodge River, a tributary of the Salt Fork of the Arkansas River that Plains Indians believed had healing qualities.

In October 1867 thousands of Plains Apache, Arapahoe, Cheyenne, Comanche, and Kiowa Indians and their headmen met to talk peace with high-ranking US Army officers and government officials—a regiment of cavalry and an artillery battery standing by just in case. With numerous newspaper correspondents on hand to cover the proceedings, three treaties the Indians hoped would assure them good land and end their warring with the whites were negotiated and signed. The first, with the Comanche and Kiowa, was signed October 21. Later that day the government executed a treaty with the Kiowa-Apache. Seven days later, the final treaty was signed with the Southern Cheyenne and Arapahoe. In the end, it all meant nothing.

The conflict with Plains Indians having continued, in 1874 members of the Kansas State Guards and local citizens built a large log stockade not far from where the treaties had been signed. During periods of heightened concern, two-hundred-plus people (along with their livestock and dogs) would take shelter inside the stockade's nine-foot walls. The fortification was never attacked and was eventually torn down. The stockade covered much of what is now downtown Medicine Lodge.

The site of the 1867 treaty negotiations, which given the number present covered a lot of area, is mostly privately owned. A four-hundred-acre park owned by the Medicine Lodge Peace Treaty Association (620-886-9815; GPS coordinates: N37° 15.92', W98° 35.58') is on higher ground, overlooking the undeveloped historic site where the treaties were signed. A historical marker (120 East Washington Ave.) on the south side of the courthouse tells the stockade's story, and the **Stockade Museum** (209 West Fowler Ave.) built in 1961 to resemble (though at a smaller scale) the 1874 fortification, houses relics and exhibits devoted to Barber County's history.

A Rainy Day in April

The hooves of their horses splashing mud, four men rode into town on April 30, 1884, during a torrential downpour. They tied their mounts behind the Medicine Valley Bank on Main Street and three of them walked in out of the rain to do some business. (The fourth man stayed outside with the horses.) One of the men ordered bank president Wylie Payne (1847–1884) to start gathering up all the money, but—in a move that would cost him his life—he went for a gun instead. (Shot by one of his robbers, he died the following day.) Cashier George Geppert raised his hands to signal submission, but one of the robbers shot and killed him anyway. However, before he died he managed to slam shut the door to the safe. The intruders had claimed two lives, but they would not be collecting any money.

Running from the bank, the robbers jumped on their horses and galloped out of town, a nine-man posse soon hot on their heels. They crossed Medicine Lodge River and headed into the gypsum hills southwest of town. Trapped in a box canyon, the would-be bank robbers surrendered and were returned to town.

As if the bold robbery attempt was not startling enough, the identity of two of the prisoners stunned the town: Caldwell city marshal Henry Brown and his chief deputy, Ben Wheeler. The other two men, John Wesley and Billy Smith, were cowboys recruited by Brown. Before they were placed in jail, a photographer took their picture. By then the rain had passed and the sun was shining, but things looked dark for the four men.

Given dry clothing and a hot meal, the prisoners spent the rest of the afternoon writing letters to their loved ones. Though they had asked for and received assurance that they would not be mobbed (lynched) as a condition of their surrender, feelings ran too high. At about 9:00 p.m. a mob forced authorities to release the prisoners. Knowing what was about to happen, the outlaws made a break for it. Brown was shot and killed, and his erstwhile deputy seriously wounded.

Wheeler tried to make a deal with the mob leaders, saying he could provide information incriminating others if only they spared him. It was a nice try, but Wheeler and his two accomplices were soon strangling at the end of ropes.

Vigilantes strung up Wheeler, Wesley, and Smith on an elm tree on Spring Creek at the foot of East 1st Avenue. Possibly unique in Wild West history, Wesley and Smith were hanged at the same time on the same rope.

Edwin Wiley Payne, the slain bank president, lies under an imposing tombstone in **Highland Cemetery** (803 North Iliff St.). The other robbery victim, George Geppert, was buried in Oakwood Cemetery in Allegan, Michigan. Also buried in Highland Cemetery is robber John Wesley (1853–1884). His modern grave marker, a flat red granite stone bordered by a metal fence, has this inscription: "A good cowboy who made a bad decision." The grave sites of Ben Wheeler and Billy Smith are lost, though they are believed to have been buried somewhere just outside the cemetery. The whereabouts of Brown's grave is also unknown. Some have speculated that his wife had him buried at Caldwell while others believe he was buried near his colleagues in crime. The cemetery is one mile east of Medicine Lodge off US 60.

The 1882 vintage building where the robbery occurred was later razed. A modern bank building stands on the site at Main Street and Kansas Avenue. A bronze plaque on the front of the building gives details of the crime that took place there.

When Marshal Brown and his confederates in crime galloped hell for leather down Kansas Avenue with a determined posse hot on their heels, they rode past a new hotel under construction, a hostelry that Payne and Geppert had been prime movers in organizing a stock company to build. The three-story brick **Grand Hotel** (124 South Main St.) would have sixty rooms, plush furnishings, and became the business and social center of the town. For a time after it opened in March 1885, it was the tallest building in Kansas west of Wichita. It still stands today, and a historical marker gives its history.

Famed prohibition crusader Carry A. Nation (1846–1911) lived in Medicine Lodge when she began her campaign against the evils of alcohol. Using a seized whiskey bottle and a pool ball, she trashed her first saloon in nearby Kiowa, Kansas. Not until she raided a saloon in Wichita did she start using the implement for which she became famous: a hatchet. Listed on the National Register of Historic Places, the **painted brick house** (211 West Fowler St.; 620-886-3553) in which Nation lived from 1889 to 1902 still stands in town.

Newton (Harvey County)

Newton began its brief reign as Kansas's most free-wheeling cow town when the Santa Fe Railroad arrived in July 1871. Since Newton lay sixty miles south of Abilene, drovers from Texas no longer had to push their longhorn herds any farther than the new rail head. With Newton suddenly the final stop on the Chisholm Trail, the usual venues of vice and violence soon popped up here like so many pimples on an unshaven teenager's face. The action began almost immediately.

Newton's saloon owners pitched in to hire a couple of toughs as special policemen, Texan **Bill Bailey** and Irishman **Mike McCluskie**. While Newton sorely needed law enforcement to temper the enthusiasm of visiting Texas cowboys, the barmen hadn't counted on the two officers getting into a political argument that graduated into a fistfight that ended with McCluskie shooting and mortally wounding Bailey. That happened August 11, 1871. McCluskie hurried out of town to avoid arrest but returned a few days later after hearing that the killing probably would be considered a matter of self-defense.

Unfortunately for McCluskie, avoiding prosecution did not afford immunity from retribution. On the night of August 19, **Hugh Anderson**, one of Bailey's Texas pals, shot and killed McCluskie. Three other friends of the late Bill began firing their six-shooters, likely intending only to keep the crowd at bay until Anderson escaped. But a young McCluskie sycophant, **James Riley**, pulled both of his revolvers and started blasting away at the Texans. Riley shot seven men and three of them ended up dying.

Even though five men had died violently in Newton in the span of only eight days—four of them in one transaction—after the initial wide-spread news coverage, the incident was largely forgotten. None of the participants had been a noted figure and none became notorious in death. When young Riley walked out of the bar that night, he disappeared into history.

Hugh Anderson was said to have been slain two years later in a revenge-motivated clash, but recent scholarship has exposed the story as fiction. He returned to Texas, followed in his father's boot steps as a successful cattleman, and lived to sixty-two. What did kill him was a bolt of lightning during a New Mexico thunderstorm.

McCluskie killed Bailey in front of the **Red Front Saloon** on Main Street in Newton. The second shooting took place in **Perry Tuttle's Dance Hall** (Main and 2nd Streets) in a district south of the railroad tracks known as **Hide Town**. That name supposedly came because the "fancy women" who danced or otherwise entertained in the area "showed a lot of hide." Neither building remains, but a historical marker relating the detail of the shootout stands at the site of the dance hall.

Those killed in the so-called **Newton Massacre** were buried in the town's **Boot Hill**, but they did not rest in peace. McCluskie's family later had his remains removed for reburial in Missouri. Roughly eight years after the shooting, Dr. J.T. Axtell dug up several bodies for medical purposes. One, he said, was that of victim Jim Martin, whom he reduced to a skeleton he kept in his office for years. What became of Martin after Dr. Axtell gave up medicine is not known. The other remains in Boot Hill were later removed to Newton's **Greenhill Cemetery** (1100 West 1st St.). It had been so long since Boot Hill last saw use that no one knew for sure who was buried there.

Even after the cowboys left, the railroad continued to shape the town as Mennonite immigrants from Germany and the Ukraine streamed into the area. The **Kaufman Museum** (27th and North Main), located on the campus of Bethel College, a Mennonite school in North Newton, focuses on that aspect of Newton's history. A paved path beginning outside the museum leads to an area north of the museum where swales hollowed out by the hundreds of thousands of longhorn cattle that traveled along the Chisholm Trail can still be seen. A stone and bronze historical marker giving a history of the Chisholm Trail at this point stands in front of the **Luyken Fine Arts Building** on the Bethel campus. Another marker describing the route the trail took through Newton stands in **Okerburg Park** (4th and Plum Streets). The base of the marker is an ornately carved capital from one of the pillars in the old Harvey County Courthouse, which was razed in 1966.

The Harvey County Historical Society bought the red brick, 1903-vintage **Carnegie Public Library** (203 North Main St.) from the City of Newton in 1973 for use as a museum and opened it a year later. In addition to its artifacts and exhibits, the building houses the society's local history archives. Among the records is a July 15, 1872, grand jury indictment charging that Perry Tuttle (whose saloon was the scene of the 1871 massacre) "did set up, keep and maintain a certain common rowdy house and brothel." The museum's blog is a treasure trove of information relating to Newton's brief but violent past and other aspects of the county's history, including background on one of its better-known sons, actor Milburn Stone—Doc Adams of *Gunsmoke* fame.

Nicodemus (Graham County)

One of the Wild West's most unusual towns, Nicodemus was settled in 1877 by former slaves who came to Kansas during Reconstruction hoping for a better life. Three hundred and eighty of them arrived from Lexington, Kentucky, to live in a place that had been described to them as a new promised land. But when they got to the townsite on the prairie, they found no trees, drought-parched soil, and rough weather—real cold in winter, real hot in summer. Still, they hung on, surviving their first winter by gathering and selling the buffalo bones that littered the plains or working for the railroad. (At the time, manufacturers ground buffalo bones for use in making fertilizer.) At first, the immigrants—known in Kansas as "exodusters"—lived in dugouts, followed by sod houses, and finally wood-frame residences. The town grew and did well economically, but when it became clear a decade later that Nicodemus would never have a rail connection, the town began a slow fade. A few descendants of the original settlers still live there, making it the only originally all-black town west of the Mississippi that continues as a community.

Nicodemus National Historic Site (304 Washington Ave.; 785-839-4233) is located south of the roadside park off US 24. A visitor's center with interpretive exhibits is in the old Township Hall, the only building operated by the National Park Service and open to the public. The other structures that are part of the historic site are privately owned. A self-guided tour is available at the visitor's center.

Oakley (Logan County)

Sensational lady sharpshooter Annie Oakley reigned as one of the top stars of Buffalo Bill's Wild West show in 1886 when town founder David D. Hoag decided to name this northwest Kansas town Oakley. But Hoag meant to honor his mother, Elizabeth Oakley Gardner Hoag, and not the Ohio-born markswoman. A transportation and agricultural center, Oakley is the Logan County seat. Lest anyone think Oakley the town is named for Oakley the performer, a historical marker (1398 West 2nd St.) sets the record straight.

Two Buffalo Hunters Named Bill

In 1868 a pair of buffalo hunters who shared the same first name—William—actively plied their trade in Logan County, years before Oakley got on the map. Both young men, **William Cody** and **William Comstock**, had a contract to provide buffalo meat to the men laying tracks for the Kansas Pacific Railroad. Both had come to be better known by their nickname, but neither felt it would do to have two Buffalo Bills. Accordingly, they decided the catchy moniker would go to the hunter who took down the most buffalo in a single day. After the crack of the last shot, William Cody had harvested sixty-nine buffalo to William Comstock's forty-six. And from then on, Cody was Buffalo Bill. Logan County's early connection with the Western icon is commemorated in a twice-life-sized bronze sculpture that stands as the center piece of the **Buffalo Bill Cultural Center** (3083 US 84; 785-671-1000) in Oakley. Created by Charlie and Pat Norton of Leoti, Kansas, and dedicated in 2004, the monument is sixteen feet high and weighs nine thousand pounds.

Oberlin (Decatur County)

Founded in 1873, the Decatur County seat of Oberlin was first called Sappa for Sappa Creek, a tributary of the Republican River. But one of the men who donated land for the townsite hailed from Ohio and the new community's name was changed to honor his hometown. The singular moment in Decatur County history would come five years after Oberlin's settling.

In the fall of 1878, the last Indian raid in Kansas occurred in Decatur County when a band of Cheyenne under Dull Knife passed through during a desperate attempt to return to their homeland. Armed volunteers left Oberlin to confront the Indians, who had killed numerous settlers in the county as they made their way north after leaving their reservation in what is now Oklahoma. The Oberlin volunteers organized into three companies, one of which encountered the Indians on September 29, 1878. They killed one and possibly wounded several others before the Indians escaped into Nebraska.

Oberlin Cemetery (US 36 and US 83), just east of town, has a tall limestone obelisk erected in 1911 in remembrance of the eighteen Decatur County raid victims. Grouped around the monument are their graves, including four members of one family. The **Last Indian Raid Museum** (258 South Penn Ave.) has exhibits on the Dull Knife raid and the overall history of Decatur County. The complex includes fifteen early-day buildings, among them the old county jail.

Pawnee Rock (Barton County)

The town of Pawnee Rock was settled in 1874. It took its name from a nearby geologic feature that was an important landmark along the Santa Fe Trail. Once more than 150 feet tall (subsequent quarrying by railroad construction crews and builders reduced its height by roughly half), the sandstone rock marked the halfway point along the trail. "Pawnee rock springs like a huge wart from the carpeted green of the prairie," one traveler wrote in 1840. While not the most pleasingly evocative word choice, the "wart" was a welcome sight to travelers. The historic site was acquired by the state in 1909. Three years later, a granite monument was dedicated to commemorate the rock's significance in the settlement of the West. **Pawnee Rock State Historic Site** (one-half mile north of US 56 and the town of Pawnee Rock; 785-272-8681) preserves the landmark.

Pittsburg (Crawford County)

Pittsburg started as a railroad town in 1876 and with ample coal deposits in the area it grew as a mining and industrial center. Named for Pittsburgh, Pennsylvania, it was originally called New Pittsburgh. The "New" went away in 1880 and in 1894 the "h" was dropped. The **Crawford County Historical Museum** (651 South US 69; 620-231-1440) focuses on Pittsburg's history.

Tombstone Factory

Many a Kansas old-timer forever rests beneath a marble tombstone cut, dressed, and engraved at **Pittsburg's Hance White & Son Marble Works**. White began making grave markers and selling cut stone here in 1892, but it's what he did in 1904 that makes him memorable. Needing more workspace, he built a spacious two-story stone structure. Since he had his office and showroom elsewhere downtown, he could have put up a plain building for his stone saws, routers, and other equipment, but he oversaw construction of an ornate piece of architecture both pleasing and unusual. He accomplished that by having thirteen facial carvings used as keystones for each of the building's arched doors and windows. So far as known, White did not leave a list of the figures he immortalized in stone. That turned speculating on their identity into something of a local spectator sport—and excellent free advertising.

Some of the faces are said to be well-known and respected personages (at least at the time), including Buffalo Bill, prohibitionist Carry Nation, Mark Twain, steamboat inventor Robert Fulton, and Christopher Columbus (or George Washington). The rest of the stones are believed to be less savory Wild West characters, including Jesse James, Belle Starr, Bat Masterson, the frontier serial killers remembered as the Bloody Benders (though some say the younger looking of the stone women might be Martha Washington and not the infamous Kate Bender), and Buffalo Joe North. The latter was supposedly lynched in Pittsburg for cheating at cards. Any possibility of a big reveal died with White in 1926. Of course, he might have told his son Paul, but he's long dead as well.

The old marble works stands at the northeast corner of 2nd and Locust Streets. White and his wife Margaret are buried in **Mount Olive Cemetery** (402 East Quincy St.) in a mausoleum with no ornamentation. The couple's son Paul is buried in Kansas City, Missouri.

Built in 1889, **Hotel Stillwell** (707 North Broadway) has accommodated numerous notables over the years, including arguably the early twentieth century's most enthusiastic admirer of the Wild West, Theodore Roosevelt. The Romanesque Revival–style hotel was named for railroad tycoon Arthur L. Stillwell, who helped arrange its financing. In 1992 the hotel was converted into an apartment building.

Republic (Republic County)

Founded in 1854 near the Republic River, this northern Kansas town was named not for the democratic republic in which it stands, but for the **Kitkehahki** or Republican band of the Pawnee people. The Pawnee, once lords of the Central Great Plains, had a large, fortified village near what is now Republic. It consisted of a series of approximately forty large, earth-covered lodges with an estimated population of a thousand Pawnee and was occupied from the late 1700s through approximately 1830. Since 1967, the archeological remnants of the village have been preserved and interpreted by the **Pawnee Indian State Historic Site** (480 Pawnee Trail; 785-361-2255) on State Highway 266, eight miles north of US 36. Near the museum is a granite monument erected in 1901 to commemorate a visit to the village in 1806 by noted Western explorer and army lieutenant Zebulon M. Pike. Subsequent historical research has brought that claim into question, but the significance of the site remains.

SALINA (SALINE COUNTY)

William Phillips, James Muir, and Alexander Campbell left Lawrence on foot in 1858 looking for a suitable place to start a new town. The site they selected on the Smoky Hill River became Salina, named for the salt marshes found along the stream. The community served as a supply point for west-bound travelers, but Phillips, a lawyer and journalist, believed that a railroad would be routed through the new town someday. Any immediate likelihood of that happening ended with the Civil War. The town endured some dark days during the war, but Phillips had been right about Salina getting a rail connection. That came about in 1867. Joseph McCoy, who would transform sleepy Abilene into a booming cattle town, had looked at Salina first, but the town's civic leaders wanted nothing to do with Texas cattle or Texas cowboys. In 1872 the business community had a change of outlook and actively sought cattle herds. Salina became a second-tier cow town, but unlike Abilene and the other noted cow towns, law enforcement in Salina brooked little foolishness. Not that the town didn't have its saloons and the other typical vice venues, but it never saw the level of violence other places did. By 1874 the trail herds disappeared, and few regretted it.

With a focus on the region's history, the **Smoky Hill Museum** (211 West Iron Ave.; 785-309-5776) opened in the old downtown post office in 1986, but some of its artifacts and documents date to the organization of the Saline County Historical Society in 1879. Out of Kansas's four hundred museums, this museum is among only a dozen that are national accredited.

Topeka (Shawnee County)

The Oregon Trail crossed the Kansas River at the future site of Topeka, but the surrounding bottomland had long been a camping place of Kansa Indians. The town that grew to a city developed from a ferry built to accommodate westward travelers. Founded in 1854 and incorporated three years later, Topeka became the capital when Kansas acquired statehood in 1861.

On the last leg of his Great Plains tour, having hunted buffalo with scout William F. Cody and Lt. Col. George Armstrong Custer, Russia's Grand Duke Alexei Alexandrovich and his traveling party of military and civilian VIPs arrived in Topeka on January 22, 1873. Accompanied by Custer and the rest of his entourage, the Russian royal was escorted to the new capitol to appear before a joint session of the legislature. Ladies leaned out of windows waving their handkerchiefs as the dignitaries approached. At the time, the state capitol consisted only of what is now its east wing. The **historic statehouse**, not completed until 1903, stands at 10th and Jackson Streets.

Operated by the Kansas Historical Society, the **Kansas Museum of History** (6425 Southwest 6th Ave.; 785-272-8681) tells the story of Kansas's rich and often bloody history. Exhibits interpret all aspects of the saga, from its Native American cultures to the development of the Atchison, Topeka, and Santa Fe Railroad. Among its numerous Wild West artifacts are the rifle that had been presented to Caldwell Marshal Henry Brown before he went bad and a pair of Custer's boots, donated by his widow, Libby.

Victoria (Ellis County)

One of the frontier military's primary missions in the 1860s was protecting railroad construction gangs as tracks moved westward across the nation. But soldiers could not be everywhere. In October 1867 Cheyenne warriors attacked a party of seven Union Pacific rail workers near present-day Victoria. The warriors killed six men but a seventh, though seriously wounded, managed to make it to Fort Hays to report the massacre. He later died of his wounds and was buried at the fort. The other six men were buried in the general vicinity of where they died. The original memorial placed at the grave site was stolen. A replacement was dedicated in 2003. The first marker later turned up in Ellsworth County and was returned to the cemetery. The graves of the six victims make up what came to be called **Union Pacific Cemetery** (3rd Street and Cathedral Avenue).

Wallace (Wallace County)

Wallace is named after **Fort Wallace**, a nearby military post established just east of the Kansas-Colorado border on the south fork of the Smoky Hill River in 1867. Fort Wallace's troops had more encounters with Indians than any other post on the frontier. Its mission complete, the post was abandoned in 1882. Though only foundations remain today, the **Fort Wallace Museum** (2655 US 40; 785-891-3564) tells the story of the fort and its role in protecting travelers on the Smoky Hill Trail and workers putting down the tracks of the Kansas Pacific Railroad. Adjacent to the museum is the restored **Pond Creek Stage Station**, originally located on the Butterfield Overland Trail about a mile from its present location.

Numbers Tell the Story . . .

On September 12, 1867, assistant surgeon T.H. Turner completed a statistical report, duly endorsed by his chain of command, that encapsulates the violent nature of the Indian Wars. Styled, "Report of Killed and Wounded Soldiers and Citizens at and in Vicinity of Fort Wallace, Kansas by Indians," the numbers that followed needed no narrative to enhance their impact. From June 4 to July 1, the doctor noted, thirty-two people had died by arrow, bullet, and occasionally, a combination of both. Of those, the first twenty-one were soldiers, including two sergeants, three corporals, one bugler, and fifteen privates. The other eleven casualties were civilians, two listed as "unknown" and one simply as "Mexican." The officer did not record American Indians casualties.

Wellington (Sumner County)

Of Kansas's nineteenth-century cow towns, Wellington is the least known. That's because local officials, with help from a local vigilance committee, succeeded in keeping the community far less boisterous than the state's other cattle trail stops. Platted in 1871, and named after the Duke of Wellington, the town became the seat of Sumner County in 1872. While rowdy Caldwell, only a twenty-mile horseback ride to the southwest, slowed down after the trail drives stopped, Wellington's status as county seat, plus the advent of rail service in 1887, kept it going.

The community effort to start a museum in Wellington began in 1963 and came to fruition two years later with the donation of a four-story building that became the **Chisholm Trail Museum** (502 North Washington Ave.; 620-326-3820). The gift came from the family of Dr. A.C. Hatcher, a physician who opened a hospital in the building in 1916. Three floors of the old medical facility are devoted to exhibits related to the history of the cattle trail, Wellington, and Sumner County. The jail was replaced with a new facility in 1900 and the county put it up for sale. It and the old county courthouse were later razed. Downtown Wellington Historic District is listed on the National Register of Historic Places and includes sixty-five historic buildings.

The privately owned **Panhandle Railroad Museum** (425 East Harvey Ave.; 620-399-8611) displays a collection of early Santa Fe Railroad equipment and artifacts gathered over the years by P.H. Wiley, who spent twenty-seven years working for Santa Fe. Wiley renovated a historic building constructed in 1886 to house his collection.

Bye, Bill

William L. Brooks's career ladder went straight down rather than up. First he drove a stagecoach, a respectable job. Then he worked as a lawman, an even more respected position. He dropped a notch when he turned to buffalo hunting, though he still sought to make an honest living. But then Brooks went to stealing mules. He and two other thieves, a lawyer named L.B. Hasbrouck and a man who went by the name of Charley Smith (later found to be an alias) were arrested by a sheriff's posse in Sumner County and jailed in Wellington. Brooks's wife came from Caldwell to visit him, which turned out to be the last time they saw each other. Later that night, on July 29, 1874, an armed mob removed Brooks and his two cellmates and lynched them from a tree about a half a mile out of town. The jail was replaced with a new facility in 1900 and the county put it up for sale. It and the old county courthouse were later razed.

Wichita (Sedgwick County)

His father came from Scotland. His mother was Cherokee. His name would become attached to one of the West's more storied transportation corridors—the Chisholm Trail. **Jesse Chisholm** established a trading post at the confluence of the Little Arkansas and Arkansas Rivers to do business with the Wichita Indians—bartering buttons, cloth, flour, sugar, and other staples for furs. The north-south trail he blazed to move his goods up from what is now the Muskogee, Oklahoma, area was the initial segment of what would become the first great cattle trail from Texas to Kansas. And his remote trading post, which he ran from 1863 until his death in 1868, would become the city of Wichita.

The same year Chisholm died, cattle herds bound for the rail head at Abilene, Kansas, began passing through Wichita. But the town had only a few hundred residents until a branch of the Santa Fe Railroad arrived in 1872. That made Wichita the more logical destination for Texas trail herds and the town blossomed like a Kansas sunflower.

A state historical marker (GPS coordinates: N37° 45.63', W97° 20.17') at a roadside turnout off North Broadway, two-tenths of a mile north of I-235, tells the story of the **Chisholm Trail**.

Cowboys on the Chisholm Trail, and Indians before them, used a large mulberry tree as a waypoint. More than two hundred years old, the tree still stands on the grounds of the **Kansas Mason Home** (Martinson and Maple Streets). A historical marker tells its story.

Old Cowtown Museum (1865 West Museum Blvd.; 316-219-1871) was founded in 1953 and maintains five restored historic buildings. A visitor's center provides interpretive information on Wichita and the Old West.

The **Wichita-Sedgwick County Historical Museum** (204 South Main St.; 316-265-9314) opened in 1939 as the Wichita Public Museum and now occupies four floors of the old Wichita City Hall. Designed by George W. Bird and William T. Proudfoot in 1890 and completed in 1892, the building is listed on the National Register of Historic Places. The museum has more than seventy thousand artifacts; the third floor is dedicated to the history of Wichita.

The Keeper of the Plains statue was erected in 1974 as an early bicentennial project. Done by Kiowa-Comanche artist Blackbear Bosin, the forty-four-foot steel statue featuring the silhouette of an Indian stands next to the **Mid-America All Indian Center** (650 North Seneca St.; 316-350-3340), a large museum focusing on the Plains Indians. In 2006 the sculpture was placed on a thirty-foot rock promontory to allow it to be seen from a greater distance.

The Original Buffalo Bill

William "Buffalo Bill" Mathewson is said not to have had much use for that other Buffalo Bill, William Cody. After all, Mathewson had the nickname first. A New Yorker, Mathewson followed the Santa Fe Trail from Independence, Missouri, in 1849 and established a series of trading posts along the route in the 1850s. In the following decade, Mathewson became a professional buffalo hunter. But he and fellow hunters took buffalo meat, not the hides. In 1867, already a seasoned plainsman and scout, he helped as an interpreter during the Medicine Lodge Peace Treaty negotiations. As a trader familiar with Native American culture, he also brokered the return of more than fifty captive women and children. He built a log cabin in newly founded Wichita in 1868 and remained there the rest of his long life. After Wichita boomed during the trail-driving days of the 1870s, he became a successful banker and later operated a streetcar company.

Despite his numerous adventures on the Plains, Mathewson wasn't much of a talker and eschewed publicity. When Cody came through Wichita in 1913, the two graybeards met for the first time and posed for a photograph. In it, Buffalo Bill the showman looks jovial. The original Buffalo Bill, staring deadpan at the camera, does not look at all enthusiastic. Three years later, Mathewson died sitting in his front porch rocking chair.

Built in 1904, Mathewson's two-story, six-room, 1,216-square-foot house (1047 Market St.) still stands. It is privately owned, but easily visible from the street or sidewalk. Mathewson's grave is in **Highland Cemetery** (1005 North Hillside Ave.; 316-337-9225; Section 1, Block 161, Grave 12), his final resting place marked by a tall monument bearing this legend: "W. Mathewson/ The Original Buffalo Bill/Last of The Old Scouts."

On the west side of the Arkansas, just across the river from Wichita, was the community of **Delano**. It had a respectable name—honoring Columbus Delano, President Grant's secretary of the interior—but that was pretty much all the respectability it could muster. Delano became the venue for the seamier saloons and brothels that catered to the Texas drovers wanting to let off steam after weeks on the Chisholm Trail. One of the bar owners was **Joseph Lowe**, better known as Rowdy Joe for having bitten off a fellow's nose during a little difficulty in Denver. In Delano, Joe got even rowdier when an argument with rival saloon operator **Edwin F. Beard**, better known as Red Beard, degraded to gun play on October 30, 1873. When the shooting stopped, Rowdy Joe had a minor neck wound and Red Beard had been punctured by two buckshot balls. (He died of an infection a few weeks later.) Two innocent bystanders also sustained wounds. Rowdy Joe was arrested but not convicted and left town as soon as he could. When the cattle drives stopped coming to Wichita, Delano went into decline. The City of Wichita took in the district in 1880.

Delano's dives operated along present-day Douglas Street. A church stands at Douglas and McLean Streets in Wichita where Lowe's saloon once did business. Red Beard was buried in **Highland Cemetery** (1005 North Hillside Ave. at 9th St.; 316-337-9225; Section 1, Lot 110, Grave 7).

When **"Jack" Ledford** ran for Sedgwick County sheriff in 1870, he had a simple campaign promise: "If I am elected . . . there will be no more horses stolen around these parts." Being an accomplished horse thief and stage robber, Ledford likely would have lived up to his promise had he assumed office. But due to irregularities that he no doubt had a hand in, the election was ruled null and void. Ledford soon enough would be null and void himself. When his young wife's former boyfriend learned that Ledford had a $2,000 price on his head in connection with stealing army horses and killing a government teamster, he notified the military where the unsuccessful candidate for sheriff could be found. Troops rode into Wichita on February 28, 1871, to take the former army scout into custody. Realizing what was afoot, the unarmed Ledford ran out the back door of George DeArmour's saloon. A friend tossed him a couple of revolvers and Ledford fortified himself in the outhouse behind the drinking establishment. When troops surrounded the one-holer, Ledford emerged with pistols blazing and quickly went down with three bullet holes in him. He died about an hour later.

The bar behind which the shooting occurred is long gone, but Ledford is buried in **Highland Cemetery** (Block 1, Lot 96, Grave 6). His standard government grave marker ignores his date of birth as well as the date and circumstances resulting in his demise. All it says is "J. H. Ledford, Co. K, 2nd MO [Missouri] LA [Light Artillery]." Thirty years after Ledford's death, a Kansas newspaper reported that his friends had raised $300 toward a monument to be placed on the spot where he was killed. If such a memorial was erected, it is not known today.

Another noted Wild West figure buried in **Highland Cemetery** (Section 2, Block 70, Lot 6) is **James Patrick Masterson**, brother of famed buffalo hunter, lawman, and newspaperman Bat Masterson. Both men and their brother Ed rubbed shoulders with Wyatt Earp. Like his brother Bat, Jim Masterson started out as a buffalo hunter, but in the spring of 1877, he and a brother opened a dance hall in Dodge City, where brother Ed Masterson was sheriff (he was killed in the line of duty the following year). Jim later became town marshal in Dodge but lost his job in 1881 following a change in city administration. From Kansas he went on to spend time in Colorado and New Mexico until appointed deputy US marshal in Guthrie, Oklahoma Territory. In that capacity, he took part in the notorious shootout at Ingalls, Oklahoma, in 1893. Only thirty-nine, he died of tuberculosis on March 31, 1895.

NEBRASKA

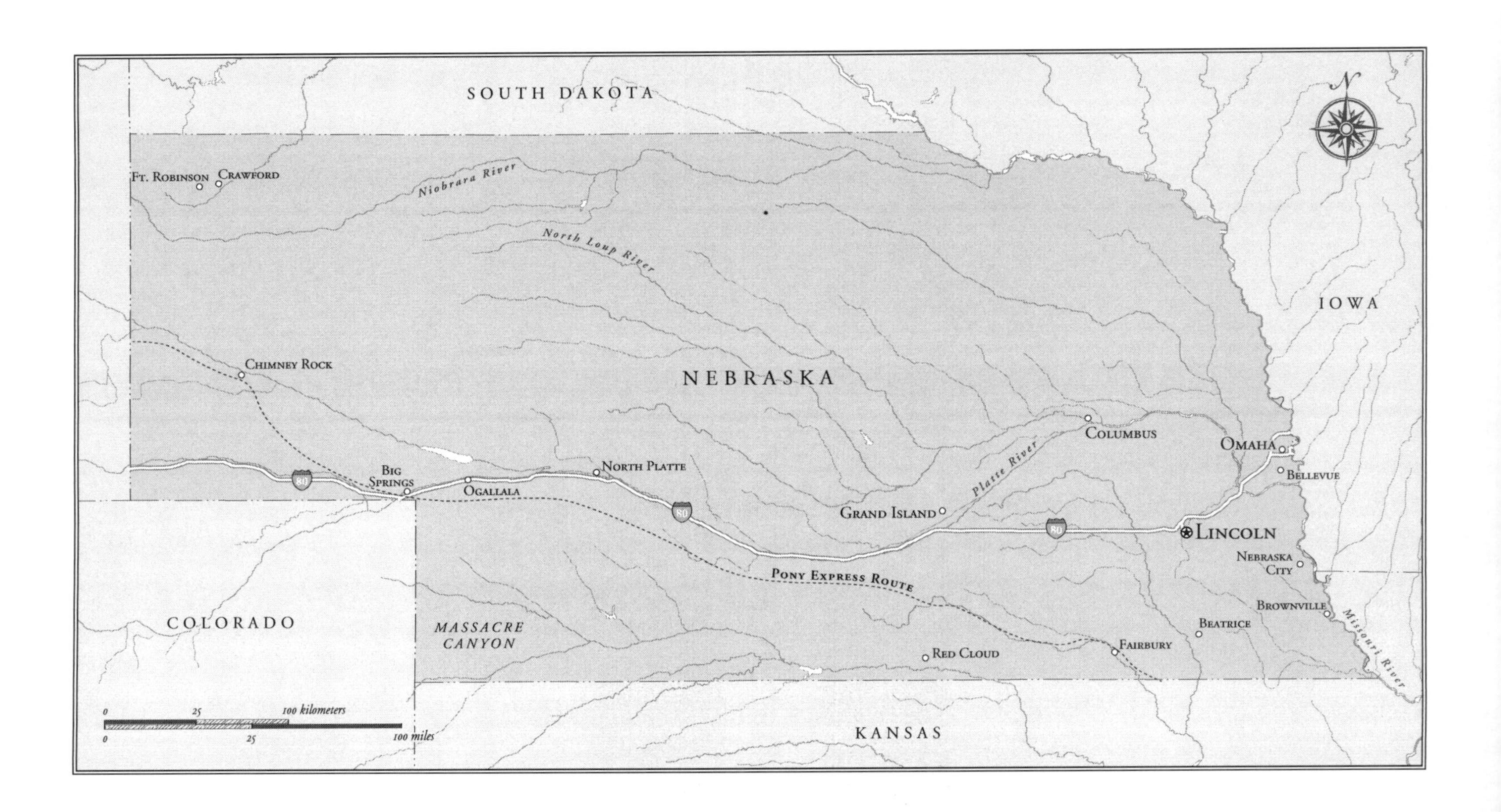
SOUTH DAKOTA
IOWA
NEBRASKA
COLORADO
KANSAS
Ft. Robinson
Crawford
Niobrara River
North Loup River
Chimney Rock
Big Springs
Ogallala
North Platte
Platte River
Grand Island
Columbus
Omaha
Bellevue
Lincoln
Nebraska City
Brownville
Missouri River
Beatrice
Fairbury
Red Cloud
Pony Express Route
Massacre Canyon
80
0
25
100 kilometers
100 miles

Alliance (Box Butte County)

In the Wild West, men deemed a lot of things worth fighting for—among them your honor, your scalp, or your town's status as county seat.

With the organization of Box Butte County in 1886, Nonpareil became the first county capital. Then, in 1891, Henningford took up the banner. But in 1899, when Alliance got the county seat, officials did not want the two-story, fifty- by forty-foot courthouse at Henningford to stand vacant so they contracted with a house mover in Lincoln to relocate the building. When that firm couldn't get it done within the stipulated time, the Burlington and Missouri Railroad—which had just reached Alliance—offered to do it. The one-hundred-ton courthouse was moved on wheels to a flatcar and then transported twenty miles to its new foundation.

The railroad-shipped courthouse served until 1913 when a larger, three-story brick building was built at 515 Box Butte Avenue.

Kenneth "Dobby" Lee thought the history of the Wild West and his area of Nebraska worth preserving. After retiring he spent the rest of his life collecting and restoring twenty-six structures dating from the 1890s to the early years of the Great Depression as part of **Dobby's Frontier Town** (320 East 25th St. at Nance Road; 308-762-4321). Ranging from an old saloon and brothel to an undertaker's establishment, the vintage buildings are full of artifacts from the frontier era. Following Lee's death at age eighty-seven in 2009, a nonprofit volunteer entity kept the attraction open.

The **Knight Museum and Sandhills Center** (908 Yellowstone; 308-762-2384) focuses on the history of Alliance and the sandhills country of western Nebraska. Beginning with Native Americans, the museum covers everything from the coming of the railroad to the "Rogues, Rascals and Visionaries" who shaped the town and surrounding area. The museum also has extensive archival records relating to Alliance and the sandhills.

The **Sallows Military Museum** (1100 Niobrara Ave.; 308-762-2385) covers military history from the Indian Wars through the war on terrorism.

Bayard (Morrill County)

When the towering geologic feature known as **Chimney Rock** came into view, travelers along the Oregon Trail knew they had made it to end of the Great Plains and the beginning of what would be a hard trek across the Rocky Mountains. While no known historically significant events occurred here, one researcher's analysis of three hundred overland travel narratives revealed that the 470-foot formation was the most-mentioned landmark on the trail. Looming over the sand hills of western Nebraska, the rock must have been even more impressive in the nineteenth century. Geologists believe it has lost roughly thirty feet in elevation over the last 150 years from wind, erosion, and lightning strikes.

Eighty acres surrounding the landmark became the **Chimney Rock National Historic Site** (9822 County Road 75; 308-586-2581) in 1956. Operated by the Nebraska Historic Society, the site is located one mile south of the junction of State Highways 26 and 92 and has interpretive displays and a video on the epic western migration.

Beatrice (Gage County)

A branch of the Oregon Trail crossed the Big Blue River at a point that would become Beatrice in 1857. But growth came slowly until Congress approved the Homestead Act in 1862. The new law granted 160 acres of free land to any head of household willing to live, build, and work on it. The West had changed forever.

Illinois-born **Daniel Freeman** (1826–1908) obtained title to his 160 acres on January 1, 1863, a short distance west of Beatrice. Millions left their homes for a new start on the frontier, but Freeman's claim was the first. The Homestead Act conveyed 270 million acres—10 percent of the land area of the nation—to claimants before its expiration in 1976. Established in 1936, the **Homestead**

National Monument (8523 West State Highway 4; 402-223-3514) stands today on Freeman's former land. The site's Heritage Center has exhibits exploring the Homestead Act's impact on immigration, native tribes, the ecosystem, agriculture, industrialization, and later Federal land policies.

Bellevue (Sarpy County)

Growing from a fur trading post established on the west side of the Missouri River in 1822, and incorporated in 1855, Bellevue is Nebraska's oldest city, and its founding marked the beginning of Nebraska settlement. West-bound travelers stocked up in Bellevue before beginning their journey. In the waning days of the Plains Indian Wars, the army established **Fort Crook** near there in 1890.

Visitors can learn about Nebraska's birthplace at the **Sarpy County Museum** (2402 Clay St.; 402-292-1880).

Big Springs (Deuel County)

First called Lone Tree for a large cottonwood that served as a waypoint on the Oregon Trail, the only thing big about Big Springs is its name. It remained only open prairie until the Union Pacific Railroad came through in 1867 and built a depot, a water tank, and a couple of houses for its workers. Located 162 miles east of Cheyenne, Wyoming, and about ten miles from the Colorado state line, Big Springs was not platted as a town until 1883.

The only thing of note that ever happened in Big Springs took place on the night of September 18, 1877, when six armed men rode up and easily took control of the depot. Disabling the station's telegraph equipment, the gunmen ordered the station agent to hang a red lantern that would bring the Union Pacific's east-bound express Number 4 to an unscheduled stop. Approaching Big Springs around 10:45 p.m., the engineer of the fast train saw the signal and, adhering to strict railroad rules, let off on the steam and set the brakes. After the train coasted to a stop, the conductor alighted to see armed bandits who rounded up the train crew and ordered the station agent to knock on the express car door. As he slid open the door, several of the men jumped aboard and began ransacking the car. They collected about $500 in cash from one of two safes—the larger of the two had a time lock and could not be opened—and were about to leave when someone opened a stack of wooden boxes, all full of twenty-dollar gold coins just minted in San Francisco.

With $60,000 in gold and another $1,300 in cash and valuables collected from the male passengers (chivalrously, the gunmen did not rob the ladies), the bandits doused the locomotive's boiler fire and rode off into the night. Stopping beneath the lone cottonwood on the north side of the Big Springs River only long enough to divide their haul six ways, the men split into groups of two and made their getaway.

While the Big Springs job is sometimes credited as being the Wild West's first train robbery, it wasn't. The Jesse James gang had achieved that honor in 1873. What could be said about the **Big Springs robbery** is that it netted its perpetrators what back then amounted to a fortune. In fact, it would be the largest loss ever for the Union Pacific (worth $1.4 million today). The leader of the gang was a young man named Sam Bass, and it was not the last time he'd make news.

A state historical marker (GPS coordinates: N41° 03.72', W102° 04.51') located in Eiker Park (US 138 and Pine Street) summarizes the robbery. The wooden Union Pacific depot is long gone, but the marker notes the robbery occurred "near here."

Built by Edwin A. Phelps in 1885 for Union Pacific railroaders and travelers, the two-story frame **Phelps Hotel** (401 Pine St.; 308-889-3246) was known as the "House of Three Chimneys." The hotel not only accommodated overnight guests, it served as the community's social center. The building is listed on the National Register of Historic Places.

Most plains sod houses did not last—the Nebraska Historical Building Survey in 1994 located only fourteen. One of them is the three-room **sod house** built in 1886 by homesteaders Wallace and Libby Waterman. Wallace's son enlarged the house in 1925 and covered the two-foot-thick sod walls with concrete. The family occupied the old residence until 1989, and the Deuel County Historical Society acquired it in 1993. A state historical marker in Eiker Park (Pine Street and US 138) outlines the structure's history. The house stands nine miles north, on the Day Road (GPS coordinates: N41° 3.72', W102° 4.51').

The Platte River Valley has been on the westward migration route since 1841. The **Overland Trail** split into two branches near future Big Springs, one following the north fork of the Platte, the other the south fork. With the discovery of gold in the Rocky Mountains in 1859, the trail along the river's south fork began to see heavier use. A state historical marker (GPS coordinates: N41° 02.05', W102° 12.67') summarizes the trail's history. There's a scenic turnout at east-bound mile marker 99 on I-80.

Brownville (Nemaha County)

Brownville was founded in 1854 by Richard Brown, who built a cabin on the west side of the Missouri River in newly created Nebraska Territory. Incorporated in 1856, Brownville became an important river port. And, since it was on the other side of a wide, formidable body of water, it made a convenient cooling off place for outlaws. Despite its citizens' early ambitions, numerous factors kept the town from growing, but during its brief heyday it was a bustling commercial and transportation center. Thirty-two Brownville structures are listed on the National Register of Historic Places. A two-story brick and stone building (116 Main St.) once accommodated the **Lone Tree Saloon,** said to have been occasionally patronized by Jesse James. Brownville has ten museums, including the **Museum of Missouri River History**. The museum is on board the *Captain Meriwether Lewis*, a 1931-vintage river dredge that resembles an antebellum riverboat. The floating museum is off Riverside Park downtown.

Calloway (Custer County)

Named for Lt. Col. George Armstrong Custer, Custer County was created in 1877. At this time, the log ranch house of Milo F. Young became the county's first courthouse. On December 17, 1880, preliminary hearings held in the structure set the stage for the trial of Texas cattleman Isom Prentice "Print" Olive and Fred Fisher for the lynching of Ami Ketchum and Luther Mitchell. After the county built a more imposing courthouse, the cabin continued for years as a private residence. In 1933 Young's estate donated the structure to the City of Calloway and workers moved it to Morgan Park. A state historical marker (200–298 North Cameron Ave.) tells the story of the courthouse.

"Man Burner"

Texas-born **Isom Prentice "Print" Olive** (1840–1886) and brothers Ira (1847–1928) and Bob (1855–1878) began ranching in Nebraska in 1877. As he had done elsewhere, Print vigorously acquired land, and soon—with an iron hand—ran the state's largest ranch. In 1878 he and his brother Bob suspected homesteaders Luther H. Mitchell (1815–1878) and Ami Whitney Ketchum (1854–1878) of stealing their cattle. After finding some of their stock on sale in Kearney, Nebraska, Bob got the Buffalo County sheriff to deputize him. He then rode out to arrest Mitchell and Ketchum for rustling. Instead, the two accused cow thieves shot him to death and fled. Print posted a $700 reward for the return of the two men to him. A sheriff more interested in money than the rule of law arrested the wanted pair and turned them over to the grieving brother. The suspects were next heard of when someone found their charred bodies hanging from a tree in Gospher County's well-named Devil's Canyon. While at least one source says Print only lynched the men and that someone else touched off a fire beneath their bodies, he nevertheless became known as "Man Burner." Print Olive and one of his men, Fred Fisher, were indicted in connection with the double lynching. Tried separately, Olive and Fisher were found guilty of second-degree murder and sentenced to life in prison. Gaining a new trial on appeal, the two were acquitted. Afterward Olive left Nebraska for the Colorado-Kansas border, leaving his brother Ira in Nebraska, where he remained and lived to age eighty. Print was not so lucky and was shot to death in Trail City, Colorado, on August 16, 1886. He is buried in Maple Grove Cemetery (1100 Matt Down Rd., Dodge City, Kansas). Ira is buried in Greenwood Cemetery (North Taft Street between Road 756 and Road 757, Lexington) while brother Bob was taken back to Texas for burial.

A state historical marker (US 70, east of Westerville, near Road 459; GPS coordinates: N41° 23.65', W99°15.44') summarizes the violent episode. Lynching victim Ami Whitney Ketchum is buried in the Kearney, Nebraska, cemetery (Avenue I and East 44th Street). Luther H. Mitchell was buried in the Central City, Nebraska, cemetery (1923 State Highway 14; Grave D8, D89, 3).

Chadron (Dawes County)

Chadron began as a stop on the newly laid tracks of the Fremont, Elkhorn, and Missouri Valley Railroad in 1885, but the northwest Nebraska town's story goes farther back. In 1837, James Bordeaux opened an American Fur Company trading post in the vicinity of future Chadron. With the American Fur Company nearing bankruptcy, in 1841 trapper Louis Chartran began operating a trading post in the area. Over the years the correct French pronunciation of Chartran, "Shattron," became corrupted as Chadron and that's how the new railroad town got its name. But if things had worked out the way pioneer homesteader **Frances "Fannie" O'Linn** wanted, the town not only would have been named "O'Linn," it would stand at a different location.

Recently widowed, O'Linn came to future Dawes County in 1884. She built a cabin on her homestead claim and a small community developed around it. When her son accidentally shot and killed himself, the settlers suggested the post office be named for him. Fannie tried to get the railroad company to route its tracks through O'Linn, but corporate officials chose a different right-of-way six miles from town. When O'Linn's legal efforts to overrule the railroad failed, she and the town moved to the new location, Chadron. There she became one of its most influential and revered citizens.

Built on the site of the American Fur Company trading post, the **Museum of the Fur Trade** (6321 US Highway 20, Chadron; 308-432-3843) is the only museum in the West devoted entirely to the fur trade that figured so prominently in the history of westward expansion. A self-guided tour of Chadron's downtown historic district is available from the Chamber of Commerce (706 West 3rd St.; 308-432-4401).

Doc Middleton's Ride

It takes a fine judge of horseflesh to compete in a thousand-mile race, and semi-reformed outlaw **Doc Middleton** (by birth James M. Riley) was one of the best. After all, he'd been stealing horses most of his adult life with a little shooting and killing to boot.

Out of Nebraska prison for several years, Doc had gone about as straight as he'd ever go—tending bar and gambling in Chadron—when John G. Maher began talking up a horse race from Chadron to Chicago. Maher offered a $1,000 prize and Buffalo Bill Cody, whose famed Wild West show was playing adjacent to the Chicago's World's Fair at the time, threw in another $500. Colt Firearms offered a custom revolver, and others pitched in various prizes for the publicity.

Of nine riders leaving Chadron June 13, 1893, seven "completed" the thousand-mile race, including Middleton. Some, including Middleton, actually rode horseback part of the way but they all cheated, covering much of the distance by train. Middleton didn't win, but he was presented a fine saddle blanket. The real winners were the stunt's promoters, all receiving ample free publicity. Middleton eventually moved to Douglas, Wyoming, where he spent his last years.

A state historical marker (195 Bordeaux St.; GPS coordinates: N42° 49.86', W102° 59.96') explains the race.

Not many small towns have two historic hotels, but Chadron does. The three-story **Blaine Hotel** (159 Bordeaux St.; 308-430-0107), built in 1888, was the starting point for the 1893 horse race. Built in 1890, **Hotel Chadron** (115 Main St.; 308-432-3380) replaced an earlier establishment destroyed by fire and is now known as Olde Main Street Inn. One of its earlier notable guests was Gen. Nelson Miles, who made the three-story brick hotel his headquarters during the investigation of the December 29, 1890, Wounded Knee Massacre. The structure is listed on the National Register of Historic Places. Both hotels continue in operation.

Wild Bunch gang member **George Sutherland "Flat Nose George" Currie** (1871–1900) grew up around Chadron and fell into cattle rustling. He got his nickname when a horse kicked him in the face. Currie ranged farther west, graduating from cattle theft to gunplay when he killed a deputy sheriff in Johnson County, Wyoming, in 1897. Three years later, on April 17, 1900, a sheriff's posse shot him to death near Moab, Utah. The outlaw was buried in Thompson, Utah, but his father later had Currie's remains reburied in **Greenwood Cemetery** (West 4rth and Linden Streets; Block 4, Lot 21, Space 7).

The **Dawes County Museum** (341 Country Club Rd.; 308-432-4999) has memorabilia related to the 1893 **Chadron-to-Chicago horse race** in addition to artifacts and exhibits dealing with area history.

Located on the campus of Chadron State College, the **Mari Sandoz High Plains Heritage Center** (1000 Main St.; 308-432-6401) focuses on the life and literature of Nebraska-born Western author Mari Sandoz (1896–1966), as well as the history and culture of the High Plains and the cattle industry. Sandoz wrote twenty-two books during her lifetime, including *Old Jules* and *Crazy Horse*.

CHAMBERLAIN (BRULE COUNTY)

The county seat town of Chamberlain began as a railroad stop in 1880 but what put it on the map in a figurative sense came in 2016 with the dedication of ***Dignity*** (off I-90 between exits 263 and 265), a fifty-foot-tall stainless-steel statue of an Indian woman in 1850s native attire standing with outstretched arms atop a bluff overlooking the Missouri River.

Designed by sculptor Dale Lamphere to honor the Lakota and Dakota people, the towering piece of public art can be seen for miles. His work, Lamphere said, "represents the courage, perseverance and wisdom of the Lakota and Dakota culture." With the approach of South Dakota's 125th anniversary of statehood, retired Rapid City businessman Norm McKie and his wife Eunabel donated $1 million to fund the statue in 2014.

Visible day or night, *Dignity* holds against her back a thirty-two-foot-wide star quilt—the Lakota symbol of honor and generosity. The blanket fashioned of 128 diamond-shaped pieces of stainless steel is designed to flutter in the wind and glisten in the sun. At night, LED lights illuminate the quilt.

Chamberlain is also home to the **Akta Lakota Museum and Cultural Center** (1301 North Main St.; 800-798-3452) on the campus of St. Joseph's Indian School.

Columbus (Platte County)

By the late 1850s it seemed almost certain the nation's first transcontinental railroad would traverse the Platte River valley in Nebraska Territory. Gambling on that, in 1856 a group of investors created a townsite company and began planning a community near the confluence of the Platte and Loup Rivers. They named it Columbus, for the Ohio city. The speculators had guessed right, but not until 1862 did Congress approve construction of a railroad that would follow what was known as the central route, taking it across Nebraska. When that happened, fewer than twenty people lived in Columbus and even by the time the tracks reached town in June 1866, it still had only seventy-five residents. But that changed in a hurry. Columbus grew rapidly in the 1870s as a railroad town and agricultural center. In 1883 a thirty-seven-year-old man who had spent much of his life on the frontier as a scout and buffalo hunter saw Columbus as the ideal location to rehearse a new enterprise, one that soon would bring the Wild West to the nation and the world.

Buffalo Bill Cody had decided to further capitalize on his celebrity by producing an exhibition that would capture the Wild West as accurately as possible, with real Indians, real frontiersmen, real firearms (albeit loaded with blanks), real buffalo, and more. With dentist and trick shot **Dr. W.F. Carver** as partner, Cody planned to debut the show in Omaha but chose Columbus as the place to block out the extravaganza and begin rehearsals. The show would be called, not too concisely, "The Wild West, Hon. W.F. Cody and Dr. W.F. Carver's Rocky Mountain and Prairie Exhibition." Later, with Carver out, it became Buffalo Bill's Wild West. Cody picked Columbus for the show's "sea trials" because it was only a short train ride to Omaha, and it was where his old friend and ranching partner **Frank North** lived. North helped recruit the show's performers, including Pawnee Indians. North's brother James, who just happened to be president of the county fair association, arranged for the rehearsal venue. After a week of run-throughs, on May 16, 1883, the train with Cody, Carver, North, and all the cast pulled out of the depot for Omaha.

Residences now cover the old fairgrounds where the show began. Frank North is buried in **Columbus Cemetery** (11th Street and 12th Avenue). A historical marker outside the Columbus Chamber of Commerce (753 33rd Ave.; 402-564-2769) summarizes the North brothers' story.

Glur's Tavern (2301 11th St.), a Columbus water hole since 1876, is said to be the West's oldest bar and is still open at its original location. Cody and his friends and associates did their drinking at Glur's when in town.

Crawford (Dawes County)

Established as Camp Robinson in 1874 but designated a fort four years later, **Fort Robinson** played a key part in the **Sioux War**. The government established the nearby **Red Cloud Indian Agency** in 1873, and that is where Chief Red Cloud and his Oglala band and other Plains Indians lived for four years. When **Chief Crazy Horse** and some nine hundred followers surrendered at the post on May 6, 1877, they also were consigned to the reservation. But on September 5, 1877, Crazy Horse was stabbed to death at the fort by another Sioux when resisting arrest. The following year, during the so-called Cheyenne outbreak, Chiefs Dull Knife and Little Wolf led their people from their reservation in what is now Oklahoma north across Kansas in an effort to return to their homeland. Captured by soldiers as they made their way through Nebraska, they were taken to Fort Robinson where they were held for some time before being told they would be returned to Oklahoma. On January 9, 1879, using a small cache of weapons they had hidden, the Indians shot their way out of confinement at the fort and tried to escape to the north. But soldiers soon caught up with them. In the fight that followed, about half the warriors were killed. Those who managed to escape were hunted down and either killed or captured. The event came to be known as the **Fort Robinson Massacre**.

With a rail connection beginning in the 1880s, Fort Robinson became even more important since its troops could rapidly be deployed where needed. The fort remained active until 1948. Operated by the Nebraska Historical Society, **Fort Robinson State Park** (308-665-2919) is three miles west of Crawford on US 20. Not only was the fort one of the most important posts on the Great Plains, it is one of the largest and best preserved. A museum in the former post headquarters tells its story. Plaques and monuments mark the scene of Crazy Horse's death and other significant historical events. The site of the Red Cloud Indian Agency is one mile west of the old fort on a park road.

Fairbury (Jefferson County)

Three men died violently on July 12, 1861, at a Pony Express stop in southeastern Nebraska known as Rock Creek Station. The affair amounted to just another Old West "difficulty" involving certain unyielding parties until Col. George Ward Nichols told the story his way in the February 1867 issue of *Harper's*.

Though published more than five years after the fact, given *Harper's* widespread circulation, the exaggerated account of what happened that summer day in Nebraska Territory gave birth to a legend. James Butler Hickok became "Wild Bill" Hickok.

Established on Rock Creek in 1857 as a stopping place and general store along the Oregon and California Trails, the owner of Rock Creek Station sold the property to David McCanles a couple of years later. McCanles settled at the station, made improvements to the property, and started ranching. When the Pony Express began carrying mail, its owners bought the station and other infrastructure but McCanles kept his ranch.

Meanwhile, Hickok arrived as an employee of either the Pony Express or the station keeper, to tend stock and handle other chores. Unfortunately for all concerned, the Pony Express was losing money and eventually went bankrupt. With the company behind on its payments, McCanles showed up on July 12, 1861, with his twelve-year-old son and two employees, James Woods and James Gordon, to demand that the property be turned over to him. The agent said he lacked authority for that and the figurative wagon rolled downhill fast from there. When the shooting stopped, McCanles and his hired hands lay dead. McCanles's son escaped and notified authorities. Hickok, the station agent, and a Pony Express rider were duly charged with murder, but in a hearing a few days later a justice of the peace ruled there was insufficient evidence to support the charges and ordered the three defendants released.

While McCanles was a hard case who had cheated on his wife and had earlier beaten up the station agent's father-in-law for no just cause, he was no outlaw leader. At least not until Colonel Nichols told the story. In Nichols's article, Hickok had not only done away with the ruthless McCanles, he'd killed ten other "desperadoes, horse thieves, murderers, and cut-throats" while he was at it.

When traffic on the once well-traveled route adjacent to Rock Creek Station faded following the arrival of the transcontinental railroad in 1867, the station fell into disrepair and eventually disappeared. In 1980, the state acquired the site and developed it as **Rock Creek Station Historical Park** (57426 710th Rd.; 402-729-5777). After archaeological investigation revealed the foundations of the station's original structures, the bunk house, barn, and cabins were reconstructed. The visitor's center has interpretive exhibits and displays artifacts recovered at the site. Trail ruts worn into the ground can still be seen in the park southeast of Fairbury. Shortly after the shooting, Gordon was wrapped in a blanket and buried along Rock Creek where he fell. McCanles and Woods were buried nearby on high ground known as Soldier's Hill. When the Burlington and Missouri Railroad crossed Soldier's Hill in the 1880s, McCanles's and Woods's remains were reburied in **Fairbury Cemetery** (56924 PWF Rd.). The two men share a gray granite marker giving only their names and date of death. Gordon's grave has been lost.

Fremont (Dodge County)

Named for solider, explorer, and unsuccessful presidential candidate John C. Fremont, the town was laid out in 1856 along the Mormon Trail, which traveled the north bank of the Platte River. A collection of barely a dozen log cabins, the community began to grow fast after the Union Pacific Railroad reached it on New Year's Eve 1865. Three years later the Sioux City and Pacific Railroad built through Fremont, followed in 1869 by the Elkhorn Valley Railroad. Housed in a home built in 1874, the **Louis E. May Museum** (1643 North Nye Ave.; 402-721-4515) covers the history of Dodge County.

Gering (Scotts Bluff County)

Rising eight hundred feet above the North Platte River, Scotts Bluff has been a landmark for centuries, first for Native Americans and later for westbound travelers working their way through nearby Mitchell Pass on the Oregon, California, and Mormon Trails. Later, the Pony

Express used the pass, soon followed by the wires of the nation's first transcontinental telegraph.

Scotts Bluff was named after Hiram Scott, a clerk with the American Fur Company. In 1828 he was traveling with a party of fur company men returning to St. Louis following the annual rendezvous, a meeting with Indians and trappers to trade supplies and other merchandise for furs. When he became ill, his colleagues left him near the bluffs that would come to bear his name. He apparently improved and tried to make it the rest of the way himself. When spring came, trappers found his body well east of where he had been left. His burial site is not known.

President Woodrow Wilson declared three thousand acres around **Scotts Bluff** a national monument in 1919. At the south end of the park, the **Oregon Trail Museum and Visitor's Center** (three miles west of Gering on State Highway 92 West; 308-436-9700) has exhibits on the western movement, geology, and the largest collection of works by William H. Jackson, the noted nineteenth century photographer of Yellowstone. The **North Platte Valley Museum and Western History Archives** (Overland Trails Road and J Street; 308-436-5411) has the world's largest collection of Oregon Trail artifacts.

Glenvil (Clay County)

Born together, they died together. Exactly when they came into the world is debated, but there's no doubt when **Elizabeth Jones Taylor** and her twin brother **Thomas Jones** ended their days—March 15, 1885.

The Jones family came to America from Wales around 1860. Elizabeth married James A. Taylor in Missouri in 1869, and she and her husband migrated west to Nebraska and went on to have three children. At some point, her parents, her brother, and two other siblings joined them on the plains, where they farmed and raised livestock.

When her husband was found dead in one of their fields in 1882, some said Elizabeth had poisoned him with potato bug dope. Then, a few years later, their hired hand disappeared under suspicious circumstances. Next, one of their neighbors was found shot to death

(Elizabeth's two sons were arrested for that killing), and then people's barns began burning down. On top of everything, folks suspected Elizabeth and her brother of stealing cattle and harboring bad characters.

No charges were ever filed against them, but the twins stood convicted in the court of public opinion. About midnight on the Ides of March 1885, vigilantes removed them from their sod house. After considerately allowing their captives time to pray, the mob marched them about one hundred yards to a bridge and hanged them.

Elizabeth Taylor and her brother are buried side-by-side between her husband and their father in **Spring Ranch Cemetery** (GPS coordinates: N40° 24.39', W98° 14.90'). Their mother was the last to die, of natural causes, and she was buried in 1889 with the rest of her family next to her possibly murdered husband. The wood-plank iron bridge from which the twins were suspended still spans the Little Blue River near the ghost town of Spring Ranch. A state historical marker (off Road 307; GPS coordinates: N40° 26.24', W98° 14.42') gives the history of Spring Ranch.

Gothenburg (Dawson County)

First settled by Swedish immigrants in 1882, Gothenburg—named for a town in Sweden—today bills itself as the Pony Express capital of Nebraska. More than two decades before the town's founding, two Pony Express stations operated in the area. One, known as **Midway Station**, stands four miles south of present Gothenburg on the Lower 96 Ranch. Still on its original foundation, the station can be viewed by appointment arranged at the **Pony Express Museum** (15th and Lake Avenue; 816-279-5059) in Ehmen Park.

The other Pony Express stop was called the **Sam MacChette Station** and was twelve miles west of town until it was moved to Gothenburg in 1931 and restored. The log building stands at 510 15th Street.

The history-minded town also has the **Gothenburg Historical Museum** (1420 Avenue F; 308-537-4212), which focuses on Dawson County's history.

On August 8, 1864, a Cheyenne war party attacked a wagon train near Plum Creek, about twenty-five miles southeast of future Gothenburg. The Indians killed eleven men and took a woman and child hostage. Eventually rescued, **Nancy Jane Morton** wrote her recollections of her ordeal, *Captive of the Cheyenne*. Years after her death in 1912, the Dawson County Historical Society published it.

Grand Island (Hall County)

Eighteenth century French fur trappers called the forty-mile-long land mass formed by channels of the Platte River "La Grande Isle." In 1857 a party of German settlers traveled from Davenport, Iowa, west to Nebraska to settle on the island. They began farming the rich alluvial soil, enduring bitter winters and clashes with Plains Indians. Two years later the discovery of gold in the Rocky Mountains in 1859 stimulated a wave of west-bound fortune seekers, and the community that had come to be called Grand Island flourished as the last place to purchase provisions to get travelers through the vast open country that lay ahead. When the Union Pacific line began moving west, the railroad developed an inland townsite in 1868 and the new community of Grand Island boomed as a Union Pacific Railroad division point. Incorporated in 1872, the city remains a transportation crossroads. With a modern building housing artifacts and artwork and an assortment of restored vintage structures, the two-hundred-acre **Stuhr Museum of the Prairie Pioneer** (3133 West US 34; 308-385-5316) focuses on the area's rich history.

Haigler (Dundy County)

Despite the Indian threat, cattle ranchers who brought longhorns up the Texas-Ogallala Trail began operating along the Republic River in the mid-1870s. When the trail migrated west fifty miles from its original route to this part of Nebraska in 1880, it passed through a canyon, which by 1881 had become known as Texas Canyon. Texans Isom Prentice "Print" and Ira Olive, along with other cattlemen, used the canyon to hold their herds until the beeves fattened. From there, the brothers and their cowhands pushed the livestock to the railhead at Ogallala. In 1883 a checkpoint was established at the canyon so brands could be examined, and the cattle inspected for disease. The last year of the trail drives was 1886, when an estimated 150,000 head of cattle passed through the canyon. A state historical marker summarizing the **Texas Trail Canyon** story stands off US 34, four miles east of Haigler.

The town was founded in 1886 but homesteaders had begun locating in the area five years before. Located in the southwestern corner of the state, Haigler calls itself the "Cornerstone of Nebraska." It has two museums, the **Haigler Cornerstone Museum and Jail** (US 34 and Porter Avenue; 308-297-3226) and, just to the south, the **Old School Museum** (US 34 and Porter Avenue; 308-297-3226). The latter occupies an old one-room schoolhouse moved to Haigler from its original rural location in 2007.

Harvard (Clay County)

In 1885 the red-brick **Harvard jail** (151–185 West Oak St.) briefly held five men charged with first degree murder in the lynching of Elizabeth Taylor and her twin brother Thomas Jones in nearby Spring Ranch, Nebraska. Newspapers at the time reported that further mob violence had been threatened if anyone was prosecuted in the case.

During World War II, the small jail, no longer in use and privately owned, was foreclosed on for unpaid taxes and sold by the city along with other real estate. A precocious sixteen-year-old bought ten lots for $15, including the old jail. Even though the property had been conveyed to a minor, the city would not buy it back. The matter went to the courts, generating national publicity. The teenager put the lot with the jail up for auction and in consideration of $10,000 in war bonds, ventriloquist Edgar Bergen bought it in the name of his puppet Charlie McCarthy. The property was then deeded back to the City of Harvard. A state historical marker tells the story of the old jail, which stands vacant.

HAYES CENTER (HAYES COUNTY)

The most notable event in Hayes Center's history happened before it even existed. Founded in 1885 and named because it sat at the center of Hayes County, it is the closest community to the setting of the most extravagant buffalo hunt in Wild West history.

In 1871 twenty-one-year-old Grand Duke Alexei Alexandrovich of Russia came to the US on an extended visit. Early in 1872 the Union Pacific Railroad and the US Army hosted a VIP buffalo hunt for the young Russian noble with Buffalo Bill Cody and Lt. Col. George Armstrong Custer as guides. With Gen. Phil Sheridan the ranking officer, a substantial military escort accompanied the duke.

The entourage, which also included the Russian's extended staff, arrived in North Platte by special train and departed in wagons and carriages for the buffalo hunting grounds. On January 13 they reached a base camp set up by the army on Red Willow Creek about fifty miles south of the Platte River. The next morning, with the duke riding one of Cody's horses and carrying a rifle the scout loaned him, Cody, Custer, and other dignitaries and staff set out to find a buffalo herd Cody knew to be in the area.

Assisted by Cody and Custer, the duke ran down a young bull and dropped it with two shots. The Russian jumped from his horse, cut off the animal's tail, and jubilantly waved it in the air. Then came the popping of champagne corks. In two days, the party killed some forty-five buffalo and an uncounted number of champagne bottles.

Camp Alexis, as it was called, was about ten miles northeast of present Hayes Center. A stone marker stands at the site, which is on private property. A state historical marker at Road 740-A and Avenue 370 summarizes the story of the hunt.

KEARNEY (BUFFALO COUNTY)

Kearney was founded in the 1860s near the fort that gave it its name. However, thanks to an early spelling error, the town of Kearney is spelled with an extra "e." A Kearney newspaper publisher wanted more for his community than two vowels in its name. In the 1860s and early 1870s, he agitated for the removal of the state capital to Kearney and, while he was at, proposed moving the nation's capital from Washington, DC, to Kearney as well. Kearney did become county seat of Buffalo County in 1874, but that's as far as it went.

The first **Fort Kearny** was established in 1846 at present Nebraska City but moved in 1848 to south central Nebraska. In addition to protecting westward travelers, the fort served as a supply depot for other frontier forts. A stagecoach station and Pony Express depot stood in the shadow of the post, and when the coming of the Union Pacific was about to make stagecoaches less important, troops from the fort protected railroad construction workers. The army abandoned the garrison in 1871. Acquired by the state in 1929, the property became twenty-nine-acre **Fort Kearny State Historic Park** (1020 V Rd.; 308-865-5305). The park has two reconstructed fort buildings, a stockade, and a visitor's center with interpretive exhibits.

Also in Kearney, the **G.W. Frank Museum of History and Culture** (2010 University Dr.; 308-865-8284) is located on the University of Nebraska campus. Some of the most interesting museums are those in a building that is itself historic. That's the case with this museum, which interprets the history and culture of Kearney and the Great Plains. In 1886, architect George William Frank, Jr. designed this three-story sandstone house for his parents. Later the house changed ownership several times before the state purchased it to serve as living quarters for Nebraska State Tuberculosis Hospital staff. The University of Nebraska acquired it in 1971 and opened it as a museum in 1976. Listed on the National Register of Historic Places, it was one of the first residences west of the Mississippi wired for electricity at the time of its construction.

One of the West's most unusual historical monuments is a large hollow steel arch spanning I-80 just outside Kearney. Buildings on either side of the interstate anchor the eight-story, three-hundred-foot **Great Platte River Archway**, which holds a museum opened in 2000 that tells the story of the Great Platte River Road. The road was a series of trails dating to the blazing of the Oregon Trail in 1841 that carried immigrants to Nebraska and the rest of the West. The archway campus also has a state-operated **Nebraska Visitors Center** (exit 275 off I-80; 308-237-1000) and family friendly attractions ranging from a replica of a homestead sod house to a fishing lake and hike and bike trails.

Kenesaw (Adams County)

The string of lonely, mostly unmarked, burial sites along the Oregon Trail through Missouri, Kansas, Nebraska, Wyoming, Idaho, and Oregon has been called the nation's longest cemetery. Due to the passage of time and the fact that settlers worried about the graves of their loved ones being robbed or disturbed by animals, only about two hundred of an estimated thirty to forty thousand burials have markers. One of the most marked is that of **Susan C. Seawall Haile**.

That the thirty-four-year-old mother of six died on July 5, 1852, is one of the few certainties in the story. She almost certainly succumbed to cholera from drinking bad water, the top cause of death along the trail.

Susan's husband buried her on a sandy knoll near the trail, left their wagon train, and went back east to buy her a marble headstone. The romantic telling of the tale has him bringing the stone back in a wheelbarrow, though historians consider that highly unlikely. No matter how the grieving widower got it there, he did. In time, souvenir hunters chipped away at that marker and a second stone marker was put up in 1900. A third marker was placed over the pioneer's grave in 1933, this one noting, "Legend Says This Pioneer Died After Drinking Water Poisoned by Indians." There was an often-used well nearby at the time of Susan's death, but the poisoning story is almost assuredly untrue. (Contrary to Hollywood, of all the ways to die in the Wild West, Indian attack statistically was the least likely.) In 1958 a small piece of land around the grave was purchased and donated to Adams County. In addition to the 1933 marker, a fourth stone marker stands at the site now along with two interpretive markers four miles northwest of Kenesaw between the 7000 block of North Denman Avenue and North Shiloh Avenue (GPS coordinates: N40° 39.33', W98° 43.45').

Lewellen (Garden County)

Of roughly a dozen clashes in Nebraska during the Indian Wars, the biggest engagement—essentially a massacre—took place along Blue Creek in what is now Garden County. On September 3, 1855, in retaliation for the slaughter of Lt. John Grattan and his small command near Fort Laramie, Wyoming, the year before, Col. William S. Harney attacked a Sioux village in the Blue Water Creek Valley. The soldiers killed eighty-six Sioux, wounded five others, and captured seventy women and children while losing only four of their own with seven wounded.

The site of the battle, at a point where Blue Water Creek empties into the North Platte River, is on private property. However, **Ash Hollow State Historical Park**, 1.5 miles west of Lewellen on US 26, overlooks the location. The park's visitor's center has an exhibit on the fight. A state historical marker (19568–19570 State Highway 92 Scenic; GPS coordinates: N41° 20.91', W102° 11.13') summarizes the incident.

Lexington (Dawson County)

A trading post established in 1860 where Plum Creek flowed into the Platte River catered to travelers on the Oregon and Mormon Trails, both of which crossed future Dawson County. Soon the short-lived Pony Express operated a station there, and when the Union Pacific arrived it 1867, the railroad built a depot and the town of Plum Creek developed. Later the name changed to Lexington. The **Dawson County Museum** (805 North Taft St.; 308-324-5340), operated by the Dawson County Historical Society, has exhibits on the county's history and culture.

Indians Derail the White Man's "Smoke Wagon"

The Southern Cheyenne soon realized the newly laid iron road that carried the white man's "smoke wagons" across the plains marked the beginning of the end of their way of life. On the night of August 6, 1867, in one of the more unusual episodes of Old West history, Indians under **Chief Spotted Wolf** first attacked a railroad handcart west of Plum Creek, killing one worker and scalping alive another worker who had played dead. A third railroader managed to escape. Later that night the Indians used tools left by railroad workers near the tracks to peel up the rails. Then they piled a stack of railroad ties on the tracks. Early on the morning of August 7, their efforts caused a west-bound freight train to derail, killing both the engineer and the firemen. The Indians looted the five overturned cars, but the rest of the train crew made it to safety. The Daughters of the American Revolution placed a marker at the site in 1940. The marker, an eight-ton boulder with a bronze plaque, was unveiled by the son of the engineer who died in the attack. It stands three miles west of Lexington off US 30 (GPS coordinates: N40° 47.44', W99° 48.49').

Lincoln (Lancaster County)

It amounted to a war of words, not bullets, but when Nebraska became a state in 1867, controversy arose over whether much larger Omaha (which had been the territorial capital) or the town that would become Lincoln (called Lancaster at the time) should be the seat of government. After assessing Omaha and other contenders, a three-member commission selected Lancaster. But a sore loser in the legislature introduced a bill renaming Lancaster in honor of the late President Abraham Lincoln. The measure passed and was signed into law. Many Confederate sympathizers in town were not happy about it, but Lincoln kept its new name.

A lot of Nebraska history was yet to be made when the Nebraska Historical Society was organized in 1878, one of the earliest such institutions in the West. The society began receiving state funding in 1883. With more than 150,000 items in its collection, the **Nebraska History Museum** (131 Centennial Mall North; 402-471-4782) covers twelve thousand years of Nebraska's history.

Nebraska City (Otoe County)

Protected by Fort Kearny (established in 1846, the fort was later moved into the interior of Nebraska), Nebraska City developed on the west bank of the Missouri River as a ferry crossing. In 1857 four townsites in the area were incorporated as Nebraska City, a community that aspired to become the territorial capital but never did. Still, it prospered as a trading center and riverboat port.

With a government contract, in 1858 the firm of Russell, Majors, and Waddell began hauling freight from Nebraska City to the army's numerous northern Great Plains forts. Supplies came upriver by steamboat and were distributed by wagon trains. Investing heavily in its Nebraska City infrastructure, the company grew into the largest shipping firm operating on the Great Plains. In 1865, its best year, Russell, Majors, and Waddell moved forty-four million tons of freight out of Nebraska City. The company's other enterprise, the Pony Express, did not fare as well. The **Old Freighters Museum** (407 North 14th St.; 402-873-3000) occupies the two-story house that served as the freight company's home office. Exhibits focus on Nebraska City's transportation history.

The **Otoe County Museum of Memories** (366 Poplar St.; 402-269-2355) is eighteen miles west of Nebraska City on State Highway 2 East. An example of innovative repurposing, the museum is housed in a former church built in 1881, its adjacent parsonage, and one other building.

Say Cheese, Jesse

The most-published photograph of outlaw **Jesse James** was taken in Nebraska City at the portrait studio of German-born photographer **Charles Christopher "C.C." Walbaum** (1812–1878) in 1875. James is thought to have sat for the photo at the urging of his friend, banker Logan F. Enyart (1831–1912), a fellow Missourian who had been a Confederate officer. Already well-known, James apparently used a fake name and Walbaum never knew he had captured the image of someone who would become one of America's best-known criminals. Walbaum died three years later at age sixty-five and is buried in **Wyuka Cemetery** (19th Street and Industrial Road; Plot OG-107-02). Enyart lies in the same cemetery.

Newton (Red Willow County)

During the Indian Wars, most fighting occurred between Indians and Euro Americans, but not always. On August 5, 1873, more than a thousand Sioux attacked 350 Pawnee in a wide canyon in present Red Willow County now known as **Massacre Canyon.** The running fight, which left some seventy Pawnee dead, was a singular event in Wild West history in three ways: It was the largest, bloodiest battle known between two North American tribes; it was the last fight between the two tribes; and it was the US Cavalry that rode to the rescue of the Pawnees and prevented more deaths.

Massacre Canyon Monument and Visitor Center (US 35; 308-334-5326; GPS coordinates: N40° 12.42', W100° 57.81') located three miles east of Trenton is a state-maintained site featuring a carved, thirty-five-foot, red granite monument erected with federal funds in 1930.

North Platte (Lincoln County)

Where the South Platte and North Platte Rivers meet, the town of North Platte began in 1866 as a Union Pacific Railroad construction camp. After the workers left for the next camp down the line, in 1867 the railroad assured the town's permanence by building a roundhouse, machine shops, and a hotel.

A high point near North Platte on the old Oregon Trail for years had a larger-than-life stone statue of a standing Indian in a war bonnet taking in what, for him, must have been a troubling view—a long line of west-bound covered wagons. Erected in 1931, the ***Sioux Lookout*** statue stood in a remote location overlooking the North Platte River, and over the years the piece had been considerably vandalized. In 2000 Lincoln County commissioners had it removed, renovated, and placed on the courthouse square in downtown Lincoln (301 North Jeffers St.; GPS coordinates: N41° 8.14', W100° 45.74'). For good measure, they had an iron fence built around it and the state placed a historical marker near it to explain the statue's significance.

An army post established in 1863 at the mouth of Cottonwood Canyon near the confluence of the North and South Platte had three different names before it officially became **Fort McPherson** in 1866. After marching from Kansas to the fort in the early summer of 1867, the Seventh Cavalry's Lt. Col. George Armstrong Custer received a dressing down there from Gen. William T. Sherman for giving rations to Sioux war chief Pawnee Killer, who duplicitously expressed peaceful intentions. In fact, a week later the chief raided Custer's command to run off his horses, but the cavalrymen repelled the attack. Troops stationed at Fort McPherson participated in various Indian War campaigns through the 1870s, including the 1879 Cheyenne breakout at Fort Robinson in Nebraska, but the post was abandoned in 1880 when the area was deemed safe.

The most visible reminder of the old fort is **Fort McPherson National Cemetery** (12004 State Spur 56A; 308-582-4433). Established in 1873 it remains in use. One mile south of the cemetery at the site of the fort's flagpole a statue of an infantry soldier placed in 1928 stands perpetual guard. The only surviving fort structure with a documented provenance is a two-room log building that served as post headquarters. Moved from its original location and restored, the building is part of the **Lincoln County Museum** (2403 North Buffalo Bill Ave.; 306-534-5640). In addition to its main building, the museum features more than a dozen historic structures including a restored 1880s railroad depot, agricultural equipment, a Union Pacific Railroad caboose, a windmill and cistern, and several historical markers.

Scout's Rest Ranch

William F. Cody began ranching in the North Platte area in 1877. Cody and family moved to the four-thousand-acre ranch in 1886, and though he was on the road a lot with his Wild West show, they lived here until 1913, when they moved back to Cody, Wyoming. In 1960 the state acquired sixteen acres of the former ranch and developed it as **Buffalo Bill Ranch State Historical Park** (2921 Scouts Rest Rd.; 308-535-8035).

By 1886 when he built a house on his ranch, Cody's Wild West show was attracting tremendous crowds and making him a lot of money. Much of that money went into this house, which locals called the **"Mansion on the Prairie."** Indeed, the Second Empire–style house was the largest in North Platte at the time.

A barn is normally purely utilitarian, a sizable wooden structure built to accommodate livestock, hold hay, and store tack along with other farming or ranching equipment. But not **Buffalo Bill's barn**, built in 1887. He had "Scout's Rest Ranch" painted in large letters on both sides of its roof, with the cupola in the center labeled "Col. W.F. Cody." Then Cody really started getting creative. At the peak of both ends of the barn is an inverted ace of spades, the card his star performer Annie Oakley favored punching bullet holes through. In addition, each of the seventy-three eaves on either side of the roof is carved in the shape of a rifle stock. Inside the barn are posters from Cody's Wild West shows, placed there by him following each season.

Fort Cody Trading Post (221 Hallagan Dr.; 308-532-8081), a roadside souvenir store with its wide range of Wild West kitsch, is an excellent example of a mid-twentieth-century tourist trap.

Guarded by a towering flat cut-out painting of Buffalo Bill with rifle in hand, Fort Cody is built of logs to look something like a frontier fort, or at least Hollywood's vision of one. The trading post does have three things for more serious history buffs: An interesting museum, a bookstore, and an impressive piece of folk art—a large, hand-carved miniature of the old scout's Wild West show.

Ogallala (Keith County)

Ogallala came to life when the Union Pacific Railroad built stock pens not far from the tracks and Texans started pushing longhorn steers to the railhead over the Western Trail, better known locally as the Texas Trail. Though often labeled the "Gomorrah of the Cattle Trail," Ogallala was not nearly as rough as its reputation had it. During its heyday (1875–1884) Ogallala had only six homicides that researchers have been able to document. On the other hand, other sources say seventeen to fourteen deaths at the hands of others occurred there. But compared with the number of people who passed through town, either arriving by train, stagecoach, or horse, any of those numbers represents a minute percentage. Still, a lot of cowboys brought a lot of cattle to town—an estimated one million head over the life of the trail. The boys patronized several score saloons, gambling halls, and brothels until trail driving became a thing of the past. A state historical marker in the 1000 block of North Spruce Street summarizes Ogallala's trail-driving era.

When Ogallala was a trail town, most of the action was along **Front Street**, so named because it fronted the Union Pacific's tracks. In 1963 a movie-set-like collection of Western-looking bars and eateries arose along the old street. With several partners, a local veterinarian owned the faux Front Street town for years, but the property changed hands in 2016. One of the buildings houses an Old West museum.

Not all the cowboys and boomtown riffraff left town when the trail driving era ended. Some stayed behind in **Boot Hill Cemetery**

(West 10th and Parkhill Drive). Before the then-un-named cemetery on a hill overlooking the South Platte River was abandoned in 1885, at least forty-eight people were buried there. After that, like many an Old West graveyard, Boot Hill was largely ignored. Over time, it became over-grown and its wooden grave markers disappeared.

The cemetery, though not its occupants, came back to life in a figurative sense in the 1960s. Local Jaycees cleaned the graveyard and placed new markers on graves that could be identified. Later, a grant from the Union Pacific Railroad provided for more improvements and additional research on the unknown burials. ***The Trail Boss***, a larger-than-life bronze statue of a cowboy atop his horse, looking beyond Boot Hill and Ogallala as if focusing on the trail back to Texas, stands at the cemetery. Sculpted by artist Robert Summers, the piece is a duplicate of one in Dallas, Texas. A state historical marker gives the history of the cemetery and the Ogallala Chamber of Commerce distributes a brochure with information on twenty-four of the people buried there.

Just Good, Clean Deadly Fun

Three cowpokes who strayed off their range for good in Ogallala were **William Brewton**, **Henry Parker**, and **William Snook**, all in their late teens or early twenties. When the drovers hit town with their herd, they proceeded to get drunk and started shooting up the place. Sheriff **Joe Hughes** arrested the men, but they escaped jail and resumed their boozy binge. When they declared no one in town could re-arrest them, the sheriff and a deputy dutifully took up the challenge. Confronting the cowboys in one of the saloons on July 9, 1879, Hughes and deputy **Jasper Southard** ordered them to surrender. Instead, Shook drew his revolver, and the sheriff, not waiting for him to pull the trigger, shot and killed him. Parker apparently tried to get to his horse, but one bullet hit his ride, the other tore into him and he died the next day. Brewer was also shot, how or by whom is not clear, but it seems to have been in the same transaction. He died on July 13.

Most of the buildings connected to Ogallala's cow town days did not survive into the twenty-first century. But a few years after the place settled down, Leonidas A. Brandhoefer, entrepreneur and banker, built a three-story, redbrick Victorian Renaissance–style house that still stands.

Health issues forced Brandhoefer to sell the house in 1888, a year after he built it. The buyer was another banker, H.L. McWilliams. The house certainly befitted someone with money. It has nine room and two baths, a curved staircase, carved fireplaces, elaborate woodwork, brass door fixtures, and walnut shutters. A household that fancy needed a maid, and she lived in the single room that fills the smaller third floor.

The Keith County Historical Society acquired the house in 1966 and converted it into the **Mansion on the Hill Museum** (1004 North Spruce St.; 800-658-4390). The mansion is listed on the National Register of Historical Places.

Omaha (Douglas County)

Named for the Omaha Indians, Nebraska's largest city dates to 1854 when speculators founded it on the west bank of the Missouri River at a crossing known as Lone Tree Ferry. With the arrival of the Union Pacific Railroad in 1866, it became an important transportation center. Its Union Stockyards opened in 1883 and the city's name became synonymous with fine beef. Known as the "Gateway to the West," in 1898 Omaha hosted a world's fair known as the Trans-Mississippi Exposition.

A supply post established in 1868, **Fort Omaha** served from 1875 to 1882 as headquarters of the US Army's Department of Platte, an area that included present Iowa, Nebraska, Wyoming, Utah, Montana, and a portion of Idaho. Noted Indian fighter Gen. George Crook commanded the department, and in 1879 played a role in a landmark legal case involving Chief Standing Bear.

"The Same God Made Us Both"

Ponca Chief **Standing Bear** and his peaceful, agrarian people lived in northeast Nebraska. As more settlers moved west, to avoid clashes, the tribe agreed to move to a reservation they mistakenly believed was near Omaha. But the government forced the tribe to relocate to Indian Territory.

In the spring of 1877, the tribe made the six-hundred-mile trek. Along the way, 150 of Standing Bear's people died. After reaching Oklahoma, unable to grow crops, by year's end starvation and disease claimed many more. Among them, Standing Bear's son, who begged before he died to be buried in his homeland.

With dozens of his followers, the chief left their new reservation in early 1879 to honor his son's request. But when they reached Omaha, the army arrested them. Though General Crook had orders to return the Indians, instead he went to a local newspaper editor who turned the case into national news. On Standing Bear's behalf, two Omaha attorneys filed for a writ of habeas corpus. In his testimony, Standing Bear held up a hand and said, "That hand is not the color of yours. But if I pierce it, I shall feel pain. If you pierce your hand you also feel pain. The blood that will flow from mine will be the same color as yours. I am a man. The same God made us both." After hearing the case federal district Judge Elmer Dundy issued a landmark ruling that Indians were persons entitled to equal protection under the law and ordered the Poncas released from custody.

The army shut down the fort in 1918 and the former post saw a variety of uses over the years. In 1975, the seventy-acre property was deeded to Metropolitan Community College. Crook and his family occupied a brick, two-story officer's quarters until he left the fort in 1882. The house (5730 North 30th St.; 402-455-9990) is now a museum.

A historical plaque affixed to a large rock outside the museum commemorates the Standing Bear case. The building where the hearing was held no longer stands but Standing Bear's name can be found on schools and parks in Nebraska and Oklahoma. Aside from a larger-than-life bronze statue (see Lincoln, Nebraska), the chief's most impressive monument is the long span across the Missouri River linking Nebraska and South Dakota, **Chief Standing Bear Memorial Bridge**.

In 1883 William F. Cody chose Omaha for the first-ever performance of "The Wild West, Hon. W.F. Cody and Dr. S.W. Carver's Rocky Mountain and Prairie Exhibition," forerunner to his famous Wild West show. The venue was the **Omaha Driving Park** (18th and Sprague Streets) and the crowd loved it. The site of Cody's first show is now a residential neighborhood. A state historical marker in Kounz Park (3500–3698 Florence Blvd.) commemorates the event.

Located in the former Union Station, a 124,000-square-foot Art Deco building opened in 1931, the **Durham Western Heritage Museum** (801 South 10th St.; 402-444-5071) focuses on Omaha's history from the time of the dinosaurs onward, including the city's role in the settling of the West. The once-busy train station closed in 1971 and was in danger of being torn down until a volunteer group prevented that and succeeded in turning the structure into a museum in 1975.

Red Cloud (Webster County)

Though born in Virginia, **Willa Cather** came with her family to Nebraska in 1883 when she was nine years old and the West was still wild. Growing up in Red Cloud, after graduating from the University of Nebraska in 1895, she went east to work as a teacher and journalist. Soon she began the transition to poet and full-time novelist that resulted in a life's work of a dozen novels, including the classic, *O Pioneers!* "The United States knows Nebraska because of Willa Cather's books," declared author Sinclair Lewis. Indeed, in the years following her death in 1947 she has come to be viewed as a canonical American writer. Cather's life story and the work she produced is the focus of the **National Willa Cather Center** (425 North Webster; 402-746-2653).

Located in the 1909 Silas Garber mansion, the **Webster County Historical Museum** (721 West 4th Ave.; 402-746-2444) covers the history of the south-central county that produced a literary master.

Sidney (Cheyenne County)

It lacked an evocative name, but for a time, Sidney was just about as wild as Deadwood. Seven years before the 1874 discovery of gold in the Black Hills of Dakota Territory, Sidney grew quickly after the Union Pacific Railroad built a depot there in 1867. With dozens of saloons, gambling venues, and houses of ill repute, Sidney was not a safe place for the milder set. Train conductors warned through passengers not to get off the train because they'd probably be robbed before they got back on. Indeed, research has documented fifty-six homicides or attempted homicides, and some one thousand criminal cases prosecuted in Sidney from 1876 to 1881. As the numbers show, Sidney had become even more lively—or deadly—as the point of departure to Deadwood when that boomtown developed.

Sidney has more than two score structures on the National Register of Historic Places. A self-guided **walking tour** is available at the Cheyenne County Chamber of Commerce (740 Illinois St.; 308-254-5851).

Established as Sidney Barracks in 1867 to protect the Union Pacific, **Fort Sidney** (955 6th Ave.; 308-254-2959) moved to its current location two year later. In 1870 the War Department designated it as Fort Sidney and the post continued to be strategically important during the Black Hills gold rush and the Sioux War. When the Cheyenne under Dull Knife escaped their reservation in Indian Territory in 1878 and tried to fight their way back to their homeland, troops at the post remained on high alert. During the episode, the Union Pacific kept a special train on standby so soldiers could quickly be dispatched in either direction on the mainline. On October 4, 1878, the troop train sped to Omaha to intercept the Indians before they reached the east-west tracks, but the Indians escaped. Another sixteen years went by before the army finally abandoned the post in 1894. The **Fort Sidney Museum**, located in the two-story former post commander's quarters (544 Jackson St.; 308-254-2150), has interpretive exhibits on the fort's history. The only other original building still standing is old powder magazine.

Sidney's **Boot Hill** (640 Elm St.) got its start in 1868 as the cemetery for Fort Sidney, but as the town grew, so did the cemetery. The army exhumed all known military graves there in 1922, removing 211 sets of remains. Last used in 1894, the old graveyard stood neglected for decades, but the cemetery has been cleaned up and touted as a destination for tourists interested in Wild West history. Signs at the cemetery document the lives of the more interesting occupants.

Valentine (Cherry County)

Named for US Senator Edward K. Valentine and not the patron saint of love, Valentine was founded in 1884, two years after the Sioux City and Pacific Railroad laid tracks through the area. Nearby **Fort Niobrara**, named for the Niobrara River, was established in 1880, and in 1890 some of the troops stationed there played a role in the Wounded Knee incident (see Pine Ridge, South Dakota).

Fort Niobrara continued as an active post until 1906. From then until 1911, it was a remount station where cavalry horses were procured and distributed. Located off State Highway 12, five miles east of Valentine, all that remains of the old fort is a large barn, foundations, and earth works. Now the **Fort Niobrara National Wildlife Refuge**, its 19,131 acres is home to a buffalo herd and other wildlife, including elk and prairie dogs. The visitor center (402-376-3789) has interpretive exhibits on the fort's history.

Centennial Hall Museum (3rd and Macomb Streets), housed in an 1897 redbrick schoolhouse, focuses on the area's history as does the **Cherry County Historical Museum** (Main Street and US 20; 402-376-2015), which occupies an old log cabin.

SOUTH DAKOTA

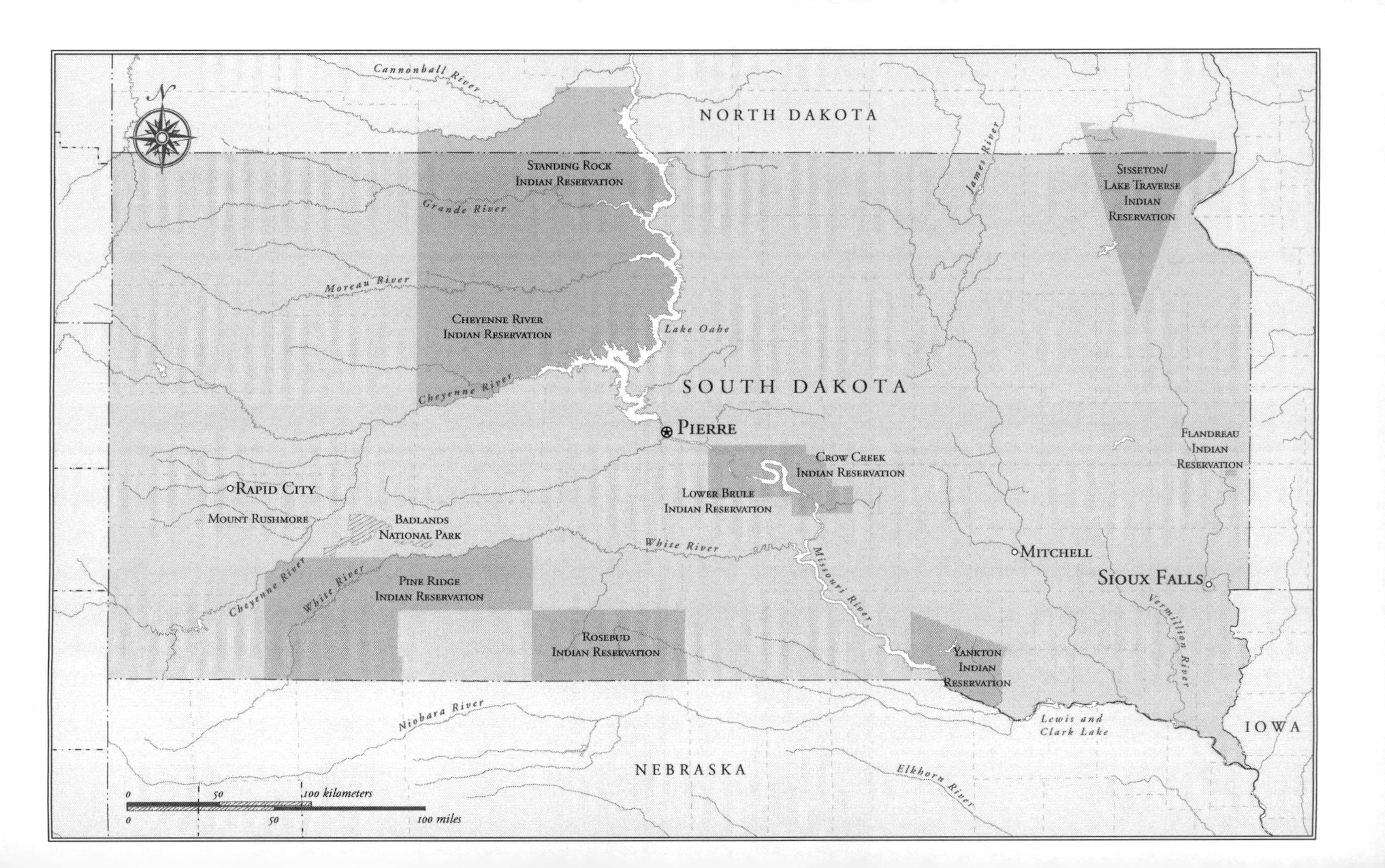
N
Cannonball River
NORTH DAKOTA
James River
Standing Rock Indian Reservation
Sisseton/ Lake Traverse Indian Reservation
Grande River
Moreau River
Cheyenne River Indian Reservation
Lake Oahe
SOUTH DAKOTA
Cheyenne River
Pierre
Flandreau Indian Reservation
Crow Creek Indian Reservation
Lower Brule Indian Reservation
Rapid City
Mount Rushmore
Badlands National Park
White River
Mitchell
Sioux Falls
Cheyenne River
White River
Pine Ridge Indian Reservation
Missouri River
Vermillion River
Rosebud Indian Reservation
Yankton Indian Reservation
Niobara River
Lewis and Clark Lake
IOWA
NEBRASKA
Elkhorn River
0
50
100 kilometers
0
50
100 miles

Belle Fourche (Butte County)

Belle Fourche (French for "beautiful forks") began when the Fremont, Elkhorn, and Missouri Valley Railroad progressed through western South Dakota in 1890. The line built a depot near the forks of Hay Creek and the Redwater and Belle Fourche Rivers, and a thriving ranch town and cattle shipping point developed.

Seven years later, the town became the setting for one of the Wild West's more controversial robberies. On June 28, 1897, five members of the Wild Bunch (debate continues as to which members) entered the Butte County Bank and ordered everyone to stick up their hands. Unfortunately for the would-be robbers, someone outside saw what was going on and spread the alarm. As armed citizens rushed to the scene, the outlaws fled, leaving behind $30,000 in the bank's safe. Four made their escape, but Tom O'Day, way too drunk to be robbing a bank, fell off his horse. He frantically commandeered a mule, but the animal wouldn't budge. Fleeing on foot, he ran into an outhouse between a saloon and the local newspaper office. Dropping his pistol down the hole, the boozy bandit emerged thinking he had succeeded in making his getaway. Instead, an armed citizen stood there waiting for him and he went to jail. No longer a bank, the two-story stone building where the holdup occurred still stands at 701 6th Avenue. Privately owned, its first-floor exterior has been modernized.

The flopped bank job was just another Old West crime until the Wild Bunch acquired their standing as one of the era's most famous outlaw gangs. Belle Fourche gained another claim to fame when the US acquired its fiftieth state in 1959. Suddenly the small town had become the exact geographical center of the nation.

The **Tri-State Museum's** collection of Western artifacts started with one man's private collection. Butte County resident Roy Williams had been collecting relics associated with the Old West for years and following his death, in 1955 his wife donated the collection and $1,000 toward development of a local museum. That became a reality, and the collection has continued to grow. In 2004 the museum moved into a new building it shares with the **Center of the Nation Visitor's Center** (415 5th Ave.; 605-723-1200 or 605-723-2010). Adjacent to the museum is a restored two-story log cabin built in 1876 by Black Hills pioneer Johnny Spaulding. The **Butte County Historical Society** (259 Jensen Rd.; 605-892-2507) offers showings of other historic structures and sites.

Custer (Custer County)

Custer, originally Custer City, was the first gold rush boomtown in the Black Hills. It developed in 1876 on the north bank of French Creek, just west of where the Custer Expedition had found a deposit of gold in 1874. From a tent camp of six men, the population of Custer jumped to a thousand-plus in a month. By its fourth month, the new town had four hundred wood-frame buildings and a thousand tents. Peaking in its fifth month, Custer's fortunes changed for the worse as word spread that prospectors had discovered richer deposits at a place called **Deadwood Gulch**, fifty miles to the north. Interest in the French Creek diggings heated up again in 1878, and the town came back to life.

Custer County's first courthouse served from 1881 to 1975. Even before county offices moved to a new location, the Custer County Historical Society had been working to transform the two-story brick building into a museum. With exhibits covering the full spectrum of the southern Black Hills's history, the **1881 Courthouse Museum** (411 Mount Rushmore Rd.; 605-673-2443) opened in 1976. One of the items on display is a Sharps & Hankins Model 1862 .52-caliber hunting rifle that had belonged to Lt. Col. George Armstrong Custer. His widow Elizabeth Custer donated it to the City of Custer in 1928.

Across the street from the museum in Way Park is the oldest surviving Black Hills structure, the restored 1875 **Flick log cabin**.

Nearby stands a monument to **Horatio Ross**, the Custer Expedition member credited with finding gold in French Creek.

Custer State Park (13329 US 16A; 605-255-4515) covers 71,000 acres in the Black Hills and has one of the nation's largest herds of buffalo.

Only four miles north of Custer, and only seventeen miles from the sixty-foot chiseled stone faces of Presidents George Washington, Thomas Jefferson, Abraham Lincoln, and Theodore Roosevelt at **Mount Rushmore National Monument**, stands an in-progress mountain carving of another American leader, Crazy Horse. Polish-American sculptor Korczak Ziolkowski began the **Crazy Horse Memorial** in 1948 at the behest of Lakota elders and worked on it until shortly before his death in 1982. After her husband's death, Ruth Ziolkowsk pushed to have Crazy Horse's face finished so that it could be seen from the site's visitor's center. She died in 2014 but her children and grandchildren have continued to work on completing the massive project, albeit slowly and as they can afford it. (The non-profit foundation handling fund-raising will not accept any government money.) When the project is finished, the pegmatite granite monument depicting a mounted Crazy Horse will be the world's largest mountain carving, 563 feet high and 641 feet long. The chief's face alone is eighty-eight feet tall, his eyes eighteen feet across.

Visitors can assess how the enormous undertaking is proceeding by comparing the mountain view with a 1/34-scale plaster model of the statue that stands outside the visitor center, which is a mile from the massive work in progress. When completed it will be four times the size of the four faces on Mount Rushmore.

Beneath the monument is a cluster of related attractions (12151 Avenue of the Chiefs; 605-673-4681), including the forty-thousand-square-foot welcome center with interpretive exhibits, the **Indian Museum of North America**, **Native American Cultural Center**, and **Ziolkowski's log home-studio-workshop**.

Fly Specked Billy

His righteous name was **James Fowler**, but dark freckles on a fair face saddled him with an unappealing nickname, Fly Specked Billy. (Where "Billy" came from is not known.) Fowler possessed a character about as unattractive as his nickname. A freighter, he arrived in Custer in 1881 and when not working, devoted his energies to drinking. On January 6, in George Parmer's Saloon, he became drunk and abusive and ended up fatally shooting one Abe Barnes. The victim's friends and other law-and-order-minded townsfolk decided that Fly Specked Billy needed hanging sooner than the legal system might get around to it. The sheriff and his deputy resisted nobly if ineffectively, and as one writer later put it, Fly Specked soon ended up "decorating a pine tree." The 1881 Courthouse Museum has an exhibit telling Fowler's story and detailing two other Custer County hangings. Fowler's grave has been lost.

DEADWOOD (LAWRENCE COUNTY)

The second in the triumvirate of famous Wild West towns (in order of their founding Dodge City, Kansas, is first, Tombstone, Arizona, third), Deadwood got its evocative name because a stand of dead trees filled the gulch that quickly became a mining boomtown in 1876 following the discovery of gold in the Black Hills. As was the case with the other two best-known Western towns, the first four letters in Deadwood proved particularly appropriate. For a time, the town supposedly averaged a murder a day. As the *Black Hills Pioneer* reported on May 13, 1878, "Murder is becoming [too] fashionable in the gulch. Before the body of one man becomes cold in the grave, the coroner is summoned to sit on the remains of another. This is a terrible, fearful state of affairs."

One of those drawn to Deadwood at the height of the boom was the already legendary James Butler Hickok, better known as Wild

Bill Hickok. He only lived there for ten days, but his mortal remains would never leave.

Wild West boomtowns had an average life of three years. That was about right in the case of Deadwood. Unlike many of its contemporaries, Deadwood did not become a ghost town, but business stayed mighty slow until 1989 when gambling was legalized. That greatly benefited the economy but starting with a fire in 1879 that wiped out most of its original buildings, over the years the town lost much of its historical authenticity. Civic leaders have made up for that, however, by maximizing what remains and playing up the town's legends and lore. In addition, the popular 2004–2006 cable television series *Deadwood* gave the town a twenty-first century boost in name recognition.

The **visitor's center** in the 1897 brick train depot (3 Siever St.; 605-578-1876) has brochures on all of Deadwood's attractions, from historic sites to modern casinos. The center also has a self-guided walking tour of downtown, where interpretive signs explain historic sites. Deadwood has a city-run trolley system (on wheels, not tracks) visitors can use to reach the various history-related venues.

One of the West's best-known figures, famous even in his lifetime, James Butler "Wild Bill" Hickok was killed on the afternoon of August 2, 1876, by twenty-five-year-old Jack "Crooked Nose" McCall as he sat playing poker in Deadwood's No. 10 Saloon. The legend is that Hickok held a pair of black aces, a pair of black eights, and a nine when a .45 round tore through the back of his head and took his life while assuring him lasting fame. Picky historians note, however, that there is no official documentation as to what cards Hickok clutched when McCall cashiered him that long-ago evening. Even so, ever since, aces and eights have been known as the Dead Man's Hand.

No. 10 Saloon (657 Main St.) is across the street from its original location, which was 624 Main Street. Three years after the shooting, the saloon was destroyed by fire. The L.H. Chase Building was built on the site in 1898 and still stands. Purchased in March 2014, the site remained vacant for two years before the new owners dressed it up and reopened it as a bar. Wild Bill—at least someone dressed up to look like him—continues to get shot in a reenactment of the killing that takes place four times a day, at least during the peak tourist season. "Jack McCall" also is regularly retried at the **Masonic Hall** (715 Main St.; 800-952-9398).

The only thing characters like Wild Bill Hickok and Calamity Jane did for Deadwood was contribute to its notoriety as a particularly rambunctious frontier boomtown. W.E. Adams did just the opposite. As a businessman, long-time mayor, and philanthropist, he helped make it a good place to work and raise a family. He also played a key role in preserving its history.

A Giant Nugget and a Mysterious Stone

William Emery Adams arrived in Deadwood at the height of its boom in 1877. The twenty-three-year-old and his older brother James built and ran a grocery store on Main Street. The fire of 1879 that wiped out most of Deadwood destroyed their store, but they rebuilt, and their business continued to grow. James eventually sold his half of the business to William and moved to California, but William transitioned from retail to wholesale sales, eventually running one of the state's grocery and produce wholesale businesses.

Adams served six terms as mayor and, active in the Chamber of Commerce, worked to monetize Deadwood's gold rush past. Not that attracting tourist dollars was his only motivation. He appreciated history for its own sake. In 1929, on the eve of the Great Depression, he bought a downtown lot and built the **Adams Museum** (54 Sherman St.; 605-578-1714). Then he donated the property to the City of Deadwood.

Now considered one of the West's top museums, two of its displays are particularly popular. One is a glittering reproduction of the 7.346-ounce gold nugget prospector Johnny Perrett, a character better known as Potato Creek Johnny, found in the Black Hills' Spearfish Canyon. Adams bought the actual nugget, which is kept in a vault, for $250 in 1934. The other artifact, known as the **Thoen Stone**, represents one of the West's most intriguing unsolved mysteries. A man named Louis Thoen claimed to have found the sandstone slab in 1887 near Spearfish, South Dakota. Carved on it are forty-six words telling a grim, but history-altering story:

> *Came to the hills in 1833 seven of us . . . Al ded but me Erza Kind killed by Indians on the high hill. Got all the gold we could carry our ponies all go by Indians. I have lost my gun and nothing to eat and Indians hunting me.*

If the stone, which lists six other gold seekers besides Kind, is for real it means that the Black Hills gold rush would have begun forty years earlier had even one of the men made it out alive. But most scholars, pointing to the fact that its discoverer just happened to make his living as a stone carver, dismiss it as a well-done hoax. Others assert that a researcher located some of the descendants of the men listed on the stone and that they reported they did have an ancestor who disappeared in the West in the 1830s.

Adams bequeathed his 1892 Queen Anne–style house to the City of Deadwood and it is operated as the **Adams House** (22 Van Buren; 605-578-3724), an adjunct to the museum. The properties are all maintained and operated by the non-profit Deadwood History, Inc. (605-722-4800), as are the **Days of '76 Museum** (18 76th Dr.; 605-578-1657) and the **Homestake Adams Research and Cultural Center**.

Deadwood's historic **Mount Moriah Cemetery** (10 Mt. Moriah Dr.; 605-578-2600), far greener and much more scenic than the Boot Hills in Dodge City or Tombstone, covers the side of a prominence overlooking the once wild and very wooly Deadwood Gulch. The high ground could pass as a mountain, but the geologic feature itself is not Mount Moriah. That's only the name of the cemetery, which comes from the Bible. Of the cemetery's 3,672 known burials, the two most famous graves are those of Hickok and **Calamity Jane** (1852–1903).

The cemetery is more than four thousand feet above mean sea level and visitors face a steep, four-hundred-step climb to get to Wild Bill's monument. For a fee, visitors can catch a shuttle bus from the downtown visitor's center to the historic cemetery. The bus stops near Hickok's grave, saving the climb. Anyone wanting even more exercise can visit the lone grave of legendary Deadwood lawman **Seth Bullock** (1849–1919), the county's first sheriff. It lies up a trail an additional 750 feet higher than the rest of the cemetery.

A mile north of Deadwood, just off US 85 races a herd of fourteen larger-than-life bronze bison being driven off a cliff by three Native American horsemen, a giant bronze sculpture believed to be the third largest in the world. It was commissioned by actor Kevin Costner shortly after he completed his starring role in *Dances with Wolves*. The work by artist Peggy Detmers is the center piece of **Tantanka: Story of the Bison** (100 Tantanka Dr.; 605-584-5678), a museum opened in 2005 devoted to the buffalo (for which the Lakota word is "tantanka") and the people whose survival once depended on the iconic animal.

De Smet (Kingsbury County)

With the Dakota Central Railroad laying tracks through what would become Kingsbury County, in 1879 Charles P. Ingalls moved to South Dakota to take a job as construction camp timekeeper. A year later, once rail service began, a town was laid out and named for Jesuit Father Pierre De Smet, a Belgian-born priest who did missionary work with Native Americans. Ingalls liked the prairie country and decided to stay. He remained for the rest of his life, but it was his daughter Laura Elizabeth who would give the town its principal claim to fame.

The Little House on the Prairie

When the Ingalls family came to South Dakota, Laura was twelve. Her father homesteaded 160 acres near the small town, and she and her siblings grew up in the Ingalls' little house on the prairie. Counting her time in De Smet following her marriage to Almanzo Wilder, future best-selling author Laura Ingalls Wilder (1876–1957) spent a dozen years in and around De Smet. Her memories would inform six of her series of *Little House* books. (They have sold forty-one million copies and counting.)

Among the sites in De Smet tied to the internationally known author are the **Surveyor's House** (103 Olivet Ave.) where the family first lived and that Wilder wrote about in her novel *By the Shores of Silver Lake*; the **Ingalls homestead** (20912 Homestead Rd.); and the **town home** Charles Ingalls built in 1887 (210 3rd St.). In reality, almost any nineteenth-century building still standing in De Smet, from the **Loftus Store** (205 Calumet Ave.) to the old school she attended, has a connection to the author. The **De Smet Depot Museum** (104 Calumet St.; 605-854-3731) covers the town's railroad history.

Fort Pierre (Stanley County)

In 1743, French explorer **Pierre Gaultier De La Verendrye** and his two sons deposited a rectangular lead tablet on a high point where the Bad River meets the Missouri River. That plate, discovered in 1913 by children playing in the area, constitutes the first written record of a European presence on the northern Great Plains. Fort Pierre is South Dakota's oldest settlement, its origin tracing to the Fort Pierre Chouteau trading post established by the American Fur Co. in 1832. The US government purchased the trading post in 1855 and converted it into an army post. While no evidence remains of the historic trading post, a stone monument marks the site.

The area's history is covered at the **Verendrye Museum** (Main Street and US 183). A gray granite historical marker erected in 1933, along with a later interpretive sign placed by the South Dakota State Historical Society, marks the site of the Verendrye plate discovery (Verendrye Drive, four-tenths of a mile west of 2nd Avenue; GPS coordinates: N44° 21.33', W100° 22.71'). The historic tablet itself is on display at the **South Dakota Cultural Heritage Center** (900 Governors Dr.; 605-773-3458) in nearby Pierre.

A sign at the end of Hustan Avenue near the present Colonel Waldron Missouri River Bridge in Fort Pierre marks the beginning of the old **Fort Pierre-Deadwood Trail**. When gold was discovered in the Black Hills, the easiest way to get there was by steamboat up the Missouri from Yankton to Fort Pierre, and from there over land for two hundred dangerous miles.

Garretson (Minnehaha County)

Garretson is a small community founded in 1889 when the Sioux City and Great Northern Railroad came through the area. But it's a legend concerning the Jesse James gang that makes the town of interest to Wild West history buffs. Following the infamous Northfield, Minnesota, raid of 1876, in which the James-Younger gang shot up the town and in the process got shot up themselves, folklore has it that Jesse and Frank James fled to what is now South Dakota. Supposedly, while being chased by a posse, Jesse jumped his horse over a chasm known as Devil's Gulch. As one article on the legend puta it, "There are more holes in this story than would eventually be in Jesse James." You can view the site and assess whether such a feat of horsemanship could even be possible by visiting **Devil's Gulch Park** (North Central Avenue and 5th Street).

Hill City (Pennington County)

Hill City was the second town settled in the Black Hills during the 1876 gold rush. A small mine, but one that produced enough gold to make it worthwhile, was the town's reason for being. At its high point, Hill City had a hotel, a sawmill, and other businesses. Bigger money was being made in Deadwood, however, and Hill City was in decline within a few years of its founding. The town had a second act in 1881 with the discovery of commercial quantities of tin in the area. At one point the Harney Peak Tin Mining Co. employed some three thousand people. When the nation's demand for tin tapered off, so did Hill City. In 1957 the figurative curtain went up on the town's third act, the opening of an attraction known in the tourist industry as a heritage railroad.

The mines in the Black Hills were served first by a narrow-gauge line and then a railroad with standard trackage. But when mining ceased, so did the railroads. In the mid-1950s, William Heckman, a public relations man who liked steam engines, and Robert Frazier, another railroad buff, organized the **Black Hills Central Railroad** to preserve working steam trains. The line opened in 1957 to carry passengers from Hill City to Keystone and as intended, became a popular attraction. New owners acquired the business in 1990.

No. 7, the railroad's oldest steam engine, rolled out of the Baldwin Locomotive Works in 1919, not 1880. But with its diamond-style smokestack it looks enough like a typical locomotive from the Black Hills gold boom era to have starred in a two-part episode of the long-running *Gunsmoke* television series and in other productions since then. To modern passengers, the venerable locomotive also sounds and feels like a nineteenth-century steam engine. Tickets available at the depot at 222 Rail Avenue or online.

Hot Springs (Fall River County)

The story of the Wild West is not solely an action-filled chronicle of discovery, conquest, and lawlessness. Entrepreneurs, from town builders to patent medicine quacks, could be as notable in their endeavors, with as interesting lives, as the more stereotypical Western figures. Hot Springs is a monument to one of those early entrepreneurs, **Fred T. Evans, Sr.** (1835–1902). A big man at six feet four, he also had big ideas.

A successful freighting company owner, he transformed a place called **Minnekahta** (Lakota for "warm water") into one of the West's earliest resorts, Hot Springs. First, in 1886, he built a grand hotel to accommodate people wanting to spend time in the town's hot springs. Evans also led the effort to bring rail service to the budding resort (which soon became the smallest American city with a union depot), and, in 1890 opened the **Evans Plunge** (1145 North River St.)—a building with a seventy- by two-hundred-foot indoor pool fed by bubbling hot springs. His first hotel burned in 1891. The following year he opened the even larger **Evans Hotel** (now a senior housing facility) (545 North River St.), five stories tall and built with native sandstone. In addition to the things he did to make himself money, he donated generously to the community.

Evans's 1899-vintage two-story Queen Anne–style house (1741 Summit Rd.) still stands but is a private residence. Evans is buried in **Evergreen Cemetery** (Cemetery Road at School Street; Section E, Block 3, Lot 5). The cemetery is on a hill on the north side of town. For a man who did so much, his tombstone bears only his name and years of birth and death.

The **Pioneer Museum** (300 North Chicago St.; 605-745-5147) has twenty-five exhibit areas dedicated to the history of Hot Springs and Fall River County.

Lead (Lawrence County)

Lead, only three and a half miles southwest of Deadwood, is another of the Black Hills mining towns dating to the gold rush days. When the easy placer gold played out, hard-rock mining began in 1877 when Californian George Hearst (father of future newspaper tycoon William Randolph Hearst) purchased the Homestake claim—the area's richest source of gold—for $70,000. Miners from the UK, Italy, and Scandinavia gave Lead a diverse ethnic population, and by the end of the nineteenth century, it ranked as one of South Dakota's largest cities. The richest area mine, the Hearst-founded Homestake, continued to produce ore until 2002. That made it the longest continuously operated gold mine in the world.

The **Black Hills Mining Museum** (323 West Main St.; 605-584-1605) offers the state's best overview of its gold mining history. The museum's centerpiece is a simulated underground mine developed by Homestake miners. Visitors also can pan for gold.

Lemmon (Perkins County)

When the US government allowed the leasing of some eight hundred thousand acres of Standing Rock Indian Reservation in 1902, cattleman George Ed Lemmon founded the town that took his name. But something that happened long before that is the area's most compelling piece of history.

In 1823 a mountain man named Hugh Glass belonged to a fur-trapping expedition headed to the Yellowstone River. While hunting alone, Glass encountered a mother grizzly bear and her two cubs. Instinctively, she attacked Glass and left him unconscious and gravely wounded. The party moved on, leaving two of their number, including a young Jim Bridger, behind to care for Glass. Thinking Glass would die, the men took his rifle and supplies and abandoned him. That marked the beginning of one of the Wild West's greatest survival stories. Eventually waking up to find maggots crawling on his wounds, Glass, despite a broken leg and other injuries, managed to make it two hundred miles to a trading post on the Missouri River called Fort Kiowa. The desire for revenge, which he ended up not exacting, is what fed his determination to live.

The tale was the basis of the 2015 Oscar-winning film *The Revenant,* starring Leonardo DiCaprio. A state historical marker stands at the still-remote site of the attack (Pasture 8 Road, Shadehill). From Lemmon take State Highway 73 thirteen miles and turn west on unpaved Hugh Glass Road. At the **Grand River Museum** (114 10th St. West; 605-374-7574) there's an exhibit detailing the Glass saga. Outside the museum is a metal sculpture depicting the bear attack.

Mitchell (Davison County)

Mitchell, named for Chicago, Milwaukee, and St. Paul Railroad president Alexander Mitchell, was first settled in 1879 and incorporated four years later. It began as a farming town and still is, which is how it ended up with one of the more architecturally unique structures built in the fading days of the wild west—the 1892 **Corn Palace**

(604 North Main St.; 605-996-8430), an ornate agricultural exhibit hall that looked more like something built in pre-revolution Russia. The original building was replaced in 1905 by a larger structure, followed in 1921 by an even bigger building. In addition to the Corn Palace, the **Middle Border Museum of American Indian and Pioneer Life** (1311 Duff St.; 605-996-2122) focuses on the multi-century history of the Missouri River Valley. (The term "Middle Border" comes from writer Hamlin Garland, who in 1917 first used it to describe the Missouri River Valley, where east and west met.)

Pierre (Hughes County)

Founded on the east bank of the Missouri River in 1880 opposite the older town of Fort Pierre, Pierre has been the capital since South Dakota gained statehood in 1889. Despite its status as the center of state government, Pierre never boomed and is the least-populated state capital west of the Mississippi. The upside is that many of its nineteenth-century buildings and houses still stand.

A Smithsonian affiliate operated by the South Dakota Historical Society, the **South Dakota Cultural Heritage Center** (900 Governors Dr.; 605-773-3458) covers the state's story from the days when the Plains Indians held it to the influx of gold miners to its development as a territory and then a state.

Arkansas Joe

When Pierre got rail service in 1880, the local economy picked up considerably. Along with the standard legitimate businesses came an influx of vice-related enterprises that soon lined Missouri Street. That's where Wisconsin-born Alexander McDonald Putello, aka **Arkansas Joe**, spent much of his time. How he came by his nickname isn't known, but as one historian later noted, "Arkansas Joe" certainly sounded catchier than "Wisconsin Alexander." A big redhead, Arkansas Joe was a drinker and troublemaker. A series of rowdy escapades, capped by an armed robbery in which Arkansas Joe grazed a victim with a bullet, led to the near-unanimous sentiment among Pierre's law-abiding citizens that Joe had to go, one way or the other. The way he departed was with two loads of buckshot after trying to shoot civic leader (and former deputy US marshal) John Hilger and other citizens who had come to corral him. Hilger graciously bought the dead man a new suit and even gave him a shave before seeing to his burial. Arkansas Joe had pretty much been forgotten until 1904, when excavation for the capitol's basement unearthed a skull with remnants of red hair. Still around, Hilger identified the skull as having belonged to Arkansas Joe. For years the cranium sat on display in the state history museum, but in the early 1970s museum staffers reburied it.

The state history museum kept secret the location of Arkansas Joe's second (if partial) burial, other than to say it was somewhere in Stanley County. A state historical marker in front of the American Legion Hall (520 South Pierre St.) marks the spot where the red-headed tough died.

Pine Ridge (Oglala Lakota County)

The government opened the **Pine Ridge Reservation** in 1877 for the vanquished Sioux under Red Cloud. The 3,400-plus-square-mile reservation south of Badlands National Park continues as the Oglala Sioux tribal home.

Until publication of Dee Brown's classic book *Bury My Heart at Wounded Knee* in 1970, what happened here in 1890 had all but been forgotten. Except by the Sioux, who lost roughly three hundred ancestors here in what some call a battle and others term a massacre. By whatever description, the events of December 29, 1890, were tragic if complicated. It began with the Ghost Dance movement, a medicine man's prophecy that if Indians followed a prescribed ritual, the Great Plains would once again be empty except for the return of vast herds of buffalo. This belief, though not shared by all Native Americans at the time, terrified the state's Euro American population, who feared yet another Indian uprising. When a band of men, women, and children under Big Foot left their reservation and headed to Pine Ridge, troops intercepted them and attempted to disarm them. On the bitter winter morning of December 29, while the Sioux were surrounded by soldiers of the Seventh Cavalry, a shot was fired. At that, the troopers opened fire at the Indians, killing them by the score.

Wounded Knee is twelve miles northwest of Pine Ridge on US 18. The Sioux killed that day were buried in a mass grave.

Lost Bird

Two days after the massacre at Wounded Knee, not far from the scene on the Pine River Reservation, someone found a baby Lakota girl wrapped in a blanket. The infant's parents had tried to flee the melee in a commandeered wagon, but it overturned. The accident left the child unconscious, and the mother, thinking she had been killed, left the baby near the wagon and escaped with the child's father.

Never claimed by her parents (who may never have known the infant survived), the child eventually was adopted by General Leonard Colby, an officer in the Nebraska state militia, and his wife, Clara Bewick Colby. Since no one knew the infant's real name, she became known as Zintkala Nuni, the Lost Bird. Though she got a second chance at life, there surely were times she wished she had died with the others that bitterly cold December day. Despite the efforts of her loving adopted mother, Lost Bird would endure a hard, short life, suffering from racial prejudice, probable sexual abuse, chronic disease, and poverty. Once she was on her own, she worked for a time as a member of Buffalo Bill's Wild West show and later as a silent movie extra and vaudeville entertainer. But she never found true peace.

Only twenty-nine, Zintka died in California of influenza on Valentine's Day, 1920. Seventy-one years later, largely through the efforts of Renee Sansom Flood (author of *Lost Bird of*

Wounded Knee) her remains were exhumed from an unmarked grave and returned to the Pine River Reservation, where she was reburied by the Lakota in **Sacred Heart Catholic Cemetery** (on the Pine Ridge Reservation near the intersection of Bureau of Indian Affairs Highway 28 and Cemetery Road).

RAPID CITY (PENNINGTON COUNTY)

John Brennan and Samuel Scott were among the thousands of gold-seekers who came to the Black Hills in search of wealth. Not successful at that, in 1876 they and nine others founded what would become western South Dakota's largest city.

Most Black Hills towns began as mining camps, but Rapid City began because it made good business sense to start a town at the natural entrance to the region that would serve as a supply center. At first, the settlement was called Hay Camp, but since its mile-square townsite lay along Rapid Creek, Rapid City seemed like a more appropriate name. Despite its strategic location, Rapid City did not grow as rapidly as the boomtowns it served, but six months after its founding a hundred-plus people had settled there. The town's growth was finally assured when it got rail service.

Founded in 1997, the **Journey Museum and Learning Center** (222 New York St.; 605-394-6923) tells the story of the 1.2-million-acre timber-covered mountains the Lakota Sioux called Paha Sapa, the Black Hills. The saga begins with their formation 2.5 billion years ago and continues through the Wild West era. The center's four collections focus on geology-paleontology, archeology, Native American, and Black Hills pioneers.

SIOUX FALLS (MINNEHAHA COUNTY)

Named for a waterfall on the Sioux River, Sioux Falls got its start in 1856 when investors purchased a 320-acre site along the river and began selling lots to settlers. The village grew to become South Dakota's largest city.

The Amidon Affair

She had packed them lunch, but when her husband and son did not come home for supper after a day in their field cutting hay, Mrs. Joseph Amidon feared something bad had happened. After anxiously waiting a while longer, the pioneer housewife hurried to the nearby village of Sioux Falls to alert a detachment of Dakota Volunteer Cavalry camped there.

The following day, August 26, 1862, soldiers found the Amidons. Joseph had been shot to death. Nearby lay his son William, his body studded with arrows. The pair had been killed by a Sioux war party under White Crow. As the people of Sioux Falls soon learned, a bloody Sioux uprising in Minnesota had spread to Dakota Territory. Two days later, Governor William Jane dispatched a courier with his order to abandon Sioux Falls and proceed to the territorial capital at Yankton. Not until the US Army established Fort Dakota in 1865 did settlers return to the Sioux River Valley.

The Amidon burial site has been lost, but in 1949 the Minnehaha County Historical Society placed a tall stone obelisk atop the bluff overlooking Sioux Falls where the pioneer family's cabin once stood. A metal historical marker telling the story of the so-called Amidon Affair was placed at the site in 1991.

Begun in 1889, the first **Minnehaha County courthouse** was designed by Sioux Falls architect Wallace L. Dow, who also drew plans for a facility at the other end of the criminal justice spectrum—the **South Dakota State Penitentiary**. When the red quartzite stone courthouse opened in 1893, its designer proclaimed it the largest county capitol between Chicago and Denver. The three-story building continued in use until 1962 when the county moved to a larger courthouse. An impressive building with a tall clock tower, it stood in danger of being torn down to make room for a parking lot until local preservationists prevailed in getting the former courthouse transformed into the **Old Courthouse Museum** (200 West 6th St.; 605-367-7079). Opened in 1974, the museum has permanent and rotating exhibits focusing on the history of the region. In a way, the longtime courthouse was a museum before it technically became one. Gracing some of its interior walls are sixteen large murals painted by Norwegian immigrant Ole Running from 1915 to 1917. Each depicts some aspect of Dakota life, its landscape, or the artist's earlier life in Norway.

In 1911 R.F. Pettigrew, South Dakota's first US Senator, purchased a Queen Anne–style house built in 1888. Following his death in 1926, his will left the house to the city. Turned into a museum, the **Pettigrew Home and Museum** (131 North Duluth Ave.; 605-367-7097) has artifacts collected by Pettigrew in his world travels, his extensive library, and exhibits on the history and culture of Sioux Falls.

Sisseton (Roberts County)

The US Army was fighting the Confederacy for the Union's survival in 1864, but in the aftermath of the Minnesota Indian uprising of 1862 the military nevertheless established Fort Wadsworth in eastern Dakota Territory. Twelve years later, in 1876, the post was renamed for the Sisseton Tribe. With the Indian Wars finally at an end, the town of Sisseton was founded in 1892 by Norwegian immigrants. Now a state park, fourteen buildings of the old fort were restored by the Works Progress Administration during the Depression. Opened in 1959, **Fort Sisseton Historic State Park** (11907 434th Ave.; 605-448-5474) is thirty-two miles west of Sisseton.

In Sisseton, the area's Norwegian heritage is documented in the three-story **Andrew Stavig House Museum** (112 1st Ave. West). The **Joseph N. Nicollet Tower and Interpretive Center** (45352 State Highway 10; 605-698-7621) documents the life and times of the French mapmaker who first explored the area in the 1830s. From the seventy-five-foot-tall observation tower built of Douglas fir logs, visitors can see three states.

Spearfish (Lawrence County)

Founded during the 1876 Black Hills gold rush, Spearfish started as Queen City but later renamed itself for Spearfish Canyon, a spectacular gorge beginning just south of town. How the canyon came to be called Spearfish is debated, but the general belief is that it is based on awareness that the Sioux used spears to harvest fish from the creek flowing through the high-walled, narrow canyon. While towns like Deadwood and Lead lived and died with the rise and decline of mining, Spearfish developed as an agricultural community and survived after the precious metal played out.

The West had plenty of wild left in 1896 when Congress allocated money for construction of a federal fish hatchery in Spearfish. One of the first such facilities in the nation, the hatchery raised trout for stocking in the Black Hills and Wyoming. Trout were not indigenous to this area, but the program proved hugely successful and trout fishing became a major aspect of the outdoor recreation industry. The hatchery complex includes the **National Museum of Fish Culture** (423 Hatchery Circle; 605-642-7730) and the nation's fish hatchery archives.

A grand opera house built in 1906 by Wyoming rancher Thomas Matthews, who had driven cattle up the trail from Texas and stayed, the **Matthews Opera House** (612 Main St.; 605-642-7973) offered live performances until the rise of the film industry forced its conversion into a movie house. Closed in 1930, it saw a variety of uses, until by the 1960s it stood vacant and deteriorating. A non-profit group restored the old show place and it reopened to its former elegance in 2006.

The **High Plains Western Heritage Center** (825 Heritage Dr., southbound exit 14, I-90; 605-642-9378) is a regional museum covering the history of five states: South Dakota, North Dakota, Nebraska, Wyoming, and Montana. Opened in 1989 and operated by a non-profit foundation, the center has twenty-thousand square feet of exhibit space focusing on the American Indian, pioneering, mining, transportation, ranching, and rodeo.

Sturgis (Meade County)

Sturgis is another Black Hills town owing its existence to the 1876 gold rush, but it was not founded until 1878, the same year the army established nearby Fort Meade. First known as Scooptown, supposedly because its residents supported themselves by scooping money from off-duty cavalry troopers who patronized its bars and bordellos, the community later was renamed in honor of Civil War Gen. Samuel D. Sturgis. With the organization of Meade County in 1889, Sturgis became county seat.

Even after its initial mission of protecting Black Hills gold mining towns from the Sioux ended, Fort Meade continued as an active military post. In 1892 the post commander ordered that "The Star-Spangled Banner" be played each day at retreat. The practice spread and is now part of the daily routine at all US Army posts across the world. The fort was abandoned in 1944 and converted into a Veterans Administration Hospital. The South Dakota National Guard still uses the former post for training. Located in the former post headquarters **Fort Meade Museum** (50 Sheridan St.; 605-347-9822) documents all aspects of the fort's long history.

Poker Alice Comes to South Dakota

Mrs. Warren G. Tubbs—better known as cigar smoking **Poker Alice**—came to Deadwood from Colorado. When her husband and professional gambling partner died in 1909, she left Deadwood for Rapid City but eventually settled in Sturgis. There she met and married her third husband, George Huckert. After he died in 1924, she never remarried. In Sturgis she operated a bar until Prohibition forced her to close it. After that, she ran a bordello catering to Fort Meade soldiers. But as the years piled up like the stacks of chips she'd once raked in, in the figurative sense, she wasn't getting the cards she used to. Frequently arrested for drunkenness or for running a house of prostitution, Alice ended up facing prison time. That's when she drew one last winning hand—a pardon from the governor due to her advanced age (she was seventy-five). Four years later, on February 27, 1930, in Rapid City, she cashed in her chips for the last time. Her body was returned to Sturgis for burial in **St. Aloysius Cemetery** (1600–1698 Main St.). The house Poker Alice lived in still stands at 1822 Junction Avenue.

Yankton (Yankton County)

Named for the Yankton Sioux, Yankton was settled on a bend of the Missouri River in 1857. Its location made it the gateway to the Northern Plains and when Dakota gained territorial status in 1861, Yankton became its capital. With regular riverboat and stagecoach service, the town flourished. In 1873, when the Seventh Cavalry regiment under Lt. Col. George Armstrong Custer first came to Dakota Territory, it camped nearly a month at Yankton before marching westward to protect workers along the route of the planned Northern Pacific Railroad. The railroad was delayed but Custer and his troops remained in the West. Yankton lost its capital city status in 1883 when the seat of territorial government was moved to Bismarck.

Jack McCall (1851?-1876), accused killer of Wild Bill Hickok (see Deadwood), went on trial in Yankton on December 4, 1876. Two days later, after hearing the case, it took the jury less than four hours to find McCall guilty. Speedy as the trial had been, fourteen months would pass before the convicted killer faced execution. At mid-morning on March 1, 1878, a cold, drizzly day, he had the honor of having his neck broken in front of a thousand people, the first legal hanging in Dakota Territory.

The trial took place in the three-story wood frame St. Charles Hotel, which stood at 3rd and Capitol Streets. That building was razed in 1890 to make room for a three-story red brick building that was for many years a hotel. A historical marker attached to this Victorian structure commemorates the trial. Now part of Yankton, the site of McCall's hanging was two miles north of town at the time. A historical marker stands at the site near the south entrance of the South Dakota Human Services Center (3515 Broadway Ave.).

McCall was buried in an unmarked grave in Yankton's **Sacred Heart Cemetery** (Douglas Avenue at East Francis Street). For whatever reason, Hickok's killer went into his coffin with the rope still around his neck. All that is known about the location of McCall's grave is that it lies in the southwest corner of the cemetery, one of only two unmarked graves there. St. Benedict Catholic Church maintains the burial ground.

Founded in 1936, the **Dakota Territorial Museum** moved to its fourth location in 2018 with its opening in the **Meade Cultural Education Center** (82 Mickelson Dr.; 605-665-3898), a three-story stone structure built in 1909 as part of what is now known as the South Dakota Human Services Center. (First known as the South Dakota Insane Asylum, the now multi-building state hospital campus traces its beginning to 1882.) The museum's first location was in the former **Dakota Territorial Council Hall** at what is now Riverside Park. In 1953, the hall was moved to West Side Park. There a larger museum was built in 1971, and that had been its home until the move to its present location.

The Saga of the *Far West*

Operating on the Yellowstone and Missouri Rivers, a 190-foot, shallow-draft steamboat named the ***Far West*** had an important part in the run-up and aftermath of the Battle of Little Big Horn. Capt. Grant Marsh, master of the *Far West*, had a contract with the military to carry supplies and provide transportation during the 1876 Sioux War. The *Far West* also served for a time during the campaign as a mobile command post. After the battle, Grant made a record-breaking run carrying fifty-one wounded soldiers to Bismarck, a trip of 710 river miles made in fifty-four hours. The arrival of the *Far West* in Bismarck on July 3, 1876, brought the first word of Custer's defeat to the rest of the nation. Seven years later, under another captain, the *Far West* hit a snag and sank near St. Charles, Missouri. Considered the *West*'s most accomplished steamboat captain, yet in near poverty, Grant died at age eighty-three in Bismarck on January 6, 1916.

A life-sized statue of Marsh stands in Riverside Park overlooking the Missouri River. The inscription reads: "Captain Grant Prince Marsh, 1834–1916, Steamboat captain, Pilot and Riverman. 'He never flinched at the call of duty'. Sculpted by Frank Yaggie 1989." While captain of the *Far West*, Marsh lived in a two-story brick house that still stands (513 Douglas Ave.). The Dakota Territorial Museum displays a model of the *Far West* and has a fork stamped "Far West" that was part of the vessel's silver service.

NORTH DAKOTA

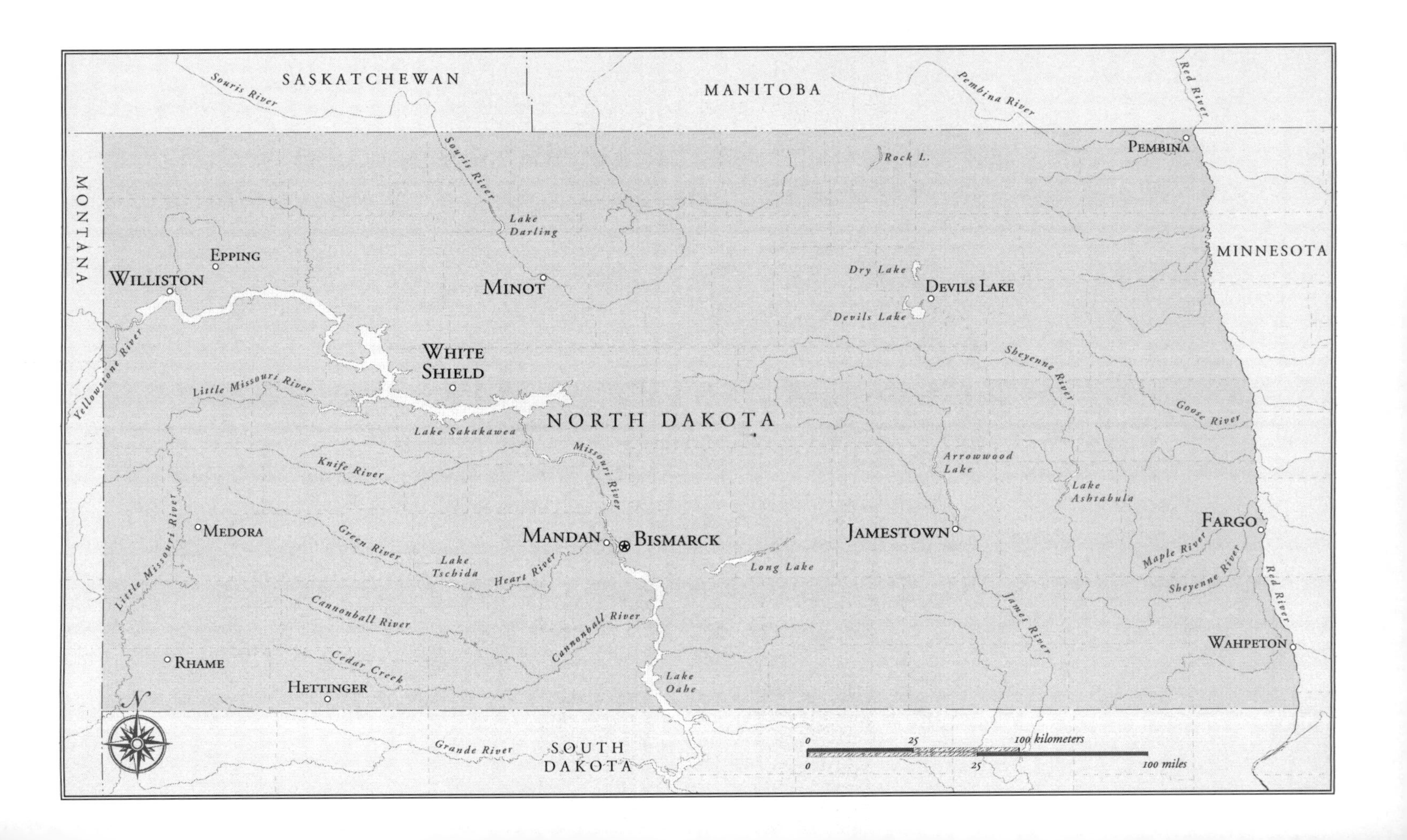
SASKATCHEWAN
MANITOBA
MINNESOTA
MONTANA
SOUTH DAKOTA
NORTH DAKOTA
Souris River
Souris River
Pembina River
Red River
Red River
Pembina
Rock L.
Lake Darling
Epping
Williston
Minot
Dry Lake
Devils Lake
Devils Lake
White Shield
Yellowstone River
Little Missouri River
Lake Sakakawea
Sheyenne River
Goose River
Knife River
Missouri River
Arrowwood Lake
Lake Ashtabula
Little Missouri River
Medora
Green River
Lake Tschida
Heart River
Mandan
Bismarck
Long Lake
Jamestown
Fargo
Maple River
Sheyenne River
Cannonball River
Cannonball River
James River
Wahpeton
Rhame
Cedar Creek
Hettinger
Lake Oahe
Grande River
N
0
25
100 kilometers
0
25
100 miles

Abercrombie (Richland County)

A small community in the state's southeast corner, Abercrombie was founded in 1884 when the Fargo and Southern Railroad laid tracks through the area. Twenty-six years earlier, in 1858, the military had established **Fort Abercrombie** a half-mile west of the future town site to protect oxcart trails used by fur traders, military supply wagon trains, stagecoach routes, and steamboat traffic on the nearby Red River of the North. Named for the officer who oversaw its construction, Lt. Col. John J. Abercrombie, the fort became known as the "Gateway to the Dakotas."

When the US Army vacated the post at the outset of the Civil War, volunteer soldiers from Minnesota garrisoned it during the Dakota war of 1862. The fort filled with settlers fleeing the conflict, and in August a large Sioux war party surrounded it. The defenders hurriedly constructed breastworks using barrels of salted pork, corned beef, and flour along with sod and firewood. The volunteers prevailed in one short but intense firefight in September when the Indians made it inside the fort's corral. Several other skirmishes took place, but the defenders succeeded in holding the fort for six weeks until five hundred volunteer soldiers showed up on September 23, 1862. Seeing they were outnumbered, the Sioux withdrew. Reoccupying the post after the Civil War, the US Army built blockhouses and a stockade to better protect the fort from any future attack. But no further hostilities occurred, and the fort was abandoned in 1877. The fort's original buildings were sold by the government and removed. During the Great Depression, the Works Progress Administration reconstructed three blockhouses and the stockade. The federal relief agency also moved the only surviving original building, the guardhouse, back to the site. Today, **Fort Abercrombie State Historic Site** (935 Broadway, Abercrombie; 701-553-8513) includes a visitor center and interpretive exhibits.

The **Richland County Historical Museum** (11 7th Ave. North, Wahpeton) covers the county's history and culture.

Bismarck (Burleigh County)

When the Northern Pacific Railroad crossed the Missouri River into Dakota Territory in 1872 the company platted a townsite called Edwinton in honor of chief engineer Edwin F. Johnson. Hoping to attract German immigrants and investment capital to the new railroad and riverboat center, the Northern Pacific soon sidetracked Edwinton and changed the town's name to Bismarck after German chancellor Otto von Bismarck. But the scheme didn't work.

What did stimulate an infusion of cash was the discovery of gold in the Black Hills in 1874. Bismarck became an important water and rail shipping point, but the influx of miners and boomtown hangers-on who descended on Dakota Territory brought big problems along with prosperity. In 1883 Bismarck became the territorial capital and with the creation of the state of North Dakota in 1889 remained the seat of government.

North Dakota Heritage Center and State Museum (612 East Boulevard Ave.) is the state's largest museum. With four substantial galleries, in addition to rotating exhibits, the museum covers everything that made North Dakota what it is, from pre-history to the present. Operated by the Missouri Valley Historical Society on a twenty-acre site adjacent to the state fairgrounds, **Buckstop Junction** (Old Highway 10; 701-328-2666) features twenty-plus restored historic buildings moved in from other areas of the state. The oldest is the store built by Bismarck baker and grocer John Yegen in 1877. Buildings range from a two-story frame hotel built in 1910 to early day outhouses.

When the army established a camp here in 1872 to protect North Pacific railroad workers, it named it **Camp Greeley** in honor of newspaper editor and unsuccessful presidential candidate Horace Greeley. A year later, the US War Department designated the post **Camp**

Hancock for Gen. George W. Hancock, commander of the military's Department of Dakota. An infantry post until 1877, it then became a supply depot and Army Signal Corps station. The army abandoned the camp in 1894.

Camp Hancock State Historic Site (101 East Main Ave.; 701-328-2666) has since been renovated and expanded, the post's log headquarters (though covered in clapboard) serves as a visitor's center with interpretive exhibits. The structure is also Bismarck's earliest surviving building.

A Monument to Journalistic Enterprise

Most historical markers commemorate pivotal events or notable figures, but a bronze plaque affixed to a granite boulder in downtown Bismarck tells the story of a story—one of the biggest newspaper scoops in US history. Late on July 5, 1876, *Bismarck Tribune* publisher Clement Lounsberry learned of Lt. Col. George Armstrong Custer's defeat at Little Big Horn. With telegraph office manager John M. Carnahan pounding the keys, the journalist spent the next twenty-four hours relaying details of the military disaster to the *New York Herald*. Transmitted 1,635 miles in dots and dashes, the fifty-thousand-word article—the length of a mid-sized book—filled fourteen columns of type. For his local readers, Lounsberry put out a *Tribune* extra containing the first published account of the battle. Mark Kellogg, a *Tribune* reporter, had been killed in the fight. At a time when a reader only had to pony up four cents for the *Herald's* latest edition, the eastern newspaper paid Lounsberry $2,500 for his story plus a $3,000 telegraph fee.

Placed on the west side of 5th Street, near the Northern Pacific Railroad depot by Sigma Delta Chi and the North Dakota Press Association, the marker (GPS coordinates: N46° 48.30', W100° 47.09') stands at the approximate site of the telegraph office, long since razed.

Little Casino was a place and a person in Bismarck. The place was considered the finest bordello in the Dakota Territory; the person was the madam who ran it—an attractive, diminutive woman whose real name was Elizabeth McClelland. Her nickname came from a then-popular card game called Casino, in which the deuce of spades was known as the "little Casino." Elizabeth had the two of spades printed on the discreet sign in front of her establishment and on her calling cards.

She arrived from Minnesota in 1873, confident Bismarck was a good place to do business. Being a busy steamboat landing as well as the terminus of the Northern Pacific, the town soon became the point of departure for prospectors and miners on their way to the gold-rich Black Hills. Even better, from her point of view, was that Fort Abraham Lincoln lay just across the river from town.

By 1874 eighteen saloons operated day and night to cater to the soldiers and western-bound travelers. Most of those establishments were on 4th Street, also known as Murderer's Gulch or Bloody 4th. But Little Casino opened her place on the better side of the tracks at 701 Front Street (where the *Bismarck Tribune* is now located).

A demure lady with a taste for elegant but conservative attire, she kept a low profile even though she did periodically have to appear in court to bail out one of her girls. Little Casino had a good income and was not reluctant to invest in her community and help those in need. To educate lawmakers on the advantages of Bismarck becoming the territorial capital, she contributed $1,200. She also invested in commercial real estate.

But when civic leaders decided on a prostitution clean-up, she lost her property to foreclosure. Moving twenty-five miles north to Wilton, North Dakota, she used her savings to get into coal mining, but never did as well as she had done as a madam. She never became penniless, but she did become a recluse, in 1916 dying old and alone, buried in an unmarked grave. During Wilton's centennial observance, a stage play based on Little Casino's life raised money for a tombstone in **Riverview Cemetery** (537–899 318th Ave. Northwest). On that headstone, "LITTLE CASINO" is arched above the deuce of spades, bookmarked by the dates 1840 and 1916. Below that is engraved "Elizabeth McClelland," followed by a brief sermon in stone: "Gone but not forgotten—ye without sin cast the first stone."

Asa Fisher, early-day Bismarck wholesale liquor dealer and banker, made a good living, but the $5,000 he got when he sold his house to the state for use as the governor's mansion was big money. Built in 1884, the two-and-a-half-story frame Victorian house was the residence of twenty governors up to 1960. Given the house in 1975, the North Dakota State Historical Society restored it to its Gay Nineties elegance and opened it to the public as the **Former Governor's Mansion State Historic Site** (320 East Avenue B.; 701-328-2666).

Sixty miles north of Bismarck is **Knife River Indian Villages National Historic Site** (one-half mile north of Stanton on County Road 37; 701-745-3300). For centuries the home of the Mandan and Hidatsa people, who lived at the site in earthen lodges, the French later operated a fur trading post here. The Lewis and Clark Expedition visited the site in 1804. This village is where the explorers first became acquainted with Sakakawea, who would become the party's interpreter as they continued their journey to the Pacific Northwest.

Devil's Lake (Ramsey County)

Settled in 1883 as Creel, Devil's Lake changed its name a year later for the large, nearby natural-water body called Devil's Lake. When nearby **Fort Totten** was established in 1867, its soldiers protected overland transportation routes and policed the Dakota reservation. The post's military mission ended in 1890 and it was turned over to the federal Bureau of Indian Affairs for conversion into a school for Indian children. Later it was used as a tuberculosis treatment facility. The well-preserved old fort became a North Dakota State Historic Site in 1960 and is listed on the National Register of Historic Places.

A visitor's center with exhibits on the fort's many uses over the years is in the post's former commissary storehouse at **Fort Totten State Historic Site** (417 Cavalry Circle; 701-766-4441), off Route 57, 14 miles south of Devil's Lake.

Epping (Williams County)

Epping pastor **Duane R. Lindberg** and a friend came up with the idea for the Buffalo Trails Museum over coffee at a local café in 1966. Lindberg and the other man were discussing the loss of historic buildings in the area when Lindberg suggested a community-supported, non-profit organization to collect and preserve old North Dakota buildings along with other aspects of local history. The eight-building museum complex includes a homesteader's log cabin, a dentist's office, a photograph gallery, a library, and an early schoolhouse. Twenty-one miles northwest of Willison on CR 6, the **Buffalo Trails Museum** (701-859-4361) constitutes most of Main Street in Epping.

Fargo (Cass County)

Fargo is named for a businessman whose enterprise played a big part in the development of the West, **William G. Fargo**, of the Wells-Fargo Express Company. Fargo also was an official with the westward-building Northern Pacific Railroad, which is what endeared him to the nascent town on the Red River just across from Minnesota. When the railroad arrived, Fargo grew rapidly with all the boisterousness associated with new railroad towns. By 1880 the population had reached 2,600-plus (many of them Scandinavian immigrants) and the city continued to grow.

Fargo's famous addition to Wild West lore can be found at **Bonanzaville** (1351 Main Ave. West; 701-282-2822). If assessed by its name only, Bonanzaville would seem like a faux Wild West tourist trap inspired by the long-running (1959–1973) TV series, *Bonanza*. But that would be wrong on two counts. First, Bonanzaville is operated by the Cass County Historical Society. The twelve-acre site features forty-one restored Old West buildings moved in from elsewhere in the area and thousands of historic artifacts. Second, the Bonanza in Bonanzaville comes from application of the word to describe the large farms around Fargo, places like the 11,000-acre Dalrymple Farm (begun in 1874) that for a time was the largest cultivated farm in the world.

Hettinger (Adams County)

Guided by Sioux and Arikara scouts, Lt. Col. George Armstrong Custer and the Seventh Cavalry (plus two infantry companies, three Gatling guns, and one cannon) made camp beneath a cliff along Hiddenwood Creek on July 8, 1874. Six days before, with 2,000 troops and teamsters, 1,000 horses, 900 mules, 110 wagons, and 300 head of cattle, Custer's command had marched out of Fort Abraham Lincoln. Joining the troops were numerous civilians, including five newspaper reporters and a photographer. The young cavalry officer, famous for his Civil War exploits, had orders to explore the Black Hills territory and find a suitable location for a new fort. Unofficially, the expedition was about proving or disproving the rumored presence of gold in the Black Hills, then part of the Great Sioux Reservation.

Professional buffalo hunters slaughtered most of the American Bison herd, but the last great hunt was an Indian affair. In June 1882, two thousand men, women, and children of the Teton Lakotas traveled on foot and horseback from Fort Yates to the Hiddenwood Creek valley and found the hills black with thousands of grazing buffalo. As they had been doing before living memory, in preparing for the hunt the men painted their faces, bodies, and horses in traditional ways. But most of the Indians pursued their quarry with rifles, not with bows and arrows. By the end of the first day, the Indians had killed two thousand buffalo. On the second day, the entire tribe worked at butchering and caring for the meat. Humps and livers were removed for feasting, and women sliced the remaining meat into thin sheets to dry and make into jerky or pemmican. On the third day, Lakota hunters killed an additional three thousand buffalo. Estimates are that fifty thousand bison had migrated to this area. A year and a half later, there were none.

Historical markers describing Custer's camp and the 1882 hunt stand at a roadside viewing area twelve miles east of Hettinger off US 12 (GPS coordinates: N45° 57.86', W102° 24.45').

The **Dakota Buttes Museum** (400 11th St.; 701-567-4429) covers the history of southwestern North Dakota, including Custer's camp and the last great hunt.

Jamestown (Stutsman County)

Jamestown began in 1871 as a tent camp for track layers as the Northern Pacific Railroad pushed westward across Dakota Territory. To protect the workers, the army established **Fort Seward**, a three-company post on high ground where Pipestem Creek flowed into the James River. Railroad president Thomas Rosser named the new railroad town for Jamestown, Virginia, and the community grew as a railroad town and county seat.

Eight years before Jamestown appeared on the Dakota Territory map, the largest Indian battle in the future state's history took place about sixty miles to the south. Nearly as many died in the Battle of Whitestone Hill as in Custer's defeat in Montana, with one major difference. In the Battle of Whitestone Hill, most of those killed were Sioux Indians.

In the aftermath of the 1862 Sioux uprising in Minnesota the army sent two large columns into what would become North Dakota. Essentially, they were on a search-and-destroy mission. On September 3, 1863, one of the columns, a large force under Brig. Gen. Alfred Sully, attacked a Sioux village of about four thousand people near a feature known as Whitestone Hill. The soldiers killed scores of Indians and took more than 150 women and children as prisoners in what was more a massacre than battle.

Military records are not ambiguous that twenty soldiers died in the fight, with another thirty-eight wounded. But no one kept an exact count of the number of Indians killed that day. Estimates range from one hundred to three hundred. If the high number is accurate, more combatants died here than at Little Big Horn. After destroying so many lives, troops spent two days at the battleground destroying all that the Indians had before the attack, including tipis, buffalo hides, travois, blankets, and their winter food supply—tons of dried buffalo meat. What the troops could not burn, they threw into a nearby lake.

In 1914, a thirty-foot granite monument with an army bugler at the top was erected on the battleground amidst the graves of the soldiers killed there. Federal Works Progress Administration laborers in 1941 built a small fieldstone cairn memorializing the Indians who died there. The state later acquired the property and maintains it as a North Dakota State Historic Site.

The battle site is twenty-three miles southeast of the small LaMoure County town of Kulm. For GPS purposes, the address is 7310 86th Street, but the site is on open prairie.

Housed in a six-thousand-square-foot log building at **Jamestown's Frontier Village** (404 Louis Lamour Ln.; 800-222-4766), the **National Buffalo Museum** (500 17th St. Southeast; 800-807-1511) tells the story of the American bison and its role in the culture of the Great Plains. Supported by the non-profit North Dakota Buffalo Foundation, the museum also oversees a herd of some twenty-five to thirty buffalo on two hundred acres along I-94.

Only foundations and basements remain of **Fort Seward** (601 10th Ave. Northwest), just off of US 281 on the north side of Jamestown. The fort was abandoned in 1877.

Louis L'Amour's Hometown

Born March 22, 1908, in the fading days of the Wild West, **Louis Dearborn LaMoore** spent his first fifteen years in and around the farming community of Jamestown. His father was a veterinarian who had been practicing there since 1882, and Louis grew up hearing stories of the recently passed frontier. Eventually changing his last name to the more interesting sounding "L'Amour," he went on to write eighty-nine western novels, fourteen short-story collections, and two nonfiction books.

Built in 1918, the **Alfred Dickey Public Library** (105 3rd Ave. Southeast) is where L'Amour developed his love of the written word. The future best-selling author got his education in the 1910-vintage **Franklin School** (308 2nd St. Southwest). The school remained open until 2000. A map showing other L'Amour-related sites is available at the **Jamestown Tourism Information Center** (404 Louis L'Amour Ln.;701-251-9145).

Mandan (Morton County)

Settled on the west side of the Missouri River at the same time as Bismarck developed on the east side, Mandan was named for the Mandan Tribe that first lived in the area. The town took off in 1882 when the Northern Pacific Railroad completed a bridge across the river.

With the Northern Pacific approaching Bismarck in 1872, the army established a fort on a bluff overlooking the Missouri at a point downstream from the town. The infantry post was named **Fort McKeen** in honor of Henry McKeen, a colonel killed during the Civil War. Later that year, Gen. Phil Sheridan inspected the post and did not like its location or its name. The general had the fort moved to a site below the bluffs and renamed **Fort Abraham Lincoln**. Sheridan also said it needed to be a cavalry post.

The collapse of the national economy in 1873 derailed plans for the new railroad for the time being but the fort continued to stand watch over Bismarck. It grew in strategic importance with the arrival of the Seventh Cavalry, a regiment commanded by Lt. Col. George Armstrong Custer. Of the Seventh's twelve companies, Custer kept six at Abraham Lincoln and divided the other companies between Fort Rice (thirty miles north of Mandan) and Fort Totten (see Devil's Lake). Custer's wife, Libby, joined him at the post in November and the couple lived in the commanding officer's quarters for the rest of their time together.

Two major events that helped shape the American West began at Fort Abraham Lincoln: the 1874 expedition headed by Custer that found gold in the Black Hills, and his May 17, 1876, departure with his troops on what would be his last campaign and the beginning of his eternal place in Wild West history.

Following Custer's death at the Little Big Horn, the post continued its strategic role in the ongoing Indian Wars. In addition, in 1879 a revitalized Northern Pacific finally began laying track that brought the need for the fort in the first place. Work on the line continued until 1883 and the army deactivated the post in 1891.

After the army left, as happened often across the West, locals capitalized on a free lumber bonanza and cannibalized the post's buildings. The state acquired ownership of the former military reservation in 1907, but not until 1934 did the Depression-era Civilian Conservation Corps (CCC) put in roads at the site. CCC workers also reconstructed two log blockhouses, built a museum and other amenities, and placed cornerstones to mark the original location of post buildings. North Dakota designated the old fort a state historical site in 1965 and began reconstructing it to its 1875 appearance. Using original plans, the state rebuilt five structures, including the commanding officer's quarters, better known as the Custer House.

Fort Abraham Lincoln State Park (4480 Fort Lincoln Rd.) is seven miles south of Mandan on State Highway 1806. Visitors may explore the post on their own or take a guided tour. There are interpretive exhibits in the museum as well as excavated foundations, markers, and monuments. Additional markers stand at the adjacent **Fort McKeen** site.

Most North Dakota towns began when the Northern Pacific rails arrived. The five-acre **North Dakota State Railroad Museum** (3102 37th St. Northwest) includes interpretive exhibits in a three-thousand-square-foot building and a large outdoor assemblage of vintage rolling stock.

Medora (Billings County)

With financial backing from his father, aristocrat and former French cavalry officer Antoine de Vallombrosa (generally referred to as Marquis de Mores) came to the Bad Lands in 1883 with what he and his father thought was a good idea: Circumvent the Chicago stockyards by building a packing plant from which he could ship refrigerated meat directly to eastern markets. He bought more than forty-four thousand acres for cattle raising, hired cowboys, and built a processing plant in Medora, a town he founded and named for his wife. He also constructed a twenty-six-room, two-story wood-frame house grandly referred to as a chateau. The marquis further invested in a stagecoach line connecting Medora with Deadwood. His wife, Madame de Mores (nee Medora von Hoffman), was daughter of a New York banker and often entertained nobility and friends from back east at the house. To accommodate his in-laws when they visited, the marquis built them a house in town and Madame Mores funded construction of a Catholic church.

Neither of Mores's two business ventures did well and in 1886 he sold his ranch, and the couple moved back to France. The marquis bitterly blamed the railroads and the Chicago beef trust for killing his enterprise, and while that probably contributed to it, the real deal killer was consumer taste. The public preferred corn-fed beef to beef raised on range grass. The Frenchman devoted most of the rest of his life to vicious anti-Semitism, capped by a crazy scheme to unite Muslims in a holy war against the British and Jews. North African tribesmen killed him in French Algeria in 1896 in an attack his family believed was an assassination planned by the French government.

The focal point of **Chateau de Mores State Historic Site** (3426 Chateaus Rd.) is the restored home with household furnishings and personal items left by the de Mores, many brought to the US from France. A visitor's center (701-623-4355) has interpretive exhibits. A bronze statue of the Marquis donated by his sons in 1926 stands in downtown Medora's **De Mores Memorial Park**. On the western edge of town is a park where the packing plant and related structures were located. The plant was destroyed by fire in 1907, leaving only its chimney still standing.

The same year the Marquis descended on the Bad Lands so did a young Easterner named **Theodore Roosevelt**. He came to hunt buffalo, but before he left, he decided to take up cattle raising and bought a ranch. In the summer of 1884, following his wife and mother's death earlier that year—both on the same day—Roosevelt bought a second ranch thirty-five miles due north of Medora, the **Elkhorn**. He spent time in its scenic solitude trying to cope with his loss, leaving the day-to-day operation of the ranch to two hunting guide friends he'd invited to move west from Maine. The two returned to Maine in 1886 and the manager of his other ranch took on the Elkhorn as well. Both operations did relatively well until the devastating winter of 1886–1887 when nearly two-thirds of his cattle died. Roosevelt abandoned the ranch in 1890 and sold the property in 1898. Historians believe Roosevelt appreciated the ranch more for its spiritually restorative landscape than as an investment. He later said he never would have become president had it not been for the time he spent there.

The **Elkhorn Ranch** site is part of **Theodore Roosevelt National Park** (315 2nd Ave.; 701-623-4466). Only the foundation remains of the old ranch house, but the ranch's isolation and striking landscape can still be experienced. To visit the ranch, the best place to start is the visitor's center at the entrance of the park's South Unit. Park staff can provide directions to the ranch site.

Two museums have exhibits and artifacts on the area's history, the **Billings County Courthouse Museum** (475 4th St.; 701-623-4829) and the **Museum of the Badlands** (195 3rd Ave.; 800-633-6721). The **North Dakota Cowboy Hall of Fame** (250 Main St.) is a fifteen-thousand-square-foot building dedicated to the preservation of the state's Western heritage and culture. The facility features interpretive exhibits and memorabilia focused on the more than two hundred Native Americans, ranchers, and cowboys who have been inducted into the hall of fame since it opened.

Minot (Ward County)

Ole Sundrie, a Scandinavian immigrant, settled here along the Souris River in northwest North Dakota in 1884. By the time the Great Northern Railroad began laying track through future Ward County, roughly forty people lived in the area. The railroad founded the town of Minot in 1886, naming it for Henry D. Minot, a Great National Railroad stockholder and friend of President James Hill, who had been killed in a train wreck. The community grew from a tent city into a town of more than five thousand inside the year. The town got its second railroad when the Minneapolis, St. Paul, and Sault Ste. Marie (less formally known as the Soo Line) reached there in 1893.

The **Railroad Museum** (19 1st St. Southeast; 701-852-7091) occupies the old Soo Line depot, built in 1912. **Ward County Historical Society Museum and Pioneer Village** (2005 Burdick Expy.; 701-839-0785) focuses on the area's history.

Pembina (Pembina County)

On the Canadian border in the upper northeast corner of the state, Pembina was North Dakota's first Euro American community. It also had the state's first post office, first school, first church, first customs house, and first homestead. Though long the homeland of Native Americans and later a fur trade center, Pembina figured in the Plains Indian Wars as the location of **Fort Pembina**. The post was established in 1869 and completed a year later. Its primary mission was to guard against Sioux incursions from Canada, where many of them had taken refuge. The fort remained active until fire destroyed many of its buildings in 1895 and the military chose not to rebuild it.

Pembina State Museum (805 State Highway 59; 701-825-6840), thirty miles southwest of Pembina, has two museums, the **Pembina County Historical Museum** (Main and Division Streets; 701-265-4691) and the **Pioneer Heritage Museum** (13571 State Highway 5; 701-265-4941) at Cavalier Icelandic State Park, five miles west of town on Route 5.

Rhame (Bowman County)

Circling the wagons to fend off an Indian attack became a Hollywood Western cliché, but sometimes it really happened. On September 2, 1864, a large wagon train crossing the open prairie in the southwest corner of what is now North Dakota—on its way to the gold fields in Montana and Idaho—came under attack by Sioux Indians angry at the intrusion on their land. When the Indians charged, the would-be miners circled their ninety-seven wagons and, with their out-numbered military escort, desperately fought to save their lives. After two days and the loss of several soldiers and civilians, the wagon train made a run for it, firing at the pursuing Indians as they tried to reach a more defensible position. Making it to higher ground, the soldiers began digging and stacking squares of sod to build a fortification with man-high walls. In honor of Private Jefferson Davis Dilts, who had been killed early in the battle, they named the redoubt **Fort Dilts**. As the siege continued, a lieutenant with fifteen cavalrymen left the makeshift fort to ride for Fort Rice for help. The soldiers made it and a large relief column galloped off as soon as possible. When the vanguard of the force rode into view on September 20, the Lakota realized the odds had changed and withdrew.

The eight-acre **Fort Dilts State Historic Site** has been maintained by the state since 1932. There are markers for the soldiers who died in the siege and remnants of the fort's walls, a partially completed well and wagon ruts still visible. To reach the site, which is on open prairie, take Fort Dilts Road 2.5 miles north of Rhame, then turn west for 1.5 miles to the site.

Washburn (McLean County)

On the upper Missouri River in the central portion of the state, Washburn was founded in 1882—but the history of the area goes back much farther to a pivotal moment in the exploration of the West.

By October 1804, traveling through what is now North Dakota, the Lewis and Clark Expedition had begun to encounter bitter cold and snow. Reaching a collection of Mandan and Hidatsa villages where the party was greeted warmly, the two captains decided it would be a good place to spend the winter. Beginning in early November the soldiers constructed a V-shaped fort of cottonwood logs with four rooms and fireplaces to accommodate the men and their supplies.

They named it **Fort Mandan**, as Clark wrote, "in honour of our Neighbours." Fresh meat was hard to come by, and the weather only worsened, but the expedition got by. "The thermometer stands this morning at 20 below zero, a fine day," Clark wrote in his journal for December 13. He and Lewis used their time interacting with the Mandans, collecting much valuable information on the geography and cultures of the northern Great Plains. It was here they acquired the services of a Shoshone woman named Sakakawea, who served as their interpreter and played an important role in the successful completion of the expedition. In early April, the keelboat that had carried the expedition to this point, manned by eleven soldiers, was sent back down the river to St. Louis laden with specimens of flora and fauna and American Indian artifacts. That same day, the rest of the Corps of Discovery resumed its western journey.

Managed by North Dakota Parks and Recreation, the **Lewis & Clark Interpretive Center** (2576 8th St. Southwest; 701-462-8535) features an exact replica of Fort Mandan as well as artifacts and exhibits related to the expedition and its peaceful dealings with the Mandan people.

White Shield (McLean County)

Named for Chief White Shield, a Seventh Cavalry scout during the Sioux War, this small community is in the Mandan, Hidatsa, and Arikara Nation on the Fort Berthold Indian Reservation. It was founded in 1954 during construction of Lake Sakakawea, which later inundated the older town of Elbowood.

Created in 1870, the **Fort Berthold Indian Reservation** is the home of the Three Affiliated Tribes. Located in central North Dakota, it covers 988,000 acres, 457,837 acres owned by Native Americans with the rest a federal wildlife area. Tribal headquarters are four miles west of New Town, the reservation's largest community. An interpretive center (336 Main St.; 701-627-2243) with exhibits on tribal history and culture can be found in New Town.

Indian Scout Post No. 1

A little-known historic Old West cemetery is cared for by an organization even less known. The cemetery has an unlikely name for a burial ground, **Indian Scout Post No. 1**. It is maintained by the Old Scouts Society, so named because the graveyard is the final resting place of several Indians who distinguished themselves as Seventh Cavalry scouts during the Sioux War.

Organized in 1979, the society's White Shield chapter is made up of descendants of Mandan, Hidatsa, and Arikara who banded together to fight their common enemy, the Sioux. They were known as the Three Affiliated Tribes.

The US Army had been hiring Indian scouts since 1866 and they were particularly important throughout the Sioux War. When the military came to Dakota Territory to protect railroad track workers, under the ancient truism that "the enemy of my enemy is my friend," dozens from the tribal confederacy joined the army as scouts. As they did elsewhere in the West, the scouts carried dispatches, found wild game and water, served as trackers and interpreters, and provided intelligence.

When Lt. Col. George Armstrong Custer commanded Fort Abraham Lincoln, he relied heavily on the scouts. They were so important that the colonel did not want them to do any fighting. But one of his first scouts, Red Bear, who Custer promoted to sergeant, was soon killed in a skirmish with the Sioux and Bobtail Bull. He died at the Little Big Horn in 1876 trying to drive off Sioux ponies prior to the battle.

The cemetery is on the Fort Berthold Indian Reservation, between White Shield and Parshall. (Check at the interpretive center for more detailed directions.) In addition to the Seventh Cavalry scouts, Indian veterans of both world wars, Korea, and Vietnam are buried here. Cemeteries at Fort Abraham Lincoln and west of Garrison on State Highway 1804 also have tribal veterans of the Sioux War.

Williston (Williams County)

What Bent's Fort was to the Santa Fe Trail, the **Fort Union Trading Post** was to the upper Missouri River and the Northern Great Plains. Established in 1828 by the American Fur Co. and continuing in operation until 1867, the trading post did a lively business with Plains Indians, taking in buffalo robes, beaver pelts, and other furs in trade for manufactured goods ranging from beads and calico to guns and ammunition. A red-roofed, two-story headquarters stood inside a high wooden stockade protected by two imposing stone bastions at opposite corners of the log enclosure. Small gun ports in each bastion would allow protected riflemen to fire in any direction, but no serious trouble ever arose between the Indians and the fur company. There would, however, eventually be trouble with one Native American who came to the trading post as a youth. His name was Sitting Bull.

After the Civil War, in 1866 the army established **Fort Buford** (15349 39th Ln. Northwest; 701-572-9034) three miles east of the soon-to-close trading post. The military's mission was to guard the well-traveled upper Missouri River and the growing number of overland travelers coming through Dakota Territory. When the old trading post was shuttered, the government purchased it and salvaged timber and stone for use in Fort Buford's construction. What soldiers did not carry off crews from passing steamboats did, using the remaining wood to fire their boilers. In only a few years, little evidence of the trading post remained.

While the fort was strategically important throughout the Sioux War, the most historical event at the post was the July 19, 1881, surrender of Sitting Bull to Major David Brotherton. The post's last mission was to protect work crews as the Great Northern Railroad laid track in North Dakota beginning in the late 1880s.

The town of Williston began in 1887 as a depot on the Great Northern called Little Muddy. When the railroad's president passed through a year later, he gave the place its drier name in honor of a friend.

The army abandoned Fort Buford in 1895. Three of the old fort's original buildings still stand—a stone powder magazine, the wood-frame officer of the guard building, and the wood-frame commanding officer's quarters. This one-story soldier-built residence is where Sitting Bull surrendered. The only other vestige of the old post is its cemetery, southwest of the post. When the army left, all military burials were exhumed and moved to Little Big Horn National Cemetery in Montana. Civilian graves dating to the time of the fort remain. Housed in the former officer quarters, the visitor's center has interpretive exhibits on the fort's history.

A half-mile east of Fort Buford (also on 39th Lane Northwest) is the state-managed **Missouri-Yellowstone Confluence Interpretive Center**. With large murals and exhibits, the center tells the story of the two rivers and their influence on the history of the West.

In 1966, almost a century after the **Fort Union** (15550 State Highway 1804; 701-572-9083) trading post closed, the National Park Service acquired the site. Based on intermittent archaeological work over a twenty-year period, the park service reconstructed the fort as it would have looked in the early 1850s.

INDEX

C

G

J

K

L

M

N

P

Y

Z

ABOUT THE AUTHOR

An elected member of the Texas Institute of Letters, **Mike Cox** is the author of more than thirty-five nonfiction books. Over an award-winning freelance career dating back to his high school days, he has written hundreds of newspaper articles and columns, magazine stories, and essays for a wide variety of regional and national publications. When not writing, he spends as much time as he can traveling, fishing, hunting, and looking for new stories to tell. He lives in the Hill Country village of Wimberley, Texas.